Silent Racism

Here on the pulse of this new day
You may have the grace to look up and out
And into your sister's eyes
And into your brother's face, your country
And say simply
Very simply
With hope
Good morning.

Maya Angelou (1993)

Silent Racism

How Well-Meaning White People Perpetuate the Racial Divide

Barbara Trepagnier

LONDON AND NEW YORK

First published 2010 by Paradigm Publishers

Published 2016 by Routledge
2 Park Square, Milton Park, Abingdon, Oxon OX14 4RN
711 Third Avenue, New York, NY 10017, USA

Routledge is an imprint of the Taylor & Francis Group, an informa business

Frontispiece from "On the Pulse of the Morning" by Maya Angelou, copyright © 1993 by Maya Angelou. Used by permission of Random House.

Chapter 2 is reprinted with permission from "Deconstructing Categories: The Exposure of Silent Racism," *Symbolic Interaction* 24, no. 2 (2001): 141–163.

Library of Congress Cataloging-in-Publication Data is available at the Library of Congress.

Designed and Typeset in New Baskerville by Straight Creek Bookmakers.

ISBN 13 : 978-1-59451-827-0 (hbk)
ISBN 13 : 978-1-59451-828-7 (pbk)

To Sam, Josie, Chris, Millie, Cecily, Claire, Zac, and Ginny

Contents

Foreword

I first came across the book *Silent Racism* through a conversation with my husband, who was a student at Texas State University. We frequently talked about my efforts to raise the issue of disproportionality in child welfare, specifically in the Texas Child Protective Services (CPS) program. He mentioned that he had heard of this book written by a Texas State University professor, Barbara Trepagnier, which might address the issue. He actually ordered the book for me.

I could not put it down once I started to read. *Silent Racism* clearly reflected some of my thoughts about leaders in child- and family-serving systems who could not come to grips with the thought that our actions might contribute to institutionalized racism, however unintentional. I was amazed at the skill Barbara had in describing white women in different stages of racist thinking. The book also stresses that owning one's own racism is necessary in order for change to occur.

Before I finished reading the book, I mentioned it to two members of my staff, a white woman—Linda Wright, a former regional director—and an African American woman—Sheila Sturgis Craig, the disproportionality manager at CPS. It happened that Linda was already reading the book. She was intrigued with it because it spoke of her personal struggle with our efforts to address disproportionality in CPS through the Undoing Racism training. *Silent Racism* makes clear that racist actions are often denied, but that when unveiled, many of those actions previously defended as nonracist are actually racist. The book really helped to validate, and put into words, things that I have known all of my life, but struggled to find the words to help others understand. So often, something appeared racist to me as an African American woman and yet my white peers just did not see it that way. Linda and I both recommended the book to Sheila and other leaders who were involved in our efforts to address disproportionality.

By the time I finished the book, I was thinking about how to engage Barbara in our efforts to address disproportionality. By this time Sheila had finished reading it, and we decided to schedule a meeting with Barbara to talk about her work and how it supports our goal of shifting to antiracist practice.

Our first meeting was held at my office in Austin, when I was the assistant commissioner for CPS. I believe I did most of the talking, about how the efforts to address the disproportionality of African American children and families started in Texas, our efforts to expand this work statewide, and the struggle associated with discussions of race and racism. I shared my personal experience of reading *Silent Racism* and how closely it depicts some of the struggles of leaders in the field of child welfare. We discussed the Undoing Racism training and some of the similarities between this training and the book. I extended an invitation to Barbara to attend an Undoing Racism workshop and to become a partner in our work by serving on the Texas Statewide Disproportionality Task Force.

Silent Racism has helped to inform our work in Texas. We have set up *Talk Backs,* where we separate women of color and white women into groups to provide opportunities for courageous conversations to occur about race and racism. The book helped us embrace the value of these types of conversations. Being able to have the conversations has led to positive changes in the CPS system's response to children, youth, and families.

I am really proud of the working relationship with Barbara that has developed as a result of my introduction to this book, and I am honored to be a part of the new chapter on disproportionality. I have no doubt that readers will find it exciting and informative. I believe that this book will impact readers both personally and professionally. Many "passionate champions" have emerged in the Texas child welfare system as a result of our commitment to systems improvements and the work depicted in the first edition of *Silent Racism.* The new chapter on lessening disproportionality will be even more beneficial for people working in child welfare or other systems where disproportionality occurs.

Joyce James, Deputy Commissioner
Texas Department of Family and Protective Services
Austin, Texas

Preface to the Original Edition

My interest in studying race issues is fueled by a salient memory of myself as a young mother in a small town in Texas during the 1960s. I remember seeing the thousands of civil rights activists in the 1963 March on Washington on television. I wanted desperately to be there but could not manage to with three young children. I felt as though I were missing out on an opportunity to publicly declare my stand against racism, to march side by side with others who cared about ending racial inequality. For many years I focused on other things besides racism, my concern about inequality buried under the routine concerns of everyday life. During those years, I undoubtedly was a bigger part of the problem than of the solution concerning racism. My commitment to racial equality was rekindled years later, and the ideas presented here are an effort to contribute now to the solution.

Support for this project has spanned almost ten years. Early encouragement for the project came from my cohort at the University of California–Santa Barbara as we made our way through the doctoral program there. Specifically, thanks go to Carol Barringer, Noreen Begorey, Rob Caputo, Susan Dalton, Lynn Gesch, Hazel Hull, Neal King, Tiffany Lopez, Wendy Marks, Martha McCaughey, Francie Montell, Greg Scott, Britta Wheeler, and all of those whose thoughts and opinions about feminism, racism, and postmodernism shaped my thinking. Thank you also to Kum-Kum Bhavnani, Sarah Fenstermaker, Avery Gordon, and Beth Schneider, whose stimulating and challenging feminist seminars provided fertile ground for growth. I am especially indebted to the members of my dissertation committee for the encouragement and support each of them gave me. Kum-Kum Bhavnani's unflagging enthusiasm for the work in progress was a constant reminder of its merit. Beth Schneider and Rich Appelbaum's thoughtful consideration of the early work is greatly appreciated, as is the respect they showed the completed dissertation. Special thanks go to Michele Trepagnier for her careful copyediting.

My colleagues at Texas State University–San Marcos have also been helpful, particularly Harold Dorton, Mona Ford, and Patti Guiffre, who read parts of the book and gave me invaluable feedback. Talks with Sally Caldwell about various aspects of the theory were also very helpful in furthering my ideas. I owe special thanks to Chad Smith for reading the entire manuscript and engaging with me on points that strengthened many of the chapters. Claude Bonazzo and Chandra Ward provided important research assistance, and Jason Lamb was invaluable as a research assistant, copy editor, and all-around support person during the final months of writing. And, to my friends Michael Bourgeois—for his feedback, suggestions, and encouragement—and Mike Boucher—for his insistence that I never give up—thank you.

Special thanks go to Sherith Pankratz, who put me in touch with Dean Birkenkamp at Paradigm Publishers. Dean's enthusiasm about the book has been unwavering. His support and that of Beth Davis and others at Paradigm were the encouragement I needed to finish the project.

Finally, I want to thank my daughters—Patti Money-Coutts, Teresa Day, Renee Trepagnier, and Michele Trepagnier—for the love and encouragement they give me.

Barbara Trepagnier
Texas State University–San Marcos

Preface to the Second Edition

I was delighted when Dean Birkenkamp from Paradigm said in August 2008 that we should start thinking about a second edition of *Silent Racism*. I had recently joined the Statewide Task Force on Racial Disproportionality in Texas and could see that many of the theoretical arguments in the first edition were evident in the work of Texas Child Protective Services (CPS). Two fundamental arguments I have seen borne out are that silent racism and racial passivity contribute to institutional racism and that an increase in race awareness decreases institutional racism. Specifically, in Texas, racial bias (that is, silent racism and racial passivity) has contributed to a disparate number of African American children being removed from their homes compared to white children—a problem in every state, not just Texas; and increasing cultural competency (that is, race awareness) along with other strategies is lowering racial disproportionality. There was no question in my mind that a case study of Texas CPS would be an important addition to the first edition of this book. I call it "Silent Racism at Work."

Racial disproportionality is not limited to child welfare. Education, the justice system, and health care produce the disparate outcomes for black and white Americans as well. Although I do not describe all of these systems in the new chapter, I include racial disproportionality in education: moving black students at a higher rate than white students out of the regular classroom into special education. The first part of the new chapter is a description of the problem in education and child welfare. The second part of the chapter is a case study of Texas CPS in relation to racial disproportionality. Many of the strategies described in the case study could easily be adapted to schools and school districts that recognize racial disproportionality as a problem.

The original chapters of *Silent Racism* remain the same in the new edition. Substantively, there was nothing I would change. The research and theory are sound, and readers—black and white—have told me that they find the ideas to be provocative, significant, helpful, and even therapeutic. If I were to change anything, it would be the tone; I would make it less academic, and I would move the references out of the text and into notes at the end of each chapter. I would also change the use of "black" to "African American" in accordance with feedback I have received from readers. But overall I am pleased with the original text, and I am very happy to be adding a new chapter that exemplifies so well the message of the first edition: We need to think differently about racism, we need to recognize it in ourselves. And if we do that, we can change institutional racism in important ways.

I am indebted to many for their contributions to this new edition of *Silent Racism*. To the men and women from Texas CPS, Casey Family Programs, and the Statewide Disproportionality Task Force that participated in the study: Thank you for your contribution to this chapter and for the important work you do for children in Texas. Thank you also Michele Trepagnier and Michael Bourgeois for your diligent work in proofreading and giving me feedback on the chapter. My heartfelt gratitude goes to Deputy Commissioner Joyce James for seeing the value of my work on silent racism and for inviting me to the table. And thank you, Dean Birkenkamp, for your enthusiasm about this work from the beginning.

Barbara Trepagnier
Texas State University–San Marcos

Chapter One

Rethinking Racism

My goal in writing this book is to encourage well-meaning white people to reconsider their ideas about racism. The title, *Silent Racism: How Well-Meaning White People Perpetuate the Racial Divide,* suggests that concerned whites are implicated in racial problems, including the disparity between blacks and whites. The title also introduces the term *silent racism,* which raises the question: Why talk about silent racism? After all, if it is silent, how could it possibly matter?

This introduction and the chapters that follow will reveal that silent racism—the racist thoughts, images, and assumptions in the minds of white people, including those that by most accounts are "not racist"—is dangerous precisely because it is perceived as harmless. The silent racism in people's thoughts, images, and assumptions shapes their perspective of reality. And a perspective that is shaped by racist thoughts, images, and assumptions—no matter how subtle they are—will produce behavior that reflects racist thoughts, images, and assumptions. But before rethinking racism, we need a clear understanding of racism within a historical context.

The definition of *racism* is somewhat complicated because it varies over time as well as from one social group to another. A common definition was adopted before the 1960s civil rights movement, when racism was thought to consist of two components: the *prejudice* of individuals—also referred to as intolerance or bigotry—and *discrimination*—behavior that treats black Americans and other races unfairly compared to white Americans.[1]

At the height of the civil rights movement in the late 1960s, a more sociological view of racism emerged among blacks. Before then, even sociologists viewed racism in terms of prejudice and discrimination (for an example see Merton 1967). A sociological view of racism means looking at an issue with a broad view, one that considers the larger social context in which an issue is embedded. Metaphorically, the difference between a sociological view and a psychological, or individualistic, view is similar to the difference between looking through a telescope or a microscope: the telescope represents the sociological view, and the microscope the psychological view. A telescope captures larger patterns that are not obtainable with a microscope. As the civil rights movement progressed, sociologists began to see the cultural and structural components of racism as an important part of the problem, especially racial inequality. In terms of effects, a psychological interpretation of racism focuses on hurt feelings (Johnson 1997), not broader material costs. And yet, racism is a cultural phenomenon that operates through social structures that produce systematic, differential effects for blacks and whites. This occurs in the economic, legal, and political systems as well as in education and health care.

The ideas presented in this book emerged from within a sociological paradigm that regards racism in the United States as a societal phenomenon that began with slavery, was sustained throughout the Reconstruction period, and persists today in the institutions of society—in other words, *systemic racism* (Feagin 2001). With these sociological insights in mind, I selected both the theoretical framework and the methodology from symbolic interactionism, a microlevel perspective within sociology. Although a microperspective, symbolic interactionism is a sociological approach, not a psychological one. Symbolic interactionists are interested in how people make sense of things; that is, how people attach meanings to their interactions and their environments and how those meanings play out in people's everyday lives. I incorporate a more critical view than the early apolitical view espoused by George H. Mead and Herbert Blumer, the founders of symbolic interactionism. Nevertheless, exploring how well-meaning white people make sense of racism entailed taking an in-depth look at the participants' thoughts about racism. Therefore, the focus of this study is the way participants define race matters and especially how they make sense of racism. My focus on the sense making of well-meaning white people regarding racism does not imply that I do not see systemic racism as the more fundamental problem; rather, my focus on the thoughts and beliefs of individuals arises from the question, Do well-meaning white people contribute to systemic racism, and, if so, what part do they play? The research project presented here, then, focuses on a small piece of the larger racism puzzle.

Definitions of Racism

White Americans and people of color in this country differ significantly in their definitions of racism (Blauner 1994). Most whites think in terms of the oppositional categories "racist" and "not racist." Whites in the "racist" category are defined as disliking or hating blacks and other minorities, and their animosity is portrayed in acts or statements that are blatantly racist (Jaynes and Williams 1989). Whites in the "not racist" category, in contrast, are defined as trying to ignore racial difference (Blauner 1994). This white definition of racism is problematic because it does not recognize racism unless it is blatant and/or intended; neither does it acknowledge institutional racism. Furthermore, the view overlooks subtle forms of racism that have emerged since the civil rights movement and that are color blind; that is, forms of racism expressed in nonracial terms that are not obviously race-identified. The white definition of racism also ignores acts of everyday racism: routine actions that often are not recognized by the actor as racist but that uphold the racial status quo (Essed 1991). For example, black women report that whites often seem surprised to find that a black person has a college degree or is a professional. This form of everyday racism—marginalization—is based in the white assumption that blacks are not educated or successful. Ignoring racism that is not hateful and intentional effectively hides the fact that white people daily perform acts of everyday racism.

Two assumptions underpin the view that white people are either "racist" or "not racist." First, most whites assume that racism is hateful; and second, most whites believe that racism is a rare occurrence. These assumptions—that racism is hateful and rare—deny that racism today is often unintended and routine. Although blatant racism like that which occurred before the civil rights movement occurs occasionally today, more often racism consists of routine acts of everyday racism that are not viewed as racist by the person performing them and therefore are not intentional. It is this unintentional racism, I will argue, that produces a good deal of institutional racism and resulting racial inequality. Yet, because this racism is not recognized by most whites, even well-meaning white people contribute to the racial divide without intending to and without knowing that they do.

In contrast to the white definition of racism, data show that blacks and other people of color see racism as permeating the institutions of society, producing racial inequality in employment, education, housing, and justice (Blauner 1994; Bonilla-Silva 2003; Feagin 2001). Women of color believe that racism "is inherent in the social system" (Essed 1991: 106). Joe Feagin (2001) devised a definition of racism based on the ideas of black intellectuals including Anna Julia Cooper, Oliver Cox, Frederick Douglass, W. E. B. Du Bois, Frantz Fanon, and Kwame Ture: racism is systemic and includes the racist practices of individuals, the economic and political power of whites over blacks, racial economic inequality, and the "racist ideologies, attitudes, and institutions created to preserve white advantages and power" (p. 16). For people of color, the definition of racism is closely tied to the recent sociological definition that racism is built into U.S. institutions and U.S. society itself.

Why do the black and white definitions of racism differ so dramatically? Definitions, like all knowledge, are shaped by culture and the social structures of society. People's definitions differ depending on where in the society individuals are located (Mannheim [1936] 1952). This is as true for people's definitions of racism as it is for other definitions. For example, before emancipation, slaves had a very different experience of the plantation than the owner because of their location *as slaves*. Later, during the segregation era when blacks were free and yet were denied entry into white establishments, they had experiences unknown to most white people. Given our racial history of slavery and segregation, it is not surprising that black and white Americans have conflicting definitions of racism.

This point is captured by W. E. B. Du Bois ([1903] 1999) in the concept of double-consciousness, which illustrates well how blacks' view of racism differs from that of whites. Du Bois writes in *The Souls of Black Folk*, "One ever feels his twoness—an American, a Negro; two souls, two thoughts, two unreconciled strivings; two warring ideals in one dark body, whose dogged strength alone keeps it from being torn asunder" (p. 11). Du Bois's poignant description, it is safe to say, describes a side of racism that does not resonate in a personal way with the experience of white people.

Rethinking racism entails rethinking the language we use to talk and to think about racism. Changing the oppositional categories "racist" and "not racist" to a continuum ranging from "more racist" to "less racist" would more accurately depict racism because it would encompass blatant racism at the "more racist" end and yet not obscure the everyday racism (Essed 1991) that is concealed in the "not racist" category. The oppositional categories in our language today hide subtle acts of racism, especially from the actors performing them, primarily because the "not racist" category implies that no harm is done. At times, everyday racism is not hateful, and it is often not intentional. And yet, everyday racism contributes to the production of institutional racism, which produces negative effects for minorities. An important function of the racism continuum would be to portray white people as racist in varying degrees, eliminating the false notion in the minds of most white people that they are not at all racist. The change to a continuum would lessen the importance of whether people *intend* to be racist and focus instead on the racist *effects* of their actions. As mentioned, the shift to a racism continuum would not diminish the importance of blatant racism that would occur at the "more racist" end of the continuum. See Figure 1.1 for the racism continuum.

Silent Racism

This study exposes racism hidden in the "not racist" category; in the process it demonstrates that white commonsense notions about racism are shaped by language that distorts the racial reality. The oppositional categories keep people from seeing a form of racism built into the fabric of society, a form of racism that maintains racial inequality. I call it *silent racism.*[2] Although the focus of this book is

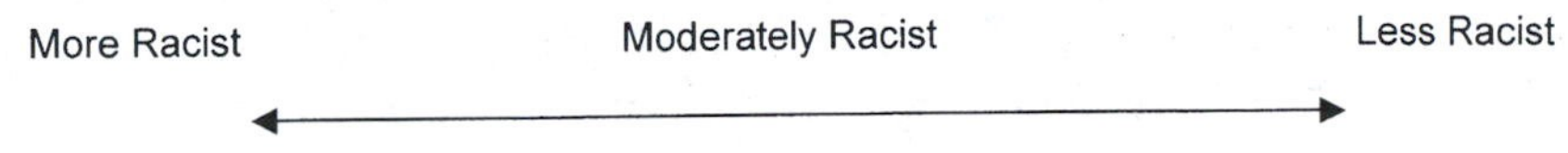

Figure 1.1 Racism Continuum

on the silent racism of well-meaning white people, that does not imply that other, more obvious forms of racism are not as important as ever. Hate crimes performed by bigots as well as the racially conservative projects of color-blind racists, both of which cause extraordinary hardship in the lives of blacks and other people of color, rightfully deserve the attention of race theorists. However, silent racism deserves attention as well, primarily because it does its damage unobserved and because it inhabits the minds of well-meaning whites—the group most amenable to changing its thinking and its behavior regarding race matters, the group most likely to stand with blacks against racism.

Two forms of silent racism emerged in the data: stereotypical images, and paternalistic assumptions. Stereotypical images are based on misinformation about blacks prevalent in the culture. Paternalistic assumptions are based on a sense of superiority found in some relationships between blacks and whites, especially hierarchical relationships that were, and perhaps still are, customary in the South. Silent racism is not the same as prejudice, which is generally perceived as bigoted attitudes held by individual whites about a minority group. Silent racism, on the contrary, is not limited to intolerant whites—it inhabits the minds of all white people whether or not they acknowledge it or are aware of it. Silent racism is more closely linked to the "images, attitudes, fictions, and notions that link to and buttress systemic racism [and] constitute a broad white-racist worldview" (Feagin 2001: 34). In addition to exposing silent racism, this study identifies passivity in white people, some of which is produced by the "not racist" category itself. Passivity emerged from the data in three forms: detachment from race matters, apprehension about being perceived as racist, and confusion about what is racist and what is not racist.

Other theorists have come to the conclusion that white people generally are racist. Blumer said in 1958 that white people as a group are racist in varying degrees. Findings here validate that statement unequivocally. Lewis Killian, in his 1990 presidential address to the Southern Sociological Society, expressed the idea as follows: "Who are the white racists—particularly in the eyes of the majority of whites who now claim to accept the principle of racial equality? It is not they themselves but those Klansmen and American Nazis and Skinheads. They themselves are innocent, for they have accepted the victories of the Civil Rights Movement" (Killian 1990: 4).

Killian uses irony to expose the fact that white people can both be racist and claim innocence. More recently Eduardo Bonilla-Silva (2003) has argued that white people generally are color blind, defined as seeing racial inequality as a result of causes other than racist practices. Most race theorists today, however, do not make this claim explicitly, leaving room for the possibility that some whites are not racist.

The decision to limit the topic of discussion to racism directed solely at black Americans when other minority groups are also routinely the objects of racism was a difficult one. In an effort to keep the discussions focused, however, I believed that limiting the topic of discussion to racism to one group was imperative. I chose racism against blacks because the literature in which this study is grounded focuses on racism toward blacks (see Blumer, Bonilla-Silva, Essed, Feagin, Frankenberg, Omi and Winant, and Wellman). In addition, data concerning racism toward Hispanics would likely have been tainted by rhetoric saturating the political climate in California in the early to mid-1990s, at the time the study was carried out.

Implementing the Study

I used small discussion groups, also called focus groups, as a format for data gathering. An advantage of this method over individual interviews is that using small, homogeneous groups is a more appropriate model when sensitive topics are discussed (Aaker and Day 1986; Churchill 1988). Because a frank discussion about racism relies upon a context of safety, focus groups were preferred for this study. I cannot know what data I might have collected in individual interviews, but I am confident that participants shared openly and honestly about their own racism in the small group format used here. I also sensed a feeling of group unity when, although joining the study entailed participating in only one discussion group, participants in several groups joked about when the group would meet again, an indication that they were open to such an idea.

After the participants for a particular group arrived, I explained that a discussion group differs from a support group in that interaction is encouraged rather than discouraged. Often, a participant was reminded of a childhood memory by another participant's comment.

Furthermore, group members were urged to engage with other participants, asking for clarification and even disagreeing with others' ideas if the occasion arose. In this way, I hoped to ensure that the groups would be dynamic, which would enhance the data. In addition, interaction within a group—called synergism—produces especially meaningful responses. For example, participants occasionally responded to another's comments by examining their own commonsense explanations. This occurred in one group when a participant, prompted by what another member of her group said, asked herself, "God, do I have any prejudices like that?" This example of synergism illustrates not only that group members are likely to be reminded of events by other members but also that participants have time in a group discussion to think about what has been said because they are not constantly under scrutiny. Observing interaction among the participants also contributed to an important finding: the importance of race awareness became evident as I noticed that several participants interrupted racism when they perceived it in their respective groups. This evidence was instrumental in the finding that race awareness is more important than whether well-meaning white people are racist.

Because I am a white woman and would be facilitating all of the focus groups, I limited the study to white women in order to ensure homogeneity in terms of gender and race/ethnicity. In addition, I was interested in looking at racism from the point of view of those performing it, and women seemed to be a logical choice because of their relative ease in engaging in open self-reflection and in articulating their emotions (Belenky et al. 1986; Spacks 1981). In addition, I wanted to explore subtle forms of racism in people who would ordinarily not be considered racist. The study flier, headlined "Women Against Racism," was expected to attract participants who were progressive in terms of race politics.

Knowledge often implies "mastery" and is associated with separation, not connection (Belenky et al. 1986: 101). One feminist scholar encourages researcher participation when she writes, "The goal of finding out about people through interviewing is best achieved when the relationship of interviewer and interviewee is nonhierarchical and when the interviewer is prepared to invest his or her own personal identity in the relationship" (Oakley 1981: 41). Although she refers to individual interviews in the preceding passage, her point is also valid for a group format. By investing my own "personal identity" in the groups, I facilitated "finding out about" participants by encouraging the process of self-exploration. During the discussions, my goal was for the participants to see me as part of the group.

Reciprocal self-disclosure refers to researchers' willingness to be open with participants about the topic under discussion in an attempt to create a dialogue rather than an interrogation by the interviewer (Bristow and Esper 1988). In Elissa Melamed's (1983) study of women and aging, also conducted in small groups, the author states, "The response to my candor was interesting. Immediately no one was neutral.... It prompted outpourings of acknowledgement, confusion, resentment, and fear" (Melamed 1983: 17). Following Melamed's model, I participated actively in all of the focus groups by becoming both a participant and a facilitator, disclosing examples of racism from my own experience when the discussion allowed.

Critics of in-depth interviewing, and of qualitative research itself, often express concern about whether researchers' bias influences the findings of their studies. Although I am clearly not neutral regarding the issue of racism, I would argue that my bias against racism did not influence the findings. Evidence of this is my acknowledgment that silent racism was identified in twenty-four participants, not all twenty-five—an example of what Weber called an *inconvenient fact* (see Weber [1918] 1958). The only participant who did not exhibit some form of racism was a quiet young woman in the pilot group. She did not share very much in her group, and she said nothing that I interpreted as racist. In addition, she was not asked if she had ever said or done anything that she later considered racist—a question that was added after the pilot study. My point is that rather than ignore this inconvenient fact in the analysis, I acknowledge and account for it, an indication of objectivity.

Facilitation of the groups consisted of asking questions intended to draw out information about topics such as early messages concerning race matters, experiences with black Americans, thoughts about the participants' own racism, and comments about their commitment to lessening racism.[3] The questions increased the likelihood that the content of the eight discussions would be somewhat consistent. However, each focus group had the flexibility to differ as participants introduced unique topics in their respective groups.

Conclusion

Throughout U.S. history a small group of white Americans has stood against the racist institutions of their day, including slavery and segregation. Perhaps the best-known antislavery activist is John Brown, an abolitionist and friend to many blacks. Brown and a small band of about twenty men, black and white, raided Harpers Ferry in 1859 in a failed attempt to provide firearms to black slaves in Virginia (Quarles 1974). Nine days later, Brown was tried and found guilty of treason. Permitted to speak in his own defense, Brown stated that the very Bible used in the court proceedings against him justified his actions and condemned slavery. On December 2, 1859, Brown was hanged and subsequently became a martyr to the antislavery cause (Fine 2001). Brown's death flamed antislavery passions, and, perhaps for the first time, abolition became a real prospect. The folk song "John Brown's Body"—initially sung by a federal regiment from Boston in 1861—is still familiar to blacks today although unfamiliar to many whites.[4] William Lloyd Garrison, another white antislavery activist at the time, was committed to a nonviolent approach against slavery until the death of John Brown. After Brown was hanged, Garrison's writing in a weekly publication thrust aside its pacifist tone, becoming more militant. Along with the efforts of former slave Frederick Douglass, Garrison and others were instrumental in furthering the abolitionist cause that eventually ended slavery.

Although blacks led the antisegregationist movement preceding the civil rights movement of the 1960s, antiracist whites played a secondary, but not unimportant, role. White antisegregationists, many from the South, took an unpopular stand against racist practices common in the South. One example is a committed ally of black Americans during the Jim Crow era, William Moore. A white postman originally from Mississippi, Moore lived in Baltimore, Maryland, when in the spring of 1963 he began a walk across five states to his home state. His goal was to deliver a letter denouncing Jim Crow laws to the governor of Mississippi, Ross Barnett, who the year before had fought desegregation at the University of Mississippi (Sterne 1968). Moore began his one-man march in Chattanooga, Tennessee, pulling a small wagon behind him. He walked through Virginia, North and South Carolina, and Georgia with a message painted on two wooden boards, one across his chest and the other across his back. One sign read, "Equal Rights for All: Mississippi or Bust," and the other said, "Black and White: Eat at Joe's" (Lipsitz 1998: ix). Moore was met with derision from whites along the way and was shot and killed on April 23, 1963, as he crossed the state line between Georgia and Alabama. Although the owner of the gun that shot Moore was arrested, he was not charged with a crime by the grand jury in Alabama. Nevertheless, some other whites in the South stood against segregation publicly as well as privately (Brown 2002).

Today, institutional racism, although not as obvious as slavery and segregation, is as pernicious as previous forms of racism. In addition, more obvious than institutional racism are racist comments and the telling of racist jokes. But today, even though taking a stand against racism does not have the serious repercussions it did in the past, rarely do whites take a stand against it.

In this chapter I have shown that the language used to talk about racism is important because it can obscure racism or illuminate it. The oppositional categories now in use—"racist" and "not racist"—obscure silent racism; a continuum ranging from "more racist" to "less racist" would illuminate it. I also have suggested that silent racism, which is rarely noticed by most whites, may be instrumental in the production of institutional racism. This could be important given that most sociologists and race theorists think that institutional racism is the cause of racial inequality.

In Chapter 2, silent racism emerges from the data in two forms: stereotypical images, and paternalistic assumptions. I present evidence that silent racism pervades the "not racist" category, illustrating how language—that is, the "racist/not racist" categories—can hide racism. An implication of this finding is that categorizing whites as either "racist" or "not racist" does not correspond with reality. Rethinking racism is important if changing the racial status quo is the goal.

In Chapter 3 I focus on passivity in well-meaning white people who sense little or no connection between their own lives and the racial status quo. The chapter also shows that the oppositional categories of racism not only hide silent racism but also produce unintended consequences that increase passivity in white people. Passivity includes apprehension about being racist and confusion about what is racist.

In Chapter 4 I proffer the theoretical argument that well-meaning white people perpetuate institutional racism through silent racism and passivity. Silent racism produces everyday racism and the racist practice that constitutes indirect institutional racism—the form of institutional racism that is not intended to cause negative effects for blacks but does so nonetheless (Feagin and Feagin 1994). Passivity endorses and encourages the racist decisions, actions, and policies of other white people. Chapter 4 also presents the theories of British sociologist Anthony Giddens and French sociologist Pierre Bourdieu to argue that individuals are implicated in the production of institutional racism and that focusing only on the macro level of analysis may provide an inadequate view of how racial inequality is produced.

I illustrate the importance of race awareness by presenting four sets of participants in Chapter 5 with various levels of race awareness. The comparisons show that high race awareness in well-meaning white people is essential to taking an antiracist stand. Furthermore, I show that correct information about racism alone does not produce the race awareness needed for an antiracist commitment. An essential component of race awareness is having close relationships with blacks and other people of color in which conversations about racism occur regularly.

I next explore the strategies for lessening institutional racism, presenting in Chapter 6 a theory of antiracist practice and the role of race awareness in that process. Participants' views about how to lessen racism are also presented as well as suggestions for facilitating race awareness workshops.

Chapter 7, the epilogue, captures the underlying theme of the previous chapters by reiterating how language, individuals, and institutional racism work together in creating the racial formation in place today in the United States. The epilogue explains that language shapes thinking by making it possible and by constraining it.

Notes

1. I use *black American* and *blacks* throughout the book because 66 percent of blacks prefer those terms, compared to 22 percent who prefer *African American* (Sigelman and Welch 1991). I also use the corresponding terms *white American* and *whites.* In addition, I follow most sociological race theorists as well as the *Chicago Manual of Style* in using lowercase letters for both *black* and *white.*

2. The term *silent racism* was first mentioned by my advisor, Kum-Kum Bhavnani, during a discussion about the early interviews for this study. I adopted the term, elaborating its meaning.

3. Questions posed to each of the participants were: What early messages did you get in your family concerning race issues? What experiences or relationships have you had with blacks? Can you think of a time when you did something that you now consider racist? What is your reaction if someone around you says or does something that is racist? What do you think needs to happen concerning racism? What role would you play?

4. Before this research, I had heard of John Brown but could not have told you who he was. I hadn't heard the song "John Brown's Body" until a black colleague who gave me feedback on this chapter sang it for me. She also informed me that where she grew up (Chicago), all the black children learned the song.

Chapter Two

Silent Racism

SILENT RACISM IS A CULTURAL PHENOMENON, not a psychological one. This does not imply that all white people are affected in a similar way, but it does imply that all whites are infected. No one is immune to ideas that permeate the culture in which he or she is raised. *Silent racism* here refers to unspoken negative thoughts, emotions, and assumptions about black Americans that dwell in the minds of white Americans, including well-meaning whites that care about racial equality, some of which are called "new abolitionists" (Winant 2004: 10). Limited to ideas in people's minds, silent racism is unspoken. It therefore does not refer to racist statements or actions referred to as everyday racism (Essed 1991); rather, *silent racism* refers to the negative thoughts and beliefs that fuel everyday racism and other racist action. Silent racism stems from the racist ideology that permeates U.S. society and inhabits the minds of all white people.[1]

Silent racism is not the same as prejudice, which refers to an individual's attitude about a particular social group. Attitudes are presumed to be composed of individual expressions that correspond closely with underlying thoughts and emotions, and they are seen as consistent over time (Jackman 1994). In contrast, silent racism refers to the *shared* images and assumptions of members of the dominant group about the subordinate group, in this case black Americans (Blumer 1958). The images and assumptions derive from the dominant ideology, which is fluid and piecemeal, transforming itself as needed (Jackman 1994).

In this chapter I will first summarize concepts similar to silent racism that are derived from the social psychology literature, namely prejudice and more recent forms of racism that have been identified: symbolic racism and aversive racism. I then turn to the contemporary sociological race theories that were instrumental in the development of silent racism as a concept. This is followed by extracts from the focus groups, specifically, the racist thoughts and feelings voiced by participants.[2] Their accounts provide evidence that the "not racist" category is filled with silent racism. (See Appendix A for a full account of the methods used in this study.) In the conclusion of the chapter I maintain that the "racist" and "not racist" categories are no longer meaningful and that they hide silent racism and its link to institutional racism.

Social Psychological Race Theories

Although largely disregarded by sociological race theorists today in favor of a macro approach, the concept of prejudice (Allport 1954) continues to be prevalent in sociological textbooks, especially introductory texts. For example, *prejudice* is defined as a "rigid and irrational" attitude toward blacks (Macionis 2001: 357) and as a "rigidly held" attitude toward minorities (Newman 2000: 395). Gordon Allport posits that the negative thoughts and feelings of whites about blacks consist of a variety of emotions and beliefs: hostility, white superiority, and disdain for those seen as inherently different from themselves. The attitudes depicted by Allport as prejudicial are seen as intractable manifestations of an authoritarian personality type, a concept developed by Theodore Adorno and his colleagues (1950) of the Frankfurt School. The concept of prejudice, while widely used by social psychologists in reference to negative attitudes of whites toward minority groups (Devine 1989; Gaertner and Dovidio 1986; Monteith 1992), no longer retains the idea that it is an immutable personality trait. Rather, prejudice is seen as closely associated with stereotypes about blacks and ethnic minorities.

Social psychologists point out that racism has not necessarily lessened since the 1960s civil rights movement as conservatives such as Stephan Thernstrom and Abigail Thernstrom (1997) claim, but has become less obvious. The new kinds of prejudice, like symbolic racism (sometimes called modern racism) and aversive racism, refer to the idea that overt racism has mutated into more subtle forms since the civil rights movement.

Symbolic Racism

Symbolic racism (Sears and Kinder 1971; Sears and McConahay 1973), sometimes referred to as modern racism (McConahay and Hough 1976), refers to racism that is fueled by a sense that blacks are being allowed to make unfair gains at the expense of whites. Symbolic racism more specifically refers to a combination of racial bias against blacks plus the conservative value of individualism (Sears 1988). Race-related policies intended to assist blacks and other minorities in achieving racial parity are objected to on the grounds that individuals should be responsible for their own welfare, not society.

Symbolic racism is expressed in voting behavior against candidates who favor racial equality. This form of racism is spurred by beliefs that blacks are too demanding, that they are getting more than they deserve, that they do not conform to traditional values, and that they want to be supported by the government (Brewer and Kramer 1985). Beliefs such as these are publicized in the media by conservative talk show hosts, increasing the negative beliefs about blacks, especially black males. The southern strategy proposed by Richard Nixon in the 1972 presidential campaign is related to these ideas. Called positive polarization, the strategy for Nixon was to pit angry white voters in the South against black voters. The strategy worked, and the South has since largely backed Republican conservative candidates, many of whom use the southern strategy.

The 1992 presidential election lends support to the concept of symbolic racism. Unlike liberal/progressive Democratic candidates, Bill Clinton distanced himself from black politician Jessie Jackson during the campaign by attacking Sista Souljah—a rap artist—thereby lessening the impression that he would cater to black demands. This strategy did not seem to cost Clinton black votes, however, and may have increased his number of white votes, helping to ensure the election victory. Clinton's strategy of moving away from Jackson, who stands for racial equality, added to his appeal with some white voters whose votes symbolically reject racial equality.

Symbolic or modern racists do not see themselves as racist; they see themselves as victims of unfair government policies regulating race matters. For them, racial discrimination ended with the passage of the Civil Rights Act of 1964 and the Voting Rights Act of 1965. Conservative values such as self-reliance and individual responsibility are used to illustrate that people (namely blacks and other minorities) who need government support are lazy and expect a government handout. It follows that symbolic (or modern) racists would defend the racial status quo. This view of racism portrays antiblack animus as deep-seated and therefore resistant to change. Silent racism, in contrast, is found not only in people who disdain support for minorities but also in well-meaning whites who are sympathetic to blacks' location in society.

Aversive Racism

Originally, *aversive racism* was defined as negative bias against blacks (Kovel 1970). More recently, the term has been expanded to include any racist feeling or thought, which—perceived by the person having it as deplorable—must be suppressed (Gaertner and Dovidio 1986). According to the current definition, aversive racism occurs when negative feelings toward blacks are denied in order for well-intentioned whites to maintain a valued self-image as "not racist." A central focus of the perspective concerns norms against discrimination. This theory posits that when the parameters of a situation are clearly defined, aversive racists treat everyone the same, black or white. However, when the situation is less clearly defined and the other person is not clearly white or black, discrimination is more likely to occur (Gaertner and Dovidio 1986). Aversive racists discriminate, but never when their discrimination would be obviously racist. Unlike symbolic racism, which is linked to conservative politics, aversive racism is closely related to self-proclaimed liberals. Aversive racism and silent racism are related in that the tendency to avoid mentioning race is acknowledged by several of the participants in this study. However, I argue that in these cases the avoidance of race is due to apprehension, which results from the negative effects of the "not racist" category rather than from animus toward blacks, as Samuel Gaertner and James Dovidio argue.

Although racism has changed over time, some scholars believe that the new racism theories do not account for the change (Bobo 1988). New theories of racism focus primarily on people's emotions and do not account for racial inequality as a structure in society. However, in making this argument, Lawrence Bobo separates individuals from structural processes such as institutional racism, a separation that is artificial.

Sociological Race Theories

Systemic racism refers to the "ideologies, attitudes, and institutions created to preserve white advantage and power" (Feagin 2001: 16). Whether the ideas, attitudes, and institutions of U.S. society were created *in order* to preserve white advantage may be disputed; however, sociological race theory clearly documents that the ideas, attitudes, and institutions of mainstream America do, indeed, preserve white advantage. My goal, suggested in this book's title, is to illustrate how well-meaning whites participate in the process, more often than not without realizing it.

That racism results from the relative group position of whites vis-à-vis blacks (Blumer 1958b, 1965) is fundamental to sociological race theory today. The sociological view is markedly different from Allport's more individualistic concept of prejudice as well as from the new racisms developed by social psychologists such as symbolic racism and aversive racism. The fundamental difference is that social psychologists see racism as a deep-seated psychological phenomenon that occurs in some whites but not in all of them. The sociological view that racism is a group phenomenon, in contrast, implies that racist thoughts and assumptions are located in the minds of white Americans as a group—that is, all whites. Sociological race theory, like sociological theory generally, takes into account the historical, cultural, and societal conditions that contribute to a phenomenon. Elements of these conditions are present in the theories that form the foundation for the ideas developed in this chapter.

Historically, the emotional aspects of racism—hostility, disgust, and particularly fear—have resided within the minds of white people over time and continue to be manifested in some form today (Kovel 1970). During slavery, physical domination was often marked by feelings of hostility that whites held toward blacks. Called *dominative racism,* hostility is the most virulent form of racism. During the Reconstruction era, feelings of disgust and/or fear by whites toward blacks emerged as segregation and legal discrimination against blacks became the law of the land. Called *aversive racism,* these emotions—especially fear—

were widely held by whites, whether or not they lived in the South. Since the civil rights movement, psychological and emotional dimensions of racism have been displaced onto economic structures and are characterized by beliefs of entitlement regarding the economic position of whites vis-à-vis blacks (Kovel 1970). Called *metaracism,* this concept became the basis for white privilege (Wellman 1977). Although each aspect of racism in this representation is identified with a specific period in time, psychological traces of the first two phases—unconscious feelings of hostility, disgust, and fear—continue to manifest themselves in the third phase.

Culturally, structures of oppression such as slavery and segregation are upheld by dominant beliefs of white Americans about black Americans (Turner and Singleton 1978). And, although dominant beliefs justify and reinforce the negative emotions toward blacks outlined earlier, progressive beliefs have at times contradicted the dominant beliefs and opposed a given structure of oppression such as slavery or segregation. Moreover, progressive beliefs may have been instrumental in producing social change when it has occurred: "Changes in the structure of oppression appear most likely to occur during, or immediately after, those periods when conflict between dominant and progressive beliefs is greatest and when progressive beliefs severely challenge the structure of oppression" (Turner and Singleton 1978: 1004). Clearly, cultural beliefs alone do not cause change in social structures; however, progressive beliefs are a key element in the process. This view lends credence to my claim that changing how race-progressive whites view racism is important in changing the racial status quo.

Societal factors central to race theory concern the interplay between individuals and institutions. The theory of racial formation (Omi and Winant 1986, 1994) views race as a fundamental organizing principle, stressing its immediacy in everyday life. The role of ideology and its focus on *process* is a distinguishing feature of this view. *Racial formation* refers to "the process by which social, economic, and political forces determine the content and importance of racial categories, and by which they are in turn shaped by racial meanings" (Omi and Winant 1986: 61). At the macro level, race is an organizing principle of social structures, such as the economy. At the micro level, individuals carry out the "rules of racial etiquette" described in the following paragraphs.

Ideology is important in the maintenance of racism in U.S. culture. And, although racial ideology in the U.S. has changed over time, the existence of an ideology regarding race has remained constant. Common sense, used here as Gramsci (1971) described it, refers to assumptions and beliefs, taken for granted and sometimes contradictory, that produce an ideological structure within which everyone operates. The prevailing racial ideology not only pervades everyone's thinking—both blacks and whites—but a "racial etiquette" is the result (Omi and Winant 1986: 62). Racial etiquette refers to the "rules shaped by our perception of race [that] determine the presentation of self ... and appropriate modes of conduct" (Omi and Winant 1986: 62). An example of racial etiquette in well-intentioned whites occurs when they rigidly *avoid* mentioning racial difference, as though it is not noticed. The theory of racial formation and racial etiquette are fundamental to the ideas that emerged from this study, especially the theory that well-meaning white people are instrumental in the production of institutional racism.

Everyday Racism

The concept of everyday racism (Essed 1991) refers to routine actions that go unquestioned by members of the dominant group, which in some way discriminate against members of a racial or ethnic category. The concept of silent racism is closely linked to this concept in that silent racism precedes everyday racism; silent racism constitutes the platform on which everyday racism is enacted. Silent racism predisposes white people to commit or collude with routine practices that are perceived by blacks as everyday racism. Silent racism is the cognitive aspect of everyday racism—in contrast to the behavioral aspect. Silent racism underpins the "broad white-racist worldview" (Feagin 2001: 34) and inhabits the minds of all white Americans.

Color-Blind Racism

Eduardo Bonilla-Silva's (2003) concept of color-blind racism is perhaps the idea most closely related to silent racism. Bonilla-Silva posits that the viewpoint that race is no longer important is an attempt to maintain white privilege without appearing racist. He identifies four frames of color-blind racism: *abstract liberalism*—the idea that liberal notions such as equality, which was a cornerstone of the civil rights movement, are now used to oppose affirmation action on the grounds that all groups should be treated the same; *naturalization*—the idea that racial patterns such as informal segregation are natural, for example, that blacks prefer to live in black neighborhoods; *cultural racism*—the idea that norms within the black culture account for racial inequality; and the *minimization of racism*—the idea that racism ended with passage of civil rights legislation.

I agree with Bonilla-Silva (2003) on the fundamental points of his theory: that all whites are influenced by the racial ideology, and therefore all whites are somewhat racist; that people who are antiracist are also racist and that therefore the category "not racist" is a misnomer; that the segment of whites least likely to exhibit racism is progressive white women who have, or have had, relationships with people of color; and that progressive whites should take their attention away from whether or not they are racist and focus on antiracist action. Nevertheless, my perspective differs from Bonilla-Silva's in that I have exposed a third form of racism in addition to the overt racism of bigots and the color-blind racism that he portrays: silent racism in well-meaning white people. In terms of the racism continuum I am posing, the blatant racism of bigots would go at the "more racist" end of the continuum, color-blind racism would take up the center of the continuum (labelled moderately racist), and silent racism would go at the "less racist" end. I do not mean to imply that the three forms of racism occupy equal space on the continuum. To the contrary, color-blind racism would indeed occupy a considerable portion of the continuum. See Figure 2.1 for a depiction of types of racism on the racism continuum.

The Study of Silent Racism

The participants in this study are young and highly educated. Over half—fourteen of the twenty-five women who participated—are

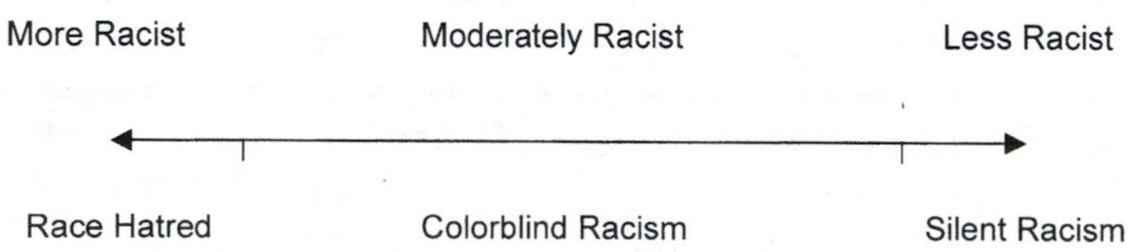

Figure 2.1 Racism on the Racism Continuum

young adults (between 18 and 29 years old); eight women fall into a middle range (34 to 47 years old); and three women are elders (68 to 76 years old). Twenty of the twenty-five participants hold college degrees. Seven of the women who have graduated from college are in graduate school, and three have master's degrees.

Other demographic data of interest include occupation and geographic region. Seven of the full-time students did not mention any other line of work. Of the remaining eighteen participants, occupations include clerical work and business (ten participants), the health and mental health fields (three), teaching (two), service (two), and full-time homemaking (one).[3]

Eleven of the twenty-five women interviewed have lived in California most of their lives. The remainder had lived in the Northeast, the South and Southwest, the Northwest, and the Midwest before moving to California. Of the demographic variables, only region appears to be relevant to silent racism: Three of the four participants who reveal paternalistic assumptions were originally from the South.

Edward T. Hall's (1959) theory of culture is pivotal in explaining the pervasiveness and operation of silent racism. Hall differentiates between formal and informal learning. Formal learning involves both teacher and student, with the teacher playing an active role in correcting the student when a mistake is made. Informal learning, in comparison, often occurs "out of awareness" (Hall 1959: 96), with the learner modeling others without either party being aware of it. People are taught formally that racism is wrong; however, people learn the negative thoughts, emotions, and attitudes that comprise silent racism by informally mimicking parents, teachers, peers, and the media. Hall's point does not imply that silent racism is unconscious. Ideas that are not in people's awareness are not necessarily in their unconscious (Hall 1959). Learning racism informally is aptly expressed by a participant named Lisa. See Appendix B for a list of participant names in each focus group with a brief biography of each participant. Lisa said:

> I was explicitly told that racism is wrong, that they (her parents) are not racist, and that I shouldn't be racist, and that anyone decent wouldn't be. Yet at the same time I got the distinct feeling that they were uncomfortable about [the black neighbors]. If I just tried to picture them meeting a black person on the street, even though I can't really remember that, I'd know the look on their faces and the way their bodies would

> tense up ... and no real explanation as to why. So I got, I think, a very deep message of underlying fear; that they intensely feared blacks.

Because Lisa's parents could not or would not tell her how they felt about blacks, she picked up the fear implied by their body language rather than through words stated explicitly. Lisa learned two lessons about blacks from her parents: a formal lesson (don't be racist), and an informal one (blacks are to be feared). It is the lessons learned informally that people do not scrutinize and that therefore are more likely to be expressed without our knowing.

There are two primary manifestations of silent racism: *stereotypical images* that set black Americans, as a group, apart from white Americans, and *paternalistic assumptions* that denote a sense of superiority in some whites in comparison to blacks.[4] Whites believe that blacks are inherently different from themselves (stereotypical images), and whites believe that blacks are inferior to themselves and need protection (paternalistic assumptions). Stereotypical images concerning black Americans result from the misinformation and false messages learned informally by most white Americans that distinguish blacks as "different." Paternalistic assumptions result from a sense of false responsibility toward black Americans that produces a condescending attitude. The fundamental difference between the two forms of silent racism is that stereotypical images are ideas about a "conceptualized group" (Killian 1990: 184), whereas paternalistic assumptions emerge in actual relationships between blacks and whites. Stereotypical images therefore are more common than paternalistic assumptions due to the fact that all whites learn negative stereotypes about blacks as a group but relatively few whites have close relationships with blacks.

Stereotypical Images

Racial stereotypes fill the definitions of white Americans, maintained through "talk, tales, stories, gossip, anecdotes ... and the like" (Blumer 1958b: 5). Statements or experiences of twenty-two of the twenty-five participants in this study portray stereotypical images concerning blacks. The stereotypes held by the participants in this study are not unique. What is remarkable is that the women who disclosed them are plausibly categorized in the oppositional categories as "not racist." Kelly began the discussion as she related the origin of her stereotypes about black Americans:

> When I think about my prejudice, so much of it is about what I've seen on television. Let's think of the mother of the fellow in the Denny trial (associated with the Los Angeles riots that followed the not-guilty verdict in the Rodney King beating case). It's so easy to look at her and think, "She's ignorant, this is possibly not a literate person." There's this whole category of people, you could think that the ghetto is full of these women who are [pause] not intelligent and not literate, because that's what you see in the news. You see people who appear not to be educated, and who are somehow or another implicated in the violence within the ghetto.

Kelly links class, race, and gender characteristics in her description of poor black women whom she presumes to be illiterate and associated with crime in some way. This depiction captures the concept of matrix of domination, which illustrates how the subordinated identities regarding race, class, and gender are inextricalby linked in the structure of society (Collins 1990) and, I would add, in the minds of well-meaning white people. Kelly seems to indicate that she is not racist against all black Americans, just poor ones. She continued,

> But I think there is a huge [black] middle class and all kinds of intelligent professional black women; I see them out on the streets every day. But what comes across in the news is [something else]. I'm delighted when—[tries to think of the name Lani Guinier] I'm confused, who did [Clinton] nominate? Anyway, he made an appointment, so that's good news. But I think there's a massive population of black middle-class women, but we don't see them. We see them on the *Cosby* show, then there's all these poor.

Kelly says that the media obscure the existence of a "huge" and "massive" black middle class, a point that has some merit—the black middle class is obscured by the media. However, Kelly overstates the size of the black middle class in comparison to the black population as a whole, a distortion that glosses over the "myth of the black middle class," a myth that does not acknowledge the economic lack of correspondence between the black middle class and the white middle class (Steinberg 1995: 179). Insightful accounts of the black middle class also illustrate important differences between the white and black middle classes (see Feagin and Sikes 1994).

Stereotypical images in the minds of white people are often expressed unintentionally. When I asked the participants if they had ever realized after the fact that something they had said or done was racist,

Martha shared the following: "Just yesterday I was tutoring a student and she pointed out that she was born in Uganda, [a fact that] made her very different—her perception of the world was international. I said, 'Gosh, that's wonderful, because when other people see you they might just think African American but really you've got this other quality.' And I didn't know whether to apologize or just take my foot out of my mouth and go on." Martha's statement indicates a devaluation of black Americans compared to Africans, exoticizing the latter. Both references—the discrediting one toward black Americans and the complimentary one toward Africans—are based on stereotypical images that saturate the racial discourse.

Martha's comment illustrates that people who are aware of racism, including their own, also adopt fragments of a racist ideology based on group position. I am convinced that the racist statement made by Martha is not related to color-blind racism, the defense of white privilege, or any of the social psychological forms of modern racism. Rather, the statement is a reflection of the culture we live in: one that discredits black Americans. Silent racism is not deep-seated or the result of psychological ambivalence. Nevertheless, the thoughts are prevalent, and they matter because they result in everyday racism as well as form the basis for indirect institutional racism, the topic of Chapter 4.

Anne spoke about a black family that lived next door to her family in New York as she was growing up. She said that Cassie, a girl her age, became a close friend, but that she was "messed up ... her [single] mom was poor and had a lot of problems, including drugs." Anne subsequently talked to her mother about her old neighbors and discovered that, in fact, Cassie had a stepfather, her family was in the middle class, and her mother was not involved with drugs. In her journal Anne expressed dismay that she had been so thoroughly affected by racist discourse that she unwittingly changed her childhood memories to accommodate it.

Unlike Kelly, both Martha and Anne expressed a high level of awareness about the stereotypes that shape their views of the world. Martha immediately recognized that her behavior had been racist, guided by the stereotypes embedded within her perspective. Similarly, Anne recognized that she had adopted stereotypes from a society that had influenced her perception of the past. Regret on Martha's part and disappointment on Anne's suggest that these participants are not defending the racial status quo, an earmark of defending white privilege or expressing color-blind racism. It also illustrates that neither of these women cling to "deep-seated" racist notions; indeed, both seem genuinely eager to give them up. Although lacking the race awareness evident in Martha and Anne, Kelly also does not exhibit a defense of white privilege. To the contrary, she is supportive of the black middle class, disparaging only of blacks in the "ghetto."[5]

Vanessa also exhibited stereotypical images; however, her example is far more egregious than those of Martha and Anne, or even Kelly. The stereotypical image expressed by Vanessa is rooted in biological determinism, exemplified in *The Bell Curve* (Herrnstein and Murray 1995). Herrnstein and Murray use racial differences in intelligence quotient (IQ) not only as justification for the material inequality between black and white Americans but also as the explanation for high unemployment and incarceration rates for black men relative to white men. Vanessa said, "And cherish the differences; respect them. And that's why . . . even this thing about the IQ tests for different races where the blacks never can come out as high on the IQ tests—they say the tests are racially biased, of course there's a whole lot of that because, when you're brought up in a home with black language, the standard language doesn't come as easy."

Sensing where Vanessa was going with her comments, I agreed with her that reading the questions on IQ tests is often difficult for some groups, but I added also that language skills are not inherent. Vanessa then added, "Sure. But so there *is* a difference among the races. Maybe the black races are not as verbally developed, and they are more developed in other ways." I intervened again at that point, asking, "If language is [just] different, why would that assumption be there, [the assumption] that they're not 'as developed?'" Vanessa replied, "I mean, even if it were, and I'm not assuming it were, but even *if* it were, that races are different—and it's quite understandable that they are because they're genetically propagated groups—races are different by definition. And it wouldn't be at all surprising if one or another trait became better in one group than another. And I don't see that [they] should be looked down on because of that." Vanessa's thinking is based on highly disputed assumptions that are presented as fact in the Herrnstein and Murray (1994) book on race differences and IQ. Vanessa's words, "I don't see that it should be looked down on because of that" seem to say that a trait such as low intelligence—a characteristic that *is* seen by most white Americans as a deficiency—should not be "looked down upon," a view that is dubious at best.

Whiteliness (Frye 1992) refers to having a white perspective. Whiteliness entails a white bias, containing white value judgments. Some stereotypical images result from seeing with a white perspective. For example, Kelly said, "I love Latin culture. I like Mexican history, anything that's Latin American. I think the differences are all really wonderful, but it's not okay to celebrate *black* cultural difference." I asked Kelly if she thought that blacks would agree with her. She responded, shaking her head, "I don't know. I just don't know." Kelly, who has studied Mexican culture, appears to have a deep appreciation of it and of how it differs from her own (white) culture. In contrast, her notion that celebrating black cultural difference is "not okay" seems to signify a deprived image of black culture, presumably due to having much misinformation about it in her white perspective. Kelly's definition of black culture clearly differs from bell hooks's (1990 and 2001) definition or any number of other black writers. Whiteliness helps explain why silent racism is pervasive in white people.

In several of the groups, I shared an experience that also illustrates the blinders of a white perspective. I said,

> I had an incident right after the Los Angeles uprisings [again, following the not-guilty verdict in the Rodney King beating case]. I talked to a black friend of mine [Ralene] and in the conversation—it's embarrassing to say this—I said, "I'm so sorry about what happened in L.A.," as if somehow the tragedy was worse for her than for me [or other whites]. I found out later that Ralene had been hurt to discover that I perceived our relationships to the event in L.A. differently simply because I am white and she is black, that being the only difference between us. I see now that our relationships to the uprising do *not* differ in the sense that I had supposed—the tragedy in Los Angeles was as much mine as it was hers.

My white perspective in this instance caused pain primarily because Ralene assumed that I knew better—that I had more race awareness than I did at the time. It is important to note that a mutual friend informed me about Ralene's distress over my misplaced sympathy; I did not figure it out for myself. My white definition of the situation, what Bonilla-Silva calls "white habitus" (2003: 104), insulated me from knowing that I had said something that would upset my friend.

A mutual friend, who is white, called and told me of Ralene's reaction. The friend has a good deal of race awareness and decided that she would intervene. The importance of intervention, either by the person experiencing the discrimination or by allies, who Goffman (1963) calls "wise ones"—that is, those who understand discrimination even though they do not experience it—illustrates the importance of race awareness.

Assuming that race issues affect only black Americans and other people of color is at the heart of whiteliness and is evidence of silent racism. Ignorance concerning race matters is a privilege of the dominant group, one that perpetuates racism. Because the repercussions of white ignorance about race matters fall upon black Americans and other minorities, not white Americans, the importance of learning about race issues goes unnoticed by whites. Educational institutions have traditionally colluded in the construction of a racist culture by affirming national identity in terms that are exclusionary and often racist (Giroux 1994). All too often, attempts to expand the curricula in U.S. schools have been limited to a fascination with differing cultural identities and a celebration of tolerance, a term that itself implies that minority groups deviate from the white norm and must be put up with as an act of charity.

Examples of other stereotypical images fueled by having a white perspective include Ruth's acknowledgment that she has at times unintentionally spotlighted race unnecessarily, such as referring to a good student in her class as "a bright black student." Ruth said that a colleague asked why she mentioned the student's race, a question that made her think about it for the first time. (Ruth's entire statement about this incident can be found in Chapter 5.) At the time of the incident, Ruth was unaware that she perceived the bright student's race as noteworthy solely because of the stereotype that black students are not as bright as white students. However, her acknowledgment of having "slipped" in her comment about the bright student in the focus group indicates that Ruth's level of race awareness had increased by the time she came to the study. Like mine, Ruth's newfound race awareness came from someone else; she did not figure it out on her own. Nevertheless, neither Ruth's nor my silent racism was so deep-seated that we could not recognize it once it was pointed out and acknowledge it rather than defend it.

Emotions and Silent Racism

Stereotypical images often have an emotional component. The fear of black men derives from the stereotype that they are dangerous and threatening (Clark 1991; Hernton [1965] 1988; hooks 1990). The historical notion of black men as "beasts" was often used to justify lynching in the South (Fredrickson 1971: 275). Jean shared the following story concerning her fear of black men:

> Two other white women and I had attended a stage show [in San Francisco] when we found ourselves in the rain, blocks from our hotel. An African American man with an airport van waved, offering us a ride. I went into a panic. I thought, "Well?" I really thought about that, you know, like, did I have a reason to be afraid? I don't have to take a taxi a lot, so I'm not used to getting into a vehicle with other people. But if he had been white, would I have felt differently about it? It made me think for weeks after that, trying to come up with an answer.

Jean's phrase "I went into a panic" signifies the emotionally charged aspect of her definition of the situation she found herself in. Individuals construct emotions, and their definitions and interpretations are "critical to this often emergent process" (Shott 1979: 1323). Whatever inner cues Jean experienced—rapid breathing, increased heartbeat, or some other sensation—she interpreted them as "fear." Jean's acknowledgment that she might have reacted differently if the driver had been white indicates that her intense emotional reaction resulted from the stereotypical image of black men as dangerous (Clark 1991). Jean considered her reaction to the van driver to be both inappropriate and troubling; she defined her reaction as a negative emotion and is aware that black men encounter such reactions repeatedly in their everyday lives (Cose 1993).

Violet also expressed her fear of black men when she said, "I know that I react more [to black men].... I'm afraid of all strange men when I walk around, but I'm more afraid of black men, especially when I encounter them in a group. I've thought about why that is, and I try not to respond. I try to censor myself so I won't feel that. I know that I don't feel it about other racial groups, so I know that it's really something." Like Jean, Violet sees her fear of black men as inappropriate and troubling. Two comments, "I'm more afraid of black men" and "I know it's really something," lend evidence to the idea that her fear of black men differs from her fear of other men and that she is aware of the difference.

Both Jean and Violet appear perplexed by the intensity of their fear, even after considerable reflection. Jean commented that she tried to "come up with an answer" for weeks; Violet said that she has "thought about why that is." Despite their efforts, their ruminations have been fruitless. Violet mentioned that she tries "not to respond" with fear when she encounters a black man, and yet both her comments and those of Jean indicate that their intention not to avoid black men is overridden by their fear of them.

In an attempt to discover the roots of Violet's fear, I prompted her further, asking if she knows where her fear comes from. She replied, "Probably my mom locking [the car] door in certain parts of town. It's something that I have thought a lot about and worked hard on, but it's also hard to work my way out of it." Violet's response, that her fear of black men may have come from her mother's behavior in "certain parts of town," indicates that her fear was learned informally and likely resulted from the stereotypical association of black men with crime or perhaps with sexual violence.

Joan, who was in Violet's group, was reminded that she had experienced a fear similar to Violet's. Joan told about a time when she and a female friend were in San Francisco. She said, "I was on Haight in San Francisco, and it was dark, and I was nervous when I realized that ... there were men around me. But when I realized they were black men around me I was *really* nervous, and I [pause], it is something that I just was."

I also asked Joan to speculate about where her fear comes from. She responded, "Maybe reality, to a certain extent. We [had] just walked through a project earlier and somebody yelled something and it scared me, so I was sort of on edge anyway." Joan's characterization illustrates that she sees her response differently from Jean and Violet. She does not consider her response to be troubling because she does not consider her fear of black men to be irrational or racist. Joan's comment in this exchange, "it is something that I *just was,*" seems to attribute the cause of her response to something outside of her. In other words, she believed that her fear was a rational response to the situation itself.

Violet spoke to Joan, making the point that "statistically, victims of crime are predominantly people of color, not white women. Black on white crime, especially concerning white women, is very [rare].... I have that kind of fear too but I classify it as irrational," Violet added. Joan then responded to Violet, "Well, I see it as irrational as far as statistics [go], but I also see it as, there I am, probably looking like I'm from out of town, and I don't have a real nose-to-the-grindstone street sense because I'm not living in the city, and I look like, I'm sure I look vulnerable, and I probably am." Joan answered Violet's attempt to reframe the fear of black men as irrational by conceding that it was irrational "as far as statistics" go, implying that there is a limit to a statistical argument. Joan then complicated the issue by introducing a new factor into the equation:

> So it's irrational in that it doesn't matter if it's a black or a white man, but just one layer gets [added] on [to] another layer. It's interesting too because what isn't rational at all is [that] what else frightens me in that situation is [if I encounter] a really scraggly white guy that's intoxicated. [That frightens me] as much as if I turn around and see black skin. What's irrational is that the drunk guy probably [really] is frightening for [good] reasons, but the black guy isn't.

Joan appeared at first to concede that the fear of black men is irrational when she added that "what *else* frightens her" irrationally is "a really scraggly white guy that's intoxicated." The comparison between a "scraggly drunk" white man and a black man (presumably not scraggly and not drunk) began as an attempt to illustrate that irrational fears are not necessarily racist. However, Joan abandoned the analogy and finished by repeating, "I don't know" several times, shaking her head from side to side as though she can no longer make sense of what she is saying. Joan's apparent incoherence may be explained by "incursions into forbidden issues" (Bonilla-Silva 2003: 54). Incoherence is not uncommon when whites speak of a particular race matter that they suddenly feel is not appropriate to talk about in the post–civil rights era.

In an effort to ease Joan's discomfort I suggested that her fear of the black men in San Francisco might have been a result of being in unfamiliar surroundings. She replied, "But if those were women—a white scraggly drunk woman or a black woman—I wouldn't have the same fear factor." The introduction of gender as a factor may have been a diversionary tactic for Joan, intended to counteract the incoherence in her earlier comparison between black and white men.

Joan's defensiveness about her remarks may also indicate a need to demonstrate that she is "not racist."

Joan is not necessarily more racist than Jean or Violet—her fear of black men is no more intense than theirs; all three women seem to have strong emotions in response to stereotypical images of black men. However, Joan's account of *why* she experienced the fear differed from the other two in that she sees the fear as rational, not irrational, and she does not see it as racist, as Jean and Violet do. Joan differs from the others in her level of race awareness, her understanding of how racism works and her implication in it. I would add that, although Joan is defensive in her account, she does not defend white privilege; rather, she defends against the possibility that she may have said something racist. Neither is her racism color-blind. Indeed, she drew a distinction between her responses to black and white men. Joan's incoherence appears to signify her discomfort in discussing an issue that is normally taboo in today's racially charged environment.

Katie also expressed irrational racism when she painted a portrait of her family that reveals a heightened suspicion of black Americans' intentions. Katie revealed the following about her relatives'—and quite likely her own—definition of blacks when she said, "A lot of white people think that black people want your things. They don't [just] want to have the same kind of stereos you do, they want *your* stereo—they want you to *not* have it." I asked Katie who "they" referred to. She answered, "I've actually heard my aunts and uncles say this kind of stuff. It's almost like a personal thing. You see a black person and you automatically perceive that they want what you have. It's like this very paranoid scared protectiveness about your things."

Katie assumed that my question about who "they" were referred to her relatives rather than the black Americans she was describing. Nevertheless, Katie then inadvertently answered my question when she added, "You see a black person and you automatically perceive that they want what you have"—a reference to blacks in general, and a blatant stereotype. The tone of the words, "they want *your* stereo, they want you *not* to have it," seems to imply that black Americans are inherently menacing, a notion that is highly inflammatory. Katie repeats her relatives' racist viewpoint without any disclaimer that would have distanced her from their beliefs.

The following exchange resulted from another comment from Katie. I include the exchange in its entirety because the other participants and I (indicated by the initials *BT*) joined forces in disputing Katie's suggestion, a situation that seems to expose the nonsensical nature of her argument to everyone except Katie:

> **Katie:** I don't know what you all are going to think of this, but I wonder sometimes, because there have been ... philosophers like Marcus Garvey who said the solution was to repatriate back to Africa.[6] To go back to where their heritage is, where ... I mean, I guess there is still neocolonialism ...
>
> **Martha:** You are talking about a whole continent. Which part?
>
> **Katie:** I know, that's true, but from where their roots came from, I guess. But I don't know if it's too late to find out for a lot of people, but sometimes I wonder, why do they stay [in the U.S.]? Why don't they give up? It would suck to have this to overcome!
>
> **Julie:** It would suck more in many places. I mean, Africa?
>
> **Katie:** Yeah, because there is so much neocolonialism that ...
>
> **Martha:** How could you try to regain the tribal culture when your whole culture has been 500 years of being in America?
>
> **Julie:** It would be easier for me to say I'll go back to Wales or something.
>
> **Martha:** And even then people would laugh at you like, "Why are you here?" I can't go back to Scotland—I'm not Scottish.
>
> **Katie:** But I just wonder.... Do you know who Marcus Garvey is?
>
> **BT:** I can see why a black American might think that, philosophically, but I think it's a very different thing for white people to consider that might be a solution.
>
> **Katie:** I know that there must be a lot of connection to where you grow up. It's almost like a sort of instinct to hang onto the place where you grew up. But it's kind of like twisted when things turn into gangs and the whole idea of turf, and claiming certain neighborhoods and all that. It becomes such a terrible place.... I mean, I guess I've just wondered that because if it was me I would leave. I would try and find someplace where it didn't feel ... maybe that's a cheap way out, just trying to find

a place where the people treat you normally instead of trying to face the gargantuan problem of trying to change a zillion people so that the people that you come into contact with don't treat you ...

JULIE: But [blacks] wouldn't be treated normally if [they] went to Africa right now.

KATIE: No, but you know, anywhere, somewhere ...

BT: The truth is, American blacks that go to Africa are [considered] American, not African.

KATIE: I was just wondering, that's all, because if it was me, I would want to leave. [It's like] they're trapped. That is what I am talking about. What can they do?

As is evident from our responses, the other participants and I were surprised at Katie's suggestion. Each of us in turn offered arguments that she countered with, "Yes, but" or "I know, but," suggesting that she continued to see repatriation as a solution, and that Marcus Garvey legitimized her argument. Despite the misinformation in Katie's "solution," it is important to note that she is concerned about racism and about her part in it. In my field notes for Katie's focus group, I wrote, "In response to the question: What does it mean to be antiracist? Katie said that it was in trying to see how she is racist, and in trying to gain knowledge of black culture through reading [black authors] and listening to black music. [Katie] added that she holds back in terms of initiating friendships with black Americans and wants to change that." It is not surprising that Katie holds back in initiating friendships with blacks. Her stereotypical images are filled with notions that would produce ambivalence, and perhaps apprehension, regarding such an endeavor. Nevertheless, Katie's concern about the issue of racism and her part in it is documented in the field notes.

The data in this section indicate that stereotypical images exist in the minds of well-meaning white people and that those stereotypes shape the participants' understanding of race matters. Some participants are aware of the stereotypes; others are not. And, as indicated, race awareness does not preclude action based on a stereotypical image. There is no reason to think that these stereotypical images remain dormant in people's minds, not influencing the actions they take.

Rather, it is logical to assume that the images and beliefs surrounding them determine the behavior following from them.

Paternalistic Assumptions

Paternalism began as a sympathetic attitude toward blacks, one first expressed in some master-slave relationships in the South (Genovese 1974). Slave owners' wives at times established "strong bonds of affection with slaves" (Weiner 1985/1986: 382). Later, liberal southern whites adopted paternalism as a way to relate to blacks with benevolent attitudes introduced into the dominant/subordinate relationship (Fredrickson 1971; Jackman 1994). Today paternalistic assumptions are found in relationships between whites and blacks and are characterized by a patronizing attitude on the part of the white person. Paternalistic assumptions are seen often in white middle- to upper middle-class families with black domestic workers (Rollins 1985). Like stereotypical images, people learn paternalistic assumptions informally; therefore, the assumptions are often outside one's awareness. Several of the participants, including myself, told of experiences rooted in this form of silent racism.

Penny told a story that illustrates the complex nature of hierarchical relationships between whites and blacks. Her account concerns the closeness between a white child and the black "nanny" who cared for the child. Penny said, "There was an interesting furor about racism in the lesbian community because a white woman who was brought up by a black woman, a nanny, wrote a song to her when [the nanny] died, and women of color had a really strong reaction to her [for] idealizing this relationship that she had, which was an inherently subservient relationship."

Vanessa, a member of Penny's group, entered into the exchange. Vanessa said, "Yeah, and the interchange—the black servant nurses the white baby, and is intimate with the little children, the little white children, in a friendly, affectionate way. And the strength of the relationship is real, and nurturing." Nodding, Penny answered, "And [the white lesbian] was probably closer to the nanny than to her mother. So it's like, where does that put that white woman in that situation? It's like, 'No, this isn't PC [political correctness], but this was my mother.'"

The question raised by Penny is a good one: Is the affection expressed in hierarchical relationships necessarily racist? I expect that the furor in the lesbian community was not about whether the relationship between the white child and the black "nanny" was structurally racist—most would agree that it was; rather, disagreement more likely concerned whether the *caring* expressed by the lesbian in her poem was itself racist. Penny said that the women of color in the lesbian community had "a strong reaction to the white woman idealizing the relationship." But how could they know that she was "idealizing" the relationship, and not merely expressing her love for the woman who raised her? The women of color in Penny's story denounced the love a white woman expressed for her black nanny because they believed it transformed the relationship into something that it was not. However, expressions of caring on both sides of the domestic/employer relationship may be valid and need not be disparaged in attempting to demonstrate that inequities also exist.

Katie, previously mentioned, also talked about an aspect of paternalistic assumptions in her focus group when she said, "I used to feel so sorry for [blacks] ... that's the attitude I grew up with. The relationship between white people and black people [is] like a master/servant relationship. For a long time we had this old black woman who came and cooked and did the laundry and stuff, which is like all of my friends, I mean they all had an old black woman who came in. It was kind of the normal thing, you know?"

The reference Katie made to a "master/servant relationship" corresponds with Judith Rollins's (1985) depiction of maternalism and deference. Rollins bases her work on Erving Goffman's (1967) idea that how people act exposes both how they see themselves and how they expect to be seen by others. Maternalism reveals not only arrogance on the part of the person displaying it but also an expectation of gratefulness from the receiver.

I shared with some of the groups the following memory about my childhood that also illustrates paternalistic assumptions:

> When I was growing up a young man named James worked for us [my family]—in fact he came to work for us when he was fifteen or sixteen. He did stuff for my dad, and he taught me [and my sisters and brother] how to drive. He became like—and I'm using the words that came right out of my family—part of our family. And when my dad died twenty-five years ago, he sat with us at the funeral. He felt that much a part of our family. That's the kind of racism that I was brought up with. It was very patronizing, and it's so slippery that it's hard to call it

> racism, but it is racism because our relationship with James was more like the relationships between good southerners and their slaves than like contemporary relations between employers and employees.

I later asked my mother (age eight-six at the time) what it meant that James was "part of our family." She said, "Your father and I treated James the same as we treated all of you kids—we trusted him and we expected him to behave. He was the *grownup kid* in the bunch" (personal communication, May 1995). James worked for my family until he was well into his thirties, and yet my mother still thought of him as "one of the kids." She continued to look upon him as "childlike," regardless of the fact that he and his wife (a teacher) had since raised three children, and he had served as a member of the city council for over fifteen years in the small town where they lived.

Hierarchical relationships like the one between my family and James are governed by asymmetrical rules that are a ceremonial expression of relative status positions (Goffman 1967). In addition, members of oppressed groups often transform the meaning of dominant/subordinate relationships into a "dependency-bond, a relationship that is justified by responses and agreed-upon rights" (Wolf 1994: 374). By sitting with us at my father's funeral, James acknowledged the morality of his relationship to our family. Clearly, the affection experienced and expressed between James and my family was sincere. Goffman (1967) says that affection and "belongingness" are earmarks of deference (p. 59). And while sincerity and affection do not mitigate the racist structure of similar hierarchical relationships, they illustrate the complexity found in some of them.

Sharon had also been raised in a family that employed a black domestic worker for many years, and she indicated that her experience differed from mine. Sharon contrasted her family's relationship with Anna to my family's relationship with James:

> We had Anna; she worked for us for years. My mother would go to work—she didn't clean house, she hated to clean. Anna did it. [Anna] was in a way part of—I mean, she came in two or three times a week and we just accepted her. I took it for granted; she was there, and we were so grateful to have somebody who worked well and did a good job. I think my mother probably paid her well, but I don't think anybody patronized her. There wasn't a feeling of her being a part of the family or anything. I mean, she would never have come to a funeral or anything like that.

Sharon explicitly stated that her family was not patronizing; in fact, she downplayed the emotional aspect of the relationship with phrases like, "We just accepted her. I took her for granted." Yet, she began, "We had Anna," a common reference to black domestic workers that implies ownership. Sharon also interrupted herself in mid-sentence when she said that Anna was "in a way part of" and then shifted to "she came in two or three times a week." It is possible that Sharon almost said Anna "was part of the family" and stopped when she realized the implication of such a statement: her family was indeed somewhat like mine. The paternalistic assumptions in Sharon's family were less pronounced than they were in my family, perhaps because she grew up in the North. Nevertheless, Sharon's words betray paternalistic assumptions, both in terms of possession and inclusion. Quite possibly, the difference in the two cases (mine and Sharon's) concerns Anna and James more than the white families they worked for. Unlike James, Anna presumably did not portray a sense of deference or the dependency bond mentioned in reference to James. In this sense, Anna did not reciprocate paternalism and James did.

Sometimes paternalistic assumptions exist in white/black friendships. In response to the question about a time when participants had said or done something that they now think is racist, Karen described an incident that illustrates paternalistic assumptions. She said, "In high school my friend Belle—who was black—and I would go places and I would try and do everything [for her], especially in establishments where it was all white. One time I asked her what she wanted, and I ordered her ice cream for her. She looked at me and said, 'I can order for myself.' And at the time I felt that I had messed up or whatever."

Karen's trying to "do everything" for Belle suggests she was operating according to paternalistic assumptions. Ordering Belle's ice cream illuminates both Karen's good intentions *and* an offensive, patronizing attitude that Belle rebuffed. Friendships are normally governed by symmetrical rules that dictate equality (Goffman 1967). Only hierarchical relationships operate according to asymmetrical rules. Paternalistic assumptions in Karen's perspective led her to define her relationship with Belle as hierarchical. From Karen's point of view, ordering Belle's ice cream was a generous gesture—one she thought would be appreciated. However, her action clearly insulted Belle because it devalued her standing in the relationship.

Karen's surprise at Belle's curt response indicates that Karen had no idea beforehand that her action would be offensive. She learned this through role-taking—seeing the situation from Belle's point of view. Karen's experience illustrates how silent racism leads to behavior that is unintentionally offensive to people of color, sometimes a characteristic of everyday racism.

Not surprisingly, Karen learned paternalistic assumptions in her family. In the following passage, Karen's comments reveal a sense of paternalism in her father, who uses the fact that Karen's mother provided childcare in their home for a black child as evidence of his family's goodwill. Karen stated, "My dad said that this was a neat experience to have a black child [in our home]. So I thought it was something special.... He would say that [racism] is wrong and that was why we have a black child here." Karen's father appeared to be eager to show that their family was *not* racist; in the process, he taught Karen that whites are benevolent when they take care of blacks.

The paternalistic assumptions illustrated here make it evident that racism sometimes arises from a sense of goodwill. At the same time, paternalistic assumptions embody Blumer's (1958b) idea that race prejudice is characterized by dominant group members perceiving themselves as superior to those in a subordinated group.

Paternalistic assumptions engender a sense of self-satisfaction in the people who operate with them. For example, another participant, Mary, told about going to lunch with a Chicana friend who picked her up at work. Mary acknowledged the following about her realization that coworkers would observe her with her friend. She said, "I found myself thinking how proud I was of myself that I have this woman of color coming to see me and that she's a friend—and I realize that I'm thinking this. It was a real humbling experience. I think there are a lot of us who think, when we're hanging around with our friends who are people of color, 'I'm so cool.'" Mary made this comment with a great deal of race awareness, which is an important step toward lessening the paternalistic assumptions.

Paternalistic assumptions were not as prevalent in the data as stereotypical images, which were evident in almost all of the participants. However, paternalistic assumptions emerge in close relationships between whites and blacks, and only seven of the participants ever had a close relationship with a black American. Because stereotypical images are held about an abstract group with no personal relationship needed for their formation, they are far more common than paternalistic assumptions.

The data concerning stereotypical images and paternalistic assumptions indicate that the silent racism lodged in white people's perspectives influences their commonsense interpretations and contributes to systemic racism. Both aspects of silent racism fit the description of what Alfred Schutz calls "natural attitudes" (see Wagner 1970: 320), which are taken for granted and go unquestioned (McHugh 1968). Natural attitudes are composed of what we know, or think we know, to be true. We assume that others share our definitions, and we act in accordance with them as if they make up the structure of reality (Garfinkel 1967). Like other natural attitudes, those comprising silent racism embody the "mental stance" taken by people in their "spontaneous and routine" pursuits (see Wagner 1970: 320). Pincus and Ehrlich (1994) express this point when they say that children born in the United States learn its prejudicial traditions and norms as part of their cultural heritage. The data in this study support Pincus and Ehrlich's claim that all whites are affected by racist ideas in the culture.

Two participants—Janice and Corrine—stand apart from the others. Janice portrays a defense of white privilege and color-blind racism. In her focus group, Janice's statements were often color-blind, meaning that she avoided or deflected any questions that required her to deal with racism. Janice's defense of white privilege and her avoidance of race when asked about it differentiate her from the other participants and make her more closely related to the participants in Wellman's and Bonilla-Silva's studies. Although other participants at times express color blindness, it is not the color-blind racism described by Bonilla-Silva. For example, when Sharon talked about Anna, the black woman that cleaned for her family, her attempt to distance her family's relationship with Anna from my family's relationship with James could be seen as her being color blind in that she portrayed the relationship as a purely economic arrangement that minimizes the role of race in domestic service.

Corrine, like Janice, also differs from the other women in the study; however, Corrine did not defend white privilege or express color-blind racism as Janice did. Nevertheless, Corrine, a quiet young woman, also did not say anything that indicates silent racism. Corrine was in the pilot focus group before the question "Have you ever done anything that you now would consider racist?" was added. Had she been asked that question, she might have been aware of a racist incident. Nevertheless, the absence of this question in Corrine's group and her reticence during the discussion group may partially explain her difference from the other participants. However, despite the inconvenient fact (Weber [1918] 1958) that Corrine did not express silent racism, the evidence is clear: Racism abounds in the "not racist" category.

Conclusion

The data presented in this chapter illustrate that silent racism is present in the minds of the well-meaning women in this study. And, because the women in this study are not likely to be more racist than other white women or white men, it can be deduced that silent racism is present in the minds of well-meaning white people generally.

Although silent racism sounds relatively harmless, it is damaging precisely because it is difficult to see, particularly by white people, including those who are well-meaning. The reason well-meaning white people do not notice their own silent racism is because they presume that they are not racist—the categories and their white perspectives tell them so. However, the presumption is faulty, and this aspect of silent racism—that is hard for white people to detect in themselves—allows it to do its damage undisturbed.

There is an important distinction between well-meaning white people and those in organizations such as the Ku Klux Klan that cannot be ignored. However, the difference should be characterized in a more realistic way than by the "racist/not racist" categories now in use. Despite the claim, either/or categories in terms of racism have outgrown their usefulness because they imply that white people who do *not* commit hostile acts against blacks or make maliciously racist statements about black Americans should be labelled "not racist." In this way silent racism and the routine acts of everyday racism resulting from it are rendered invisible despite the fact that they sustain the racist culture that produces them. The oppositional categories also harbor symbolic racists and color-blind racists whose arguments against policies that would support racial equality are presented in nonracial language.

The oppositional categories should be replaced with a continuum that more accurately portrays racism in white Americans today. Expanding the binary categories "racist" and "not racist" into an unbounded continuum labeled "more racist" and "less racist" would both illustrate that racism is a matter of degree—some is egregious and some is subtle—and illuminate the fact that, like the women in this study, no one is literally "not racist." The racism continuum would suggest that racism is sometimes routine, informing the conduct of people going about their everyday lives. Rethinking racism in this way, while implicit in many sociological race theories (Blumer 1958; Bonilla-Silva 2003; Essed 1991; Feagin and Vera 1995; Omi and Winant 1986; Wellman 1993), has not been proposed explicitly in the racism literature until this study (see Trepagnier 2001). As a consequence, racial common sense in the public imagination—which employs the oppositional categories—has lagged far behind race theory rather than reflecting it. Explicitly stating that the "not racist" category is inaccurate, as I suggest, contradicts what most whites hold as racial common sense. Nevertheless, racially progressive whites will welcome the suggestion of a racism continuum, knowing perhaps that without realizing it, they have racist thoughts at times and may act on them.

The suggestion that the racism categories be changed to a continuum rests on the assumption that racism is a process, just as deviance is a process (Pfuhl and Henry 1993). The process approach dictates that change be taken into account, a point concerning the meanings attached to the racism categories. Before the civil rights movement, most white Americans were racist, and the few who were not blatantly racist were ostracized, often called communists. Almost the opposite is the case today in that most whites are perceived as "not racist," and today it is the racist who is ostracized. If we continue to label racists as deviant when racism is systemic and all white Americans both contribute to it and benefit from it, then the labeling system should be changed. As it stands, the oppositional categories are part of the problem—a big part.

In addition to changing how people think about racism, the shift to a racism continuum would have significance in terms of what people do. The concept of silent racism gives well-meaning white people permission to explore their own racism. Instead of asking, "Am I racist or not?" progressive whites will ask, "How am I racist?" Becoming clearer about one's connection to racial inequality may increase race awareness to a small degree. This, in turn, although it will not erase silent racism, should lessen everyday racism that often goes unnoticed by the white people who perform it. Any change that results from rethinking racism is expected to occur at the "less racist" end of the racism continuum. No change is expected at the "more racist" pole or even at the midpoint of the continuum. However, my goal is not to change how blatant racists or even color-blind racists think about racism. Rather, my goal is to change how white liberals and progressives think about racism. Liberal and progressive whites, despite their good intentions, are neither well informed about the historical and cultural impact of racism on blacks nor clear about what is racist. It is not surprising that as a group, white progressives do not stand up and demand racial equality.

Theoretically, the exposure of silent racism at the "less racist" end of the continuum identifies a phenomenon that has previously gone unnamed, a phenomenon that is pivotal in the production of institutional racism. In the next chapter, another piece of the racism puzzle—one closely related to silent racism—is described: the passivity of well-meaning white people.

Notes

1. For a discussion of effects of the racist ideology on blacks, see, among others: Bell 1992; Du Bois [1903] 1999; hooks 1989, 1990, and 2004; and Roediger 1991. For a discussion of strategies of blacks in dealing with antiblack discrimination, see Feagin and Sikes 1994.

2. In the original draft of this and other chapters, I used the familiar pronouns "our" and "we" in an effort to include myself as a well-meaning white woman that is at times racist. However, after numerous discussions with colleagues I removed the familiar references because of their awkwardness.

3. Bonilla-Silva (2003) argues that white working-class women are the least likely group to exhibit color-blind racism. This study confirms his finding in the sense that most of the women were not married at the time of the study (85 percent), and that alone would predict that they are not likely to be in the middle or upper-middle class (Sidel 1998), despite their high level of education. I can also add that the most race-aware women in the study are working-class women who also happen to be lesbians.

4. It may be an artifact of the study that guilt did not come up often in the discussions and is not included in the concept of silent racism. The women who volunteered to be in the study knew from the flier or from the person who recommended the study to them that participants would talk about racism, including their own. Presumably people who feel guilt and shame would avoid such a study. An alternative explanation is that participants sensed permission to talk about their own racism, a situation that did not induce guilt.

5. It is possible that a number of participants in this study would have defended white privilege or exhibited color-blind racism if they had been asked questions similar to those in Wellman's and Bonilla-Silva's studies (see note 2 in Appendix A for a few examples).

6. Marcus Garvey was a black separatist minister from Jamaica who preached in the 1920s that black Americans should leave the United States and return to Africa (Marger 1994).

Chapter Three

Passivity in Well-Meaning White People

DATA PRESENTED IN THE PREVIOUS CHAPTER demonstrated that silent racism permeates the "not racist" category. In this chapter I argue that the exposure of silent racism renders the "not racist" category meaningless. Readers will see that in addition to hiding silent racism, the "not racist" category conceals passivity regarding race issues. Passivity not only inhabits the "not racist" category but appears to be partly created by the category itself; that is, passivity is often an unintended consequence of the category "not racist."

Passivity

Passivity regarding racism is not well documented in the race literature. The exception is Joe Feagin (2001), who briefly mentions "bystanders" as a category of white racists that "provide support for others' racism" (p. 140), and who in his work with Hernán Vera and Pinar Batur (2001) suggests that "passivity is a first step in learning to ally oneself with white victimizers against black victims" (p. 49). The latter study deals primarily with passivity in the face of antiblack violence. This follows much of the literature on bystanders, which is based largely on the "anonymous crowd" that colluded with the atrocities of the World War II Holocaust (Barnett 1999: 109). Our interest concerns the passivity of well-meaning white people who collude not with violent acts but with subtle forms of racism.

Ervin Staub (2003), the foremost scholar regarding the bystander role, defines bystanders as people "who are neither perpetrators nor victims" (see Goleman 2003: 29). Bystanders are present in situations where a person or a group is the target of a negative act or statement, whether or not the victim is present at the time. Passivity in bystanders appears to have multiple causes, including alienation from victims, identification with perpetrators, and fear of repercussions. And, although bystanders are neither victims nor perpetrators, their reaction in the situation is important. Passive bystanders differ from "active bystanders" (Staub 2003: 3) in that passive bystanders do nothing in the face of injustice or discrimination; active bystanders interrupt the unjust behavior or discrimination.

Most passive bystanders feel little or no connection to the victim (Barnett 1999). In-group/out-group differentiation may play a part in the passivity of bystanders because it is easier not to come to the aid of people who are in some way outsiders (Staub 2003). Intergroup theory posits that a primary function of groups, or categories, is to enable their members to distinguish themselves from members of other groups. Categorical differentiation is a means of cognitive sorting that facilitates information processing (Brown 2002). The sorting procedure "sharpen[s] the distinctions between categories and, relatedly, blur[s] the distinctions *within* categories" (Brown 2002: 397, emphasis in original). The resulting emphasis on similarities with in-group members and on differences with members of the out-group cause the in-group to be seen positively in comparison to the out-group. According to intergroup theory, differential categorization accounts for members of out-groups being seen in a less positive light than fellow in-group members and helps explain why people are more likely to be passive bystanders when targets of discrimination are different from themselves. Some have critiqued intergroup theory because it tends to make discrimination appear as though it is a natural occurrence and therefore cannot be avoided (see Fiske 1989).

The just world hypothesis may help explain passivity as well. The *just world hypothesis* refers to the idea that victims of injustice get what they deserve. The premise is that people want a world that is orderly and predictable. And if the world is orderly and predictable, it is also just. In order to sustain this belief, people must either come to the aid of victims of injustice or decide that the victims deserve the treatment they receive. Given that out-group members—people that are different in some way—are more likely to be seen as deserving of discrimination than in-group members, people's level of belief in the just world hypothesis is in inverse relation to the degree of empathy held for the group under attack (Staub 1992). The silent racism in people's minds would tend to support the white belief that blacks in some way deserve discrimination.

Another reason some people are passive bystanders is out of loyalty to the person doing the discriminating. Fear of causing embarrassment or anger may discourage interrupting racism, even if the bystander disapproves of the behavior. Shifting from being a passive bystander to an active one takes moral courage (Staub 2003). This is particularly true in situations where a power differential is in play, such as when one's boss tells a racist joke or makes a racist decision. In this case ambivalence (Smelser 1998) is likely to occur, and the decision of whether to intervene will be weighed against the cost of doing so.

The role of bystanders is important because they have a good deal of influence in how a given situation will proceed (Staub 2003). For example, when people make racist statements and bystanders remain passive, the passivity is perceived as collusion with the exposed racist point of view. This perception, right or wrong, empowers people to persist in their racism. By contrast, when bystanders actively interrupt racist statements, the balance of power shifts away from those making racist statements in support of the target group, blacks or other people of color. This means that despite the connotation of the terms "bystander" and "passivity," neutrality is not an option. Doing nothing creates an alliance with the perpetrator, regardless of the bystander's intention (Barnett 1999). In other words, bystanders, by virtue of being present during a racist incident, align either with the target of discrimination by interrupting the discrimination or with the perpetrator by remaining passive.

A final point about the bystander role is in order. The tendency to remain passive in the face of discrimination tends to continue once the pattern is set (Staub 2003). By the same token, taking an active bystander role by interrupting racism may also become easier with practice.

The data discussed in the next section relate to passivity in the participants. The first form of passivity results from feeling estranged from the target of discrimination because of detachment. Two additional sources of passivity emerged in this study, both of which are latent effects of the "not racist" category: apprehension about being perceived as racist, and confusion about what is racist.

Detachment from Race Issues

The "not racist" category distances well-meaning white people from racism by implication: White people who see themselves as "not racist" are unlikely to see their connection to race or racism. Sharon expressed a sense of detachment from race issues several times during the discussion in her group. The first example was in response to the question, "What do you think needs to happen in order for racism to end?" Sharon said, "Racism has no connection to my life." Later, when asked if she had ever been told by someone else, or realized herself, that she had said or done something racist, Sharon again appears detached. She said, "I can't think of anything. I'm sure there must be, but I can't think of anything. It didn't hit me." Sharon would not regard her indifference as problematic in any way. Rather, as she stated, "Racism has no connection to my life." But Sharon's thinking is faulty: we are all intimately connected with issues of race (Frankenberg 1993).

Sharon's detachment from race issues makes her a passive bystander when confronted with others' racism. For example, when asked, "What do you do when you are around someone who has made a racist remark or tells a racist joke?" Sharon responded, "Nothing, usually." The indifference characterized by Sharon is akin to willful blindness, a term used in reference to the perpetrators of white-collar crime such as Ken Lay, the president of Enron. Lay claims no knowledge of criminal behavior that he and others greatly profited from. Similarly, detachment from race matters serves white people who benefit from the racial status quo. Sharon's detachment from race issues is more striking than any other participant's, although others demonstrated disconnections as well. For example, Karen, in Sharon's focus group, also said that she usually does nothing when confronted with others' racism.

Detachment from racism is not limited to people like Sharon, who came to this study accidentally and who knows very little about racism. Penny is more representative of well-meaning white people who are concerned, yet passive. Penny senses that she should interrupt racism, but she openly admits that often she does not. When Penny answered the question about what she does if someone tells a racist joke or makes a racist comment, her answer illustrates passivity. Penny said, "Ideally, I would say, 'I don't laugh at that.' Do I say it? [That] depends on how grounded I'm feeling that day or what my relationship, my role in the group, is.... Then you get into the whole thing about, 'Oh, I didn't say it.' And 'I'm complicit.' It can be quite a conundrum." Penny, unlike Sharon, has good intentions about interrupting racism and feels bad about not doing it. Penny mentions that her role in the group could affect her reaction as a bystander. Bystanders who identify with the perpetrator or inhabit a subordinate role in relation to the perpetrator are less likely to take an active role for fear of disapproval or alienation (Staub 2003).

Vanessa said in response to the question about being around someone telling a racist joke, "I probably just don't laugh," an interesting response because the word "probably" casts her answer as a hypothetical statement rather than a statement of fact. A hypothetical answer instead of a factual one about one's behavior is likely to indicate avoidance of the question, perhaps due to being unsure about how the inquiring party might react. Nevertheless, whether Vanessa "just doesn't laugh" or laughs politely, her answer appears to indicate a measure of detachment.

Racist comments and jokes that go uninterrupted implicate the listener as well as the actor. The only way to not comply with racism when it occurs is to interrupt it. It is not correct to think that racism only occurs in interactions between whites and blacks or other people of color. To the contrary, those interactions may demonstrate less racism than comments that occur between or among white people when no blacks are present. Interrupting racism is as important at these times as it is when blacks are present, primarily because not to do so is perceived by perpetrators as encouragement of their racism.

Unintended Consequences

The "not racist" category appears to produce two unintended consequences: apprehension about being perceived as racist, and confusion about what constitutes racism. Both of these consequences result in passive behavior in white people. Differentiating manifest consequences—those that are obvious and intended—from latent consequences—those that are not obvious and not intended—is important in order to avoid confusion between "conscious *motivations* for social behavior and its *objective consequences*" (Merton 1967: 114, emphasis in original). A failure to distinguish between intended and unintended consequences results in flawed theoretical assumptions.

The putative intended function of the oppositional categories is to distinguish between antiblack racists and well-meaning white people who are presumed not to be racist. The unintended consequence is that the "not racist" category produces passivity, which is manifested in two ways: apprehension about being seen as racist, and confusion about what is racist.

Apprehension About Being Seen as Racist. Everyday rules regarding race matters, known as "racial etiquette" (Omi and Winant 1986: 62), are imbued with myriad meanings regarding race and racial difference that produce apprehension in white people. Several participants said that they felt apprehension about being perceived as racist. Elaine articulated her self-consciousness in dealing with black/white difference when she shared a story about meeting Dorothy, the friend of a friend, at a barbecue. Elaine said, "I opened the door and she's *black.* Oh! And I was just so mad at myself, and embarrassed for thinking that. I mean like, 'Oh, did that show?' Really worrying about it; just never getting past that."

Elaine's surprise that Dorothy was black was only exceeded by her embarrassment about being surprised. Based on her past experience, Elaine expected to see only white people at the barbecue. The racial etiquette that Elaine learned in her "all white" upbringing seems to have left her unsure about how to navigate a social setting that included both whites and blacks. The phrase "Did that show?" indicates that Elaine was afraid Dorothy might have noticed her surprise and interpreted it as racist. Apprehension about being perceived as racist troubled Elaine quite a bit, as evidenced by the comment, "Really worrying about it; just never getting past that." Elaine elaborated her discomfort by explaining how she makes sense of her reluctance to initiate friendships with black women. She said, "I do tend to socialize with people that are like me. . . . It's comfortable, it's easy, the knowns outweigh the unknowns. I think working against racism includes that fear of offending someone or fear of saying/doing the wrong thing and not being conscious of this.... I'm gonna make a mistake and I don't want to have to worry about that."

Elaine's comments do not imply that she thinks it is right to avoid situations in which she might make a misstep, as in her response to Dorothy. Nevertheless, she acknowledges that she often takes the easier path in developing friendships rather than the path that is more likely to provoke her anxiety about race difference. Her apprehension is important because of its own consequences: a tendency to avoid interactions with people of color. Ironically, as we will see in Chapter 5, having close ties with blacks and other people of color is important in developing race awareness—something that would lessen Elaine's apprehension.

Elaine added, "Racism has such a stigma attached to it that yes, we fear it. We don't want to be associated with [it]—we are not supposed to be making any mistakes." The "not racist" category produces fear of losing one's status as not racist and, in the process, lessens the tendency to question ideas about racism.

Karen made a related point in her group when she said, "I sometimes feel a barrier in approaching black women, in that I feel that they don't want to deal with me, and so I feel like I'm being respectful by keeping my distance, or something. I feel more comfortable letting them make the first move instead of me going over and starting conversations." Karen's reluctance to initiate friendships, or even conversations, with black women so they won't have to "deal with her" may relate to the incident described in Chapter 2 when Karen's black friend, Belle, rebuffed Karen's attempt to order her ice cream for her. Belle had not said why she was upset about the incident, and Karen did not ask. Consequently, Karen assumed it was simply because she was white, not realizing that it was because she had expressed a paternalistic assumption.

Apprehension about being perceived as racist keeps well-meaning white people from finding out more about racism. Anita made this point when she said, "[The] fear of saying anything that's going to label you racist ... you're not really dealing with. Well, is it or isn't it [racist], and why do I feel like that?" Lucy makes a similar point when she says, "Something that gets in my way [of dealing with my own racism] is feeling that I've got to be cool, or good, or maybe it's feeling like I try too hard or I care too much. I think it gets in my way because it prevents me from ... acknowledging that I am human." I think what

Lucy means by "acknowledging that [she is] human" refers to the inevitability that she will at times be unwittingly racist. Humans make mistakes, and sometimes those mistakes are because of misconceptions or ignorance regarding racism. The need to be seen by oneself and others as "not racist" hinders becoming more aware of race matters. Moreover, people with low race awareness are not likely to be active bystanders who interrupt others' racism; rather, people with low race awareness are likely to be passive bystanders, encouraging racism.

Loretta also indicated apprehension about being perceived as racist. She said, "People silencing themselves out of the fear of not saying the right thing [means] not being able to talk, and therefore not being able to change. Making actual change may mean making a mistake, saying the wrong thing, and having somebody call you on it and having to own that." Loretta's statement shows insight into the paradox of being unable to discuss racism for fear of being perceived as racist. Loretta's comment also shows insight into the danger of seeing racism as deviant. The original definition of *political correctness,* now known as PC, was "internal self-criticism" among liberals (Berube 1994: 94). For example, liberals hoped to raise awareness about biases in language—such as the use of sexist language—because biases in language reinforce biases in society (Hofstadter 1985). Conservatives co-opted the term, mocking liberals by casting political correctness as an attempt to limit the freedom of speech. Today political correctness is widely perceived as destructive, rather than as it was originally intended: an attempt not to be offensive (Feldstein 1997).

Passivity resulting from the apprehension about being perceived as racist is evident in the preceding stories of the well-meaning white women. The fear of being seen as racist paralyzes some well-meaning white people, causing them to avoid meeting and interacting with blacks. This is significant—and ironic—because forming close relationships with blacks and other people of color is the most important step they can take to lessen their apprehension.

Confusion About What Is Racist. Confusion about racism is epitomized by uncertainty and embarrassment and is sometimes related to being apprehensive about being seen as racist. People who see themselves as not being racist often presume that they should know what is racist and what is not, even when they are not sure. Confusion about what is racist is closely related to passivity in that it suppresses action. In the following comments, participants share experiences demonstrating confusion.

Anne spoke of her confusion about whether referring to people as "black" is in itself racist. Anne reported a conversation she had with her mother in reference to a baseball announcer during a New York Yankees game. When her mom asked who announced the game, Anne said that it was Bill White. "My mom asked me, 'Who's Bill White?' I didn't want to say he was black—I thought it would be racist." Anne attempted to avoid using color as a marker for distinguishing among the sports announcers, believing that mentioning his race would have been racist. After describing many details about Bill White—color of hair, size, and so on—Anne could not think of any other way to distinguish him and finally told her mother that he was "the black announcer." This raises an important point of discussion: Was Anne's telling her mother that Bill White was "the black announcer" racist? Was it the same as Ruth, who earlier said she had a bright "black" student in her class? (See Chapter 2.)

I classified Ruth's comment as racist, as did the friend that interrupted it, pointing out that Ruth's reason for mentioning that the student was black was related to the fact that he was bright. However, that is not the case in Anne's situation; saying that Bill White was the black announcer was not related to any negative stereotype but was instrumental in identifying him to her mother.

Some would argue that using "black" as an identifying characteristic is always racist because it reinforces the notion that blacks are racialized and whites are not. This view is called *otherizing* and is thought to marginalize blacks and other minorities. However, sometimes identifying someone as black is pertinent to the context of a situation. To say he was "the black announcer" was not racist in Anne's situation because it was instrumental in that context and in no way reproduced a stereotype about blacks. I agree that white people virtually never use *white* in the same way. Nevertheless, avoiding the word *black* simply because its use is not equivalent to the use of the word *white* seems like faulty logic to me.

While discussing this issue with a black colleague, I was given this response: "Sometimes a person will apologize for saying the word *black* even when it is appropriate to include for clarity. Very often I have had whites apologize for even uttering the word. It's as if, for them, the word *black* is gaining status with *nigger* as a racially sensitive word."

Avoiding the use of *black* because it might be racist results from confusion about what is racist. Using *black* as an identifying characteristic is racist when its use is associated with a racist stereotype or if it is tacked on solely because a person is not white. However, rigidly avoiding *black* unnecessarily when its use would serve a purpose is tantamount to pretending that race does not exist or was not noticed, a prime example of racial etiquette (Omi and Winant 1986).[1]

Anne's reluctance to "utter the word" *black* indicates some hesitation about saying the word at all. Anne may have received a message as a child similar to the one Lisa received from her parents. Lisa said that she was told explicitly not to notice race differences. Lisa said that in addition to telling her "colors don't matter," her parents added, "[but] don't ever say the word *black,* don't say the word *Mexican,* and don't ever refer to a person's color. It's offensive to say those words." Lisa said that when she was ten, she and her family moved into a housing project where she would be in close proximity to black children. Since Lisa would undoubtedly play with black children—her new neighbors—Lisa's parents were perhaps trying to prepare her for that experience. By cautioning Lisa to ignore difference—a difference they also denied was there—Lisa's parents wanted to both protect her from any repercussions they thought might occur from pointing out difference *and* teach her about equality. However, parents' double messages about race and racism can cause confusion in their children in terms of what is and what is not racist. In Anne's case, confusion contributed to her apprehension about being racist, which had a paralyzing effect. Avoiding any mention of race or the word *black* rather than acknowledging one's confusion keeps people from understanding what is and what is not racist.

In a related incident, Penny, who grew up in the 1960s, spoke of asking her mother about a house that looked "different" from the ones in their neighborhood—she said that it was pink and had iron grillwork across the front. Penny stated, "My mother said, 'Oh, that's where Egyptians live.' [My mother] didn't think that I'd ever meet Egyptians, and so it was okay for me to think that Egyptians were different." The logic that Penny attributes to her mother's comment—that it was okay to think that Egyptians were different because it was unlikely that Penny would meet any—indicates the lengths to which Penny's mother went in avoiding a discussion about race difference with her children. Although Penny did not recall receiving an explicit message to "not notice" race, it appears that her mother saw the acknowledgment of difference *itself* as problematic and perhaps racist, a confusion of what is racist and what is not.

Although the reluctance to mention race can be referred to as being colorblind, the instances here do not meet the definition of *color-blind racism*: a racial ideology that "explains contemporary [racial] inequality as the outcome of nonracial dynamics" (Bonilla-Silva 2003: 2). Color blindness derives from a racist ideology that is at times racist but that is not necessarily always racist. The individuals described in this section are only color blind in that they did not want to draw attention to race difference for fear it would be racist to do so. However, I would characterize the reluctance to mention race as confusion about what is racist rather than as racism per se.

Confusion was also evident in Heather's description of an incident that occurred in her high school circle of friends. However, Heather's confusion is not coupled with apprehension. Heather said,

> I just remembered a very good friend of mine in high school who was half black—his dad was black and his mom was white—and he was blond, with blue eyes. There was an incident [in high school] that was really sticky. One of our friends didn't even know that David's father was black, and she made a very bad mistake by telling a joke about a black man and a Jewish man in an airplane—an awful, awful joke that just did not go over [well].... I think part of it was that [David] was such a blond guy. And his father had a Ph.D. in some hard science and has taught at [a major university]; he was on the faculty and then went to work at a laboratory. [David's] mom is a nurse.

Heather characterized the "sticky" incident as "a mistake" and that the friend telling the racist joke "didn't even know that David's father was black." What seems to be problematic for Heather is that David had inadvertently heard the racist joke, not the fact that the joke was racist. This interpretation is substantiated by Heather's comment that the "mistake" resulted from David being "such a blond guy" whose father has a Ph.D. and whose mother is a nurse. Heather's confusion about what is racist concerning the joke incident is likely to result from her not thinking the incident through, and, as a result, excusing her friend's racism by seeing it as harmless rather than as racist.

Confusion was also evident in a statement Alyssa made in her focus group:

> I think that everyone should be noted for their differences and celebrate their differences, instead of just ignoring, and looking through them and saying, "You know, I don't see color." Because you do [see color]. Everyone sees it. You may not think negatively of it, but when you think of the fact that you notice that a person is black, you think it's something bad. But I don't see that as something being bad—you can celebrate a difference.

The confusion in Alyssa's notion of celebrating difference becomes evident when she states inconsistent views centered on the pronoun *you*: "you may not think negatively of it" and "you think it's something bad." Alyssa seems to notice the apparent contradiction between these two thoughts when she quickly distances herself from the second statement by adding, "*I* don't see it as something bad." The confusion in Alyssa's thinking (that noticing race difference is "good" and that being black is seen as "something bad") presumably remains intact in her thinking, perhaps below her awareness. Holding contradictory beliefs without scrutinizing them may explain how many white people harbor racist thoughts about blacks and other people of color without being aware of it.

Loretta talked about the celebration of difference, but without the confusion exhibited by Alyssa. She said, "We can have a kind of 'feel good' cultural diversity yet not be antiracist. We [can] all talk the same talk, isn't this great, and cultural diversity is great. I [can] go to a food fair and taste [different food] and that's great, on one level. But if the reality is that economically only certain people are getting jobs ... and people of color are getting paid less than white people ... then there is still going to be racism." Loretta does not embrace the celebration of difference uncritically, as Alyssa does. Her critical assessment of the concept exposes the danger of celebrating the different cultural traditions of black and white Americans without acknowledging the history of racial oppression in the United States and the current racial inequality that continues today.

Confusion in well-meaning white people does not produce passivity as directly as detachment from race issues does. Neither does confusion produce passivity in the same sense that apprehension about being racist does, through the avoidance of contact. However, confusion is linked to passivity indirectly in that white people who are confused about racism are not likely to take a stand against it; one must be able to conclusively define an act as racist in order to feel justified in contesting it. Only white people who are clear about the historical legacy of racism in the United States, who understand how institutional racism operates, and who sense their own complicity with a system that benefits them to the detriment of people of color are likely to be active in interrupting racism when they encounter it. In this way, confusion along with detachment and apprehension is the antithesis of antiracism. For this reason, I consider it racist and place it just inside the midpoint toward the less racist end of the racism continuum. See Figure 3.1 for passivity on the racism continuum.

The aforementioned data support the claim that the "not racist" category itself produces several latent effects that bring about passivity in well-meaning white people. Just as silent racism produces institutional racism, passivity produces collusion with racism. Said differently, everyday racism could not stand without the participation and cooperation of well-meaning white people. However, before discussing how silent racism and passivity are key ingredients in the production of institutional racism, there is another topic to consider: possible unintended consequences of replacing the oppositional categories with a racism continuum.

One More Unintended Consequence

Would racism increase if people came to believe that all white people are somewhat racist? This concern—that some whites who now suppress their racist thoughts would presume to have permission to express them—is well founded. We saw this effect in Chapter 2 when Vanessa expressed the racist belief that black Americans are essentially different from white Americans. I questioned Vanessa's point that blacks and whites are inherently different, using the analogy of how supposed inherent gender difference between men and women have traditionally been used as a rationale against change for women. Vanessa responded,

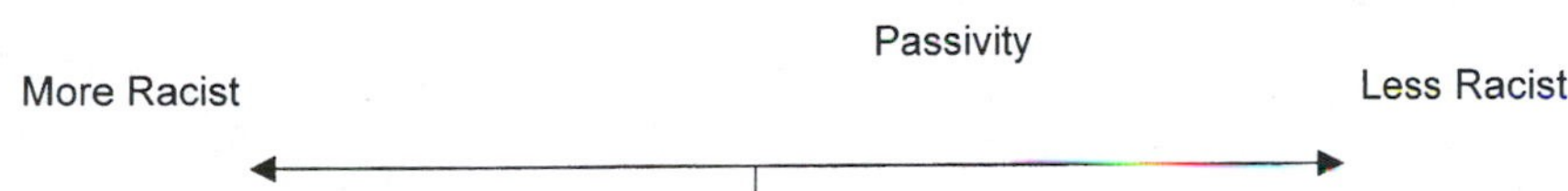

Figure 3.1 Passivity on the Racism Continuum

"Exactly. I just feel safe in saying this; I've never said it anyplace else.... As a psychologist, I wouldn't dare say what I said [laughter from several group members], but I really do question what people are so quick to say, that all races have to be equally endowed."

Vanessa acknowledged that she has never voiced the opinion before, and that she "felt safe" in saying in the focus group what she "wouldn't dare say" any place else. The idea raised by Vanessa may exemplify what would result if the sanctions against acknowledging racist thoughts were eliminated. In other words, is expressing suppressed racist thoughts a greater harm than the harm caused by their suppression?

Despite her belief in biological race differences, Vanessa expressed pride in her antiracist heritage when she told about her great-grandparents who helped "slaves escape to the North." Vanessa invokes both racist and antiracist sentiments, shifting between the two. The term *drift* can be used to explain juvenile delinquents' movement between two cultures, "convention and crime" (Matza 1964: 28). Similarly, that the focus groups granted permission to talk about race and racism likely explains Vanessa's "drift" into racism. In her journal entry, Vanessa further explained her statement concerning biological determinism:

> I felt a kind of exhilaration in being able to talk openly about a loaded subject. Also, being with others who seemed to totally share my general [antiracist] attitudes on racism was a pleasure. I soon began to view them all with admiration as the stories came forth. Although I told of attitudes and beliefs the others might not agree with offhand, I had the feeling it was a good place to share them—[I thought] they would be fairly considered.

Vanessa appears to offset her statement about biological determinism by stating that she had never said it "anyplace else," that she "wouldn't dare," and that she felt "safe" in saying it in the focus group. *Neutralization* refers to a set of techniques intended to rationalize or justify delinquent behavior (Sykes and Matza 1957). Vanessa's use of a neutralization technique illustrates her awareness that what she said is not acceptable under normal circumstances. Her statement verifies the concern that removing the "not racist" category and its tendency to silence those in it would increase the expression of racist ideas. However, concern about this effect is based on the dubious assumption that suppressed racism is preferable to overt racism. I maintain that even if statements like Vanessa's increased, the benefit of increasing race awareness would outweigh that consequence because the increased race awareness is essential to decreasing the production of institutional racism. The drift into racism demonstrated by Vanessa should not be reason to dismiss rethinking the oppositional categories; on the contrary, Vanessa's statement is evidence that more open discussion about racism is needed. The expression and discussion of racist ideas would be more conducive to understanding racism than the confusion and apprehension that now govern white people who care about racism but feel paralyzed when faced with it.

In the 1950s, whites who stood up against racism were labeled "deviant"; today, the opposite is true: whites who are overtly racist are labeled "deviant." Labeling theory posits that the process of naming people "deviant" pertains to social rules that define deviance (Becker 1963). The deviance literature states that rules concerning who is deviant (and by implication who is not deviant) are imposed from outside, by moral entrepreneurs. In the case of the labels "racist" and "not racist," however, many white people who see themselves as "not racist" impose the rules on themselves. And yet, if the function of the "racist" category is to identify and therefore punish racists, then racism is sustained by the very social regulation intended to curtail it. Furthermore, the label "not racist" produces passivity in well-meaning white people, the supposed allies of blacks and other people of color. Labels imply essences—ways of being rather than merely ways of acting (Katz 1975). This is particularly true in the case of the racism labels; white racists are perceived as qualitatively different from whites presumed to be "not racist." If all whites are somewhat racist, this distinction is false, serving only to protect silent racism, everyday racism, and institutional racism.

Conclusion

Passivity is common in well-meaning white people. It is marked by detachment that produces a bystander effect in white people who find themselves in the face of others' racism. In addition, passivity results from apprehension about being seen as racist and from confusion about what is racist—both unintended but direct effects of the "not racist" category. This chapter's central thesis is that *passivity works against racial equality*. Well-meaning white people who are passive bystanders quietly watch America grow more divided over race issues. Yet, these are not innocent bystanders. They profit from the racial divide; they reap the same advantages received by those performing racist acts that they silently witness. The well-meaning whites who are the least aware of this fact feel little or no discomfort about the situation—they do not recognize the benefits that institutional racism affords them. The well-meaning whites who are detached have a measure of race awareness and feel bad about the situation as well as about their own passivity. Other passive bystanders are apprehensive—afraid to make a move for fear that they may be seen as racist. And still others are confused or misinformed, even though most do not recognize their confusion.

Both silent racism and passivity in well-meaning white people, some of which is produced by the category system, are instrumental in the production of institutional racism, described in the next chapter.

Note

1. I would like to thank Glynis Christine and Chad Smith for their conversations regarding this topic.

Chapter Four

The Production of Institutional Racism

CHAPTERS 2 AND 3 DESCRIBED THE CONCEPTS of silent racism and passivity, both of which are instrumental in the production of institutional racism. And because silent racism and passivity are found in well-meaning white people, institutional racism is frequently produced by whites who do not intend to produce it but do so nonetheless.

This chapter begins with the sociological concept of institutional racism, including the effects it produces and the theories that have developed around it. Several of the theories imply the role of actors (people who take action); however, none bridges the micro/macro gap satisfactorily. In other words, none of the theories explains how the action of individuals produces societal patterns of racial inequality. I will present a theory of institutional racism that forges a link between social institutions and the actors who sustain them. The theory also explains how institutional racism is carried out largely by people who have no intention to produce it. Grounded primarily in the work of Pierre Bourdieu ([1994] 1998), the theory demonstrates how silent racism produces both racist practice and everyday racism in organizations and institutions. Social network theory (Whitmeyer 1994) is also utilized to argue that passivity regarding others' racist practices contributes to institutional racism. The ideas gleaned from these theorists and others illustrate that silent racism and passivity are essential in the production of institutional racism, an insight that shifts the focus from individuals' intentions onto what they do and what they do not do, regardless of intention.

Institutional Racism

Sociologists have recognized institutional racism—a form of oppression structured into the fabric of society—since the mid-1960s, when civil rights activists Stokely Carmichael—later known as Kwame Ture—and Charles Hamilton (1967) introduced the term. Since then, institutional racism as a concept has been expanded to include the role of cultural beliefs as integral to the process (Blauner 1972; Bonacich 1972, 1976; Kovel 1970; Omi and Winant 1986, 1994; Turner and Singleton 1978; Van der Berghe 1967). Despite these changes, sociology has been slow to explain the role of actors involved in the production and maintenance of institutional racism.

A breakthrough in sociological race theory, institutional racism has remained a compelling macrolevel concept primarily because it demonstrates the important idea that racism permeates society through its institutions; that is, the concept reveals that racism is systemic. In accomplishing this, institutional racism illustrates that racism is more than the prejudice of individuals. The difficulty, however, is that the concept implicitly disconnects individuals from institutions. This false separation results in institutional racism being undertheorized in terms of the mechanism through which institutions produce racial inequality.

Institutions, as defined by sociologists, are the set of ideas or expectations about how to accomplish the various goals of society, such as the socializing of a society's young, meeting the economic needs of society's citizens, and protecting members of society from outside threat (McIntyre 2002). The norms and expectations surrounding families, religion, education, the economy, and the government differ somewhat from one society to another, making each society distinctive from other societies. When the ideas and expectations that constitute any institution in a given society has racist undercurrents due to past and present social relations, institutional racism occurs in the organizations associated with that sector of society. Patterns that result from following the expectations surrounding institutions eventually become habitual, making behavior somewhat predictable, although not determined. These behavioral rules provide a measure of social control, mediated through the institutions mentioned above. Through the socialization process, children are taught to act within the institutions of their parents. In this way, institutions become legitimate (Berger and Luckmann 1966) and influence people's behavior.

Although the idea is historically rooted in the ideas of Frederick Douglass, W. E. B. Du Bois, and Frantz Fanon, the term *institutional racism* first emerged toward the end of the civil rights movement in the writings of Carmichael and Hamilton (1967). These authors posit that more damaging effects for blacks as a group come from U.S. institutions than from bigoted white individuals. This occurs because institutions favor the dominant group—white Americans—over black Americans and other minorities. Racial inequality results when U.S. social institutions such as the criminal justice system, education, and the economy put people of color at a disadvantage while simultaneously giving white people an unwarranted advantage.

Carmichael and Hamilton maintain that much institutional racism is invisible, especially to those benefiting from it. They also argue that institutional racism does not necessarily reflect any deliberate or malicious intent on the part of members of the dominant group. In reference to "respectable" white people who would never bomb a church or burn a cross, the authors point out that "they continue to support political officials and institutions that would and do perpetuate institutionally racist policies. Thus *acts* of overt, individual racism may not typify the society, but institutional racism does—with the support of covert individual *attitudes* of racism" (Carmichael and Hamilton 1967: 5, emphasis in original). At the time it was introduced, institutional racism offered an alternative view to the the narrow psychological assertion that prejudice explains racism. Moreover, since the late 1960s, sociological theories have leaned heavily toward the structural concept of institutional racism and away from the role of individuals as an explanation of racial inequality.

Effects of Institutional Racism

The legacy of slavery as well as the Reconstruction and Jim Crow eras was not eliminated by the Civil Rights Act of 1964 and the Voting Rights Act of 1965. Vestiges of racism produced by white Americans of all stripes—the far right, the new right, neoconservatives, neoliberals, and new abolitionists—is carried out daily, producing harmful effects for black Americans. A few of the negative effects are listed here, some of which are linked to well-meaning white people like the ones in this study. The forms of institutional racism mentioned in this section do not come close to covering all of the ways institutions produce racist effects. For a more comprehensive record, see Brown et al. (2003) and Feagin and Sikes (1994). However, the negative effects produced by well-meaning white people are important because they are produced unintentionally by people who, if their race awareness were increased, would produce fewer negative effects themselves and would interrupt others' racist acts.

The negative effects of institutional racism begin before blacks and other minorities enter the labor force. People of color face scarcity in terms of contacts with white people already in workplaces where they may wish to be employed. Many well-meaning whites avoid initiating relationships with blacks, some because of fear, others because of apprehension about whether blacks would welcome them as acquaintances. And, not only are ties important in learning about better jobs, but people who get jobs through social ties also tend to experience more job satisfaction as well (Breaugh 1981; Lin, Vaughn, and Ensel 1981).

Once in the labor force, blacks continue to experience institutional racism in the social relations they experience. The social relational approach relates individuals' social relations—that is, how individuals interact—to job satisfaction and indirectly to promotion opportunities (Baron and Pfeffer 1994). Feeling comfortable with coworkers eases tension and the stress that often occurs in the workplace. In addition, information sharing, especially for newcomers in the workplace, is important for achievement on the job (Hackman 1976; Ibarra and Andrews 1993; Jacobs 1981).

Social categorization in terms of in-group and out-group characteristics could be a pivotal issue when administrators consider prospective candidates for new positions within the organization (Baron and Pfeffer 1994). Not only would white administrators see white candidates as more differentiated than black candidates, but silent racism would influence their decisions as well. Take, for example, Vanessa's view that blacks are inherently different from whites and that difference in language skills is due to biological factors. If someone with Vanessa's white perspective were an administrator, her inflammatory viewpoint would undoubtedly influence decisions about any position requiring good language skills. Even Ruth, who is relatively race aware, inadvertently referred to a black student as bright as if it were remarkable. Views like these produce everyday racism and racist practice that result in institutional racism.

Institutional racism is even more evident in the criminal justice system, as it is especially hard on young black males (Brown et al. 2003). Sentencing differentials for drug offenses, for example, are striking: Whites go to federal prison half the number of times blacks go and spend less time in federal prison once they are sent. This trend holds for Latinos as well as blacks. Institutional racism is also evident regarding penalties for property crimes. Controlling for the facts that the rate of crime is higher in poor black neighborhoods and that crime in these neighborhoods is routinely performed by young blacks, practices that favor whites account for a disproportionate conviction rate of blacks over whites (Brown et al. 2003). Furthermore, controlling for prior offenses and seriousness of a given crime, black offenders are twice as likely as their white counterparts to be committed to a juvenile institution or sent to an adult court for adjudication (Bishop and Frazier 1996). The decisions that underlie this pattern could very well be acerbated by a view of the black family—especially poor, single-parent black families—that is influenced by silent racism. Remember Kelly, who viewed the black mother she saw on TV as "ignorant" and "somehow or another implicated in the violence within the ghetto." A person with Kelly's view is likely to see putting young blacks who get in trouble with the law into a facility where professional assistance is available as a better alternative to leaving them in families that might encourage criminal behavior. Misguided notions such as Kelly's result in a self-perpetuating cycle as the young people are pushed further into a system that labels them "delinquent" and treats them as adult criminals.

The death penalty, which is under scrutiny in some states due to the number of inmates proven by DNA evidence to be innocent of the crime that condemed them, is the ultimate form of discrimination in the criminal justice system. The most striking distinction, again, concerns sentencing, which operates on two fronts. First, defendants accused of killing a white victim are four times more likely to receive the death sentence as those accused of killing a black victim. And second, black defendants are more likely than white ones to receive the death penalty, regardless of the race of the victim. Lack of adquate legal representation accounts for some of this pattern. However, silent racism makes conviction more likely when circumstantial evidence is all the prosecution has to offer.

One study of middle-class blacks found that racism has a cumulative effect on the blacks and other people of color that are its targets (Feagin and Sikes 1994). Racism is experienced as blacks go about their daily lives, not in extraordinary circumstances. In addition to racial strain at work, it is experienced when shopping at the grocery store and when driving in the "wrong" neighborhood. Because racism is routine, it occurs throughout society, which gives blacks few safe havens where they are not exposed to it.

Finally, institutional racism is not limited to disadvantages that accrue to blacks and other minorities. It also includes the "miseducation of white children" (Knowles and Pruitt 1969: 46), which teaches that racial equality has been achieved despite gross evidence to the contrary. As white children grow up, they rarely discover the truth about racial inequality. This is evident in the women in this study, including myself. Even in college, where exposure to new ideas is expected, students can proceed from matriculation to graduation without ever having their assumptions about race being challenged.

Theories of Institutional Racism

Race theorists have utilized the concept of institutional racism first articulated by Carmichael and Hamilton in various ways. Examples include the following: White Europeans founded American institutions, and the guiding principles of the institutions reflect the whiteness of their creators, with members expected to "think and act in white ways" (Hacker 1992: 23). The result is that institutional racism constrains racial or ethnic minorities much the way a birdcage constrains the bird inside (Frye 1992). Looking solely at a single wire of the cage cannot reveal the network of wires that constrict the imprisoned bird. The term *systemic racism* portrays racism as permeating all of society, including but not limited to its institutions (Feagin 2001). *Racialization* suggests the idea that racism is a process that binds people and the institutions of society, both of which utilize race as an organizing principle (Omi and Winant 1986, 1994). And since institutional racism is an ideology that permeates organizations and institutions, to escape it one would have to escape society itself, an impossible feat (Dworkin and Dworkin 1999). All of these aspects of institutional racism are compatible with the theory constructed in this chapter. The difference between these portrayals of institutional racism and the theory to be outlined here is that, in this chapter, the focus shifts from the institutions and their effects on people of color to the role of well-meaning white people in the process. A few race theorists dismiss the concept of institutional racism, arguing, for example, that racism as portrayed by the "institutionalist perspective" is a "mysterious" notion, and that the approach does not explain the origin of racism or how it operates (Bonilla-Silva 2001: 26–27).

Several of the race theories mentioned in Chapter 3 are pertinent here in that they are the foundation for a theory that highlights the role of individuals in the production of institutional racism. For example, the historical theory of racism, which captures dominative racism, aversive racism, and metaracism, illustrates how individuals' racism evolves as institutions in society change over time (Kovel 1970). That psychological and emotional aspects of aversive racism continued to manifest even though aversive racism was transformed into metaracism is useful when thinking about the irrational fear of black men evident in a number of the participants in this study. This point is pivotal when considering how racism within police departments operates, especially in terms of white police officers' actions toward black suspects (Bolton and Feagin 2004).

The cultural approach illustrates that structures of oppression are linked in significant ways to cultural beliefs, and that progressive beliefs are important to social change (Turner and Singleton 1978). This insight informs the claim that beliefs held by progressives and the action following from those beliefs are important in changing the racial status quo.[1] The theory of racial formation is also important to the theory presented here because it highlights the importance of ideology on the process of racial formation (Omi and Winant 1986, 1994). The idea that race is an organizing principle of social structures and that individuals carry out the "rules of racial etiquette" (1986: 62) is borne out by both silent racism and passivity.

Two forms of institutional racism interest us here: *direct* institutional racism refers to actions within an organization that intentionally harm a member of a minority group and that are known about and supported by the organization (Feagin and Feagin 1994). The harm that results from direct institutional racism is intended by the organization and by the members who carry it out. *Indirect* institutional racism, in contrast, "is carried out with no intent to harm" the members of the subordinate group affected (Feagin and Feagin 1994: 122).

The theory outlined in this chapter is related to indirect institutional racism in two ways: indirect institutional racism has become more prominent as overt forms of racism have diminished since the civil rights movement, and indirect institutional racism concerns the population of interest in this study—well-meaning white people. This is also the group that is most likely to change its thinking regarding racism.

The Production of Institutional Racism

The proposed theory does not presume to explain all institutional racism. However, like silent racism itself, which has long been overlooked, the theory focuses on the population that is thought to be the least likely to produce institutional racism. The production of institutional racism described here, then, involves persons who are well-meaning white people, not those who are overtly racist or even those who are color-blind racists. This does not imply that overt racists and color-blind racists do not produce institutional racism but that they are not the focus here. In addition, the production of institutional racism refers to *action* that is not intended to do harm to blacks or other people of color; that is, action that is not chosen by the actor for that purpose.

In forging a theory of institutional racism, I must first broach the topic of combining the concept of actors and the idea of social structure. The once-divided camps of micro and macro sociologists have been under scrutiny by sociologists interested in forging a link between the two (Alexander 1987; Collins 1988; Ritzer 1990). An example is "methodological relationism," which refers to studying how individuals and structures interact (Ritzer and Gindoff 1994: 163). Although much race theory has been written about the micro approach (the racism of individuals) and the macro approach (institutional racism), the focus here is on both: the role of individuals in the production of institutional racism, a relational approach.

The debate in the United States over the micro/macro link is cast in Europe as the *agency-structure* debate (Ritzer and Gindoff 1994). Although "micro and agency" do not correspond perfectly, just as "macro and structure" do not, the distinction is largely philosophical rather than empirical (Ritzer and Gindoff 1994). Because our concern is the mechanism that explains how individuals produce institutional racism, the debate is not a primary concern here. The point is important, however, because the theoretical foundation for the theory begins with the theory of structuration developed by British sociologist Anthony Giddens (1984) and borrows liberally from the work of European sociologist Pierre Bourdieu ([1972] 1978).

The theory of structuration closes the gap between actor and structure that gives us a map showing how the actions of individuals and the functioning of institutions fit together. Because race theorists have largely fallen either into the micro or the macro camp, their theories have exhibited the theoretical artifact that Giddens seeks to expose. Giddens's work is especially important for race theory because the dichotomy between institutional racism and individual actors has reinforced the false notion that white people *as individuals* are not implicated in the phenomenon of institutional racism and racial inequality. The title of Bonilla-Silva's book, *Racism Without Racists* (2003), captures this paradox. The theory of structuration illustrates that racism must be and is instituted by individuals.

Giddens (1979) proposes that neither structure nor agency occurs in isolation. Structuration is a process that occurs *between* social structure and individual actors; it is "the mutual dependence of structure and agency" (p. 69). For Giddens, individuals have the *capability* to make choices (1981), although they do so rarely and only when routines are breached. Therefore, in Giddens's theory of structuration, everyday acts are not thought through and decided upon beforehand; action generally takes place without thoughtful awareness on the part of the actor. This use of the concept of agency differs from what many North American theorists propose: that *agency* not only refers to individuals' ability to make meaningful choices but that virtually all decisions are thought through and made deliberately.

For Giddens, actors' knowledge of the system within which action occurs—as well as knowledge about expectations in the system—make structuration possible. When the theory of structuration is applied to institutional racism, we can see that white actors within the institutions of society take action based on their knowledge (white understanding) of the norms and expectations associated with the institution. Because action goes largely unexamined by the actor, it reproduces the white institution. Bourdieu offers several concepts that further implicate the role of well-meaning white people in the production of institutional racism.

Bourdieu's Theory of Practice

Bourdieu's ([1972] 1978) theory of practice—another word for *action*—helps explain the mechanism for how well-meaning white people produce institutional racism. Since the 1980s, numerous disciplines, including sociology, have developed theories of practice that seek to explain how the action of individuals affects social structures and institutions (Ortner 1994). The goal of these various theorists has been to "understand where 'the system' comes from—how it is produced and reproduced, and how it may have changed in the past or be changed in the future" (Ortner 1994: 390). This is precisely our goal: to understand where institutional racism comes from, how it is produced and reproduced, and especially, how it might be changed. Bourdieu modestly refers to his theory of practice as a "thinking tool" (Jenkins 1992: 67), which is also useful for our purposes—a tool that will help us think about and understand how well-meaning white people's silent racism produces (and reproduces) institutional racism.

For Bourdieu, practice is what people *do* and is not tied to an actor's intention. In other words, "practice happens" (Jenkins 1992: 70).[2] This does not imply that practice occurs accidentally or randomly. Practice is structured, but it happens, nevertheless, without being entirely in the awareness of the actor. Like Giddens, Bourdieu sees practice as the result of actors' understanding of things—what Bourdieu calls *practical logic* and Giddens calls *practical knowledge*. This means that well-meaning white people who produce institutional racism do so without intention. I do not make this point so that well-meaning whites are excused for their part in the production of institutional racism; rather, I make it in order to expose the fact that well-meaning white people contribute to the problem of institutional racism and to racial inequality.

Bourdieu's depiction of practice is contingent on the concepts of *habitus* and *field.* Simply put, *habitus* refers to people's conception of reality. More specifically, it is a set of dispositions that does not cause a given action but does "incline" an actor to take certain action (Butler 1999: 114). The word *habitus* is Latin for "habit," the notion that ideas are taken for granted, not necessarily thought through. For Bourdieu, speech illustrates how habitus works. People generally do not think through the precise words they will use in a given conversation; they improvise. Most people take part in conversations effortlessly, using speech spontaneously and often automatically. This is because speech is taken for granted, just as habits are taken for granted. Bourdieu says that people carry out most social interactions in a similar fashion—automatically, and without thinking.

Sociologically, acting from habit was apparent in the writing of both Emile Durkheim and Max Weber (Camic 2000). Only later was the concept eschewed by American functionalists striving to set sociology apart from psychology. Talcott Parsons (1949) in particular avoided Weber's use of *habit* as traditional action—action taken without thinking—and focused instead on action determined by the norms of society. Parsons's effort to frame sociological theory as a structural explanation for action in contrast to psychological theory—especially the behaviorist claim that action is an automatic response to stimuli—had the effect of casting all action as voluntaristic, and therefore deliberate (Camic 2000). The symbolic interactionist counterclaim that action is not always determined by the norms of society but often relies on human agency sets up an either/or dichotomy. The result is that *action* came to be viewed by American sociologists as either determined by norms of society or the result of human agency, both of which avoid action as habit. The resulting micro/macro divide is evident in race theory, and my goal is to bridge that divide by introducing actors—in this case, well-meaning whites—into the production of institutional racism.

Bonilla-Silva (2003) borrows the term *habitus* when he speaks of a "white habitus that creates and conditions [white people's] views, cognitions, and even sense of beauty" (p. 123). This quote impies that the white habitus, which embodies white people's view of the world as well as their view of themselves in relation to others, is central to white people's actions. If the white habitus is filled with silent racism that is taken for granted, the action following from it will necessarily reflect that silent racism. This action is what I call *racist practice.*

Field, a concept related to habitus, refers to a network of social positions, which themselves are embedded within dominant, subordinate, and equivalent power relations (Bourdieu [1980] 1990). A social field becomes embued by race in any situation where race or racism is invoked, regardless of who is present in the field. For example, everyday racism does not necessarily occur between black and white individuals. To the contrary, much everyday racism is carried out among white people (Feagin 2001). This occurs often in casual conversation or with jokes that would not be stated in the presense of a person of color but are performed "in private" (Bonilla-Silva 2003: 56). Because of our collective history, all U.S. organizations have a racial component. This means that the field embodies race and that the possibility for racist practice is likely. Moreover, as if the white habitus were not enough to produce racist practice, the social field contributes as well. The field puts "demands" on the habitus (Butler 1999: 117), altering it at a given moment; put differently, the habitus adapts to the field. For example, the social field in a bank where red-lining is an accepted practice has a field in which racist practice would be the path of least resistance (see Johnson 1997). *Not* to take the path of least resistance would require a deliberate act because it would entail departing from existing expectations.

It is safe to say that practice not only happens but that practice matters. In this regard, it is useful to delineate what practice is not. *Practice* does not refer to individuals' enactment of societal norms and values, so practice is not determined. Neither does *practice* imply agency, the idea that action is chosen. Rather, *practice* refers to action that occurs without thought. Through practice, people produce effects that reinforce social institutions. Much of institutional racism, clearly that which is not intentional, results from racist practice made up of thoughtless actions based on silent racism that was learned unawarely and is acted upon unawarely.

The view that racist practice produces institutional racism is pertinent to a debate among social psychologists, described herewith.

Social Psychology and Practice

Stereotyping is closely related to differential categorization, the process described in Chapter 3. Differences among members of the out-group are minimized in the sorting process, whereas differences between members of the in-group are recognized, making out-group members appear to be more similar to each other than they really are (Fiske and Taylor 1984). The frames for organizing information of out-groups are less complex than those for organizing information of in-groups. More differentiation therefore occurs in in-groups (Jussim, Coleman, and Lerch 1987).

Some studies within the social psychology literature support the idea that the spontaneous activation of well-learned responses may cause whites who reject negative stereotypes about blacks to inadvertently act in accordance with the stereotypes due to an automatic response (Devine 1989). Others in the field refute this finding, arguing that people are not "wired to categorize" (Fiske 1989: 251) and that stereotyping need not be a given, that people can individuate out-group members instead of stereotyping them if they try. The concern is related to discrimination cases, which rely heavily on intent in order for discrimination to be proven, a very difficult barrier to overcome.[3] If a plaintiff cannot prove that discrimination was intended, he or she has little chance of winning a discrimination case. This view favors human agency in that it assumes that people who stereotype are making a choice to do so because other options are available for them. By stereotyping, then, people exhibit intent. The remedy is for people to concentrate and make the hard choice by "valiantly" choosing to individuate instead of choosing to stereotype (Fiske 1989: 267).

However, John Bargh (1999), also a social psychologist, disagrees with the claim that stereotyping can be interrupted by will, arguing that successful attempts to interrupt stereotypical thoughts had been accomplished in the laboratory and would be impossible to replicate in the real world. Bargh lists four conditions, all of which must be met if an attempt to interrupt stereotyping in people's lives is to succeed. First, people must be aware of particular stereotypes they hold in order to interrupt them; second, they must be aware of how a given stereotype impacts their thinking and action if they expect to interrupt it; third, they must be overly vigilant in noticing when a stereotype is triggered; and fourth, they must have the goal of interrupting a given stereotype in mind at the moment it is triggered (Bargh 1999). These conditions place an impossible burden on people in their everyday lives, making interrupting stereotypes highly unlikely. I am in agreement with Bargh: compliance with the conditions he identifies would entail an inordinate reliance on human agency, an assumption underlying Fiske's remedy. Some even say that trying to suppress stereotypes may have an opposite, ironic effect by activating the very stereotypes one is trying to suppress (Bodenhausen and Macrae 1996; Wegner 1994).

Although I agree that interrupting automatic stereotyping is not feasible, I am more optimistic than Bargh, who says that little can be done realistically to lessen stereotypical thinking. If we think of stereotypes as being embedded in the white habitus, and if we assume that racist practice proceeds from the white habitus, then we see why racist practice is not likely to be disrupted by being vigilant. However, suppressing stereotypes may not be the only way to lessen them; increasing race awareness by increasing the number of close ties with blacks may be another, better way. The challenge is to change the white habitus.

Critique of Bourdieu

The critique of Bourdieu ironically does not diminish the utility of his ideas for explaining the production of institutional racism. Criticisms of Bourdieu's theories include their being overly structural, especially for blurring the line between the structural and the cultural (Apple 1982; Giroux 1983; MacLeod 1987)—a critique that Bourdieu rejects (1989)—and for his disregard of human agency (Margolis 1999; also see Mehan 1992). The criticism that Bourdieu blurs the line between structure and culture may be what is needed regarding race theory. The misleading separation of structure and culture lessens the explanatory power of theories regarding institutional racism, forcing theories into either a macro- or a microlevel analysis. Explaining how institutional racism operates as a process entails the inclusion of culture. Structure without culture is static and cannot produce anything, including racism. Taking the relational view adopted here, culture and structure are inextricably linked. Sociologists agree that a change in structure produces a change in culture; however, a more interesting question is: If large enough, would a change in culture also produce a change in structure?

In terms of the criticism that Bourdieu disregards human agency, I would argue that the inclination of some social psychologists to stress the role of human agency in racist behavior obscures the racism of well-meaning white people, setting them apart from overt racists, just as the oppositional categories do. Bourdieu's focus on unintended action offers important insights that are useful to race theory in explaining the important role of well-meaning white people in the production of institutional racism.

In arguing that racist practice happens without thought, I do not claim that racist practice is inevitable because of cognitive processes. Nor do I suggest that racist practice is unavoidable because silent racism exists in the white habitus. However, to say that racist practice is not inevitable or unavoidable is different from saying that it is not predictable. And because practice results from actors' understanding of things, racist practice appears to be strongly linked to people's level of race awareness. Practice is not intended to accomplish particular ends; therefore, it is plausible that the lower one's race awareness, the higher the likelihood of practice having unintended racist consequences. If that is correct, then the converse is true as well: the higher one's race awareness, the lower the likelihood of practice having unintended racist consequences. Moreover, the higher one's race awareness, the higher the likelihood of antiracist practice, action that interrupts others' racist practice. Notice that agency is not part of this equation. Rather, when the white habitus contains a clearer understanding of race matters, the practice that emerges from it is not as likely to produce institutional racism and may in fact decrease it.

Not all racist action taken by well-meaning white people is taken through habit, even though much of it is. Everyday racism, which is performed with more intention than racist practice, also contributes to institutional racism. Symbolic interactionism helps to explain how the purposeful action of well-meaning whites also contributes to the production of institutional racism.

Symbolic Interaction and Everyday Racism

The difference between racist practice and everyday racism concerns intention. Racist practice is action that is not intended; everyday racism is intended action although there may be no intention that the action have racist effects. The emphasis on human agency sets symbolic interactionist theory apart from Bourdieu's theory of practice.

Everyday racism is similar to racist practice in that both arise from the silent racism in people's minds. However, everyday racism, unlike racist practice, is intended behavior. This is made clear through the symbolic interactionist concept of definition of the situation. W. I. Thomas argued in 1923 that the definition of the situation is a "stage of examination and deliberation" that precedes any "self-determined act of behavior" (p. 42). Actors interpret a situation through self-communication, using what is noticed in the present and drawing on relevant information from the past. According to symbolic interactionist theory, the deliberation process entails human agency. It is important to note that although everyday racism occurs through deliberate acts, the actor may be unaware that a particular act would be racist. This point contradicts the commonsense (and false) notion that people's intention regarding an act determines whether the act is racist. Ignorance of what is racist is not a safegaurd against performing everyday racism.

An individual's definition of a situation precedes any action he or she may take. The Thomas theorem captures this point: "If [people] define situations as real, they are real in their consequences" (Thomas and Thomas 1928: 572). In the Thomas theorem, "consequences" refers to whatever action results from the actor's definition of a given situation (see Ball 1972). Thus, unless what is noticed is problematic—in some way at odds with people's expectations—they are likely to use their definitions as a reliable guide to action, including those definitions embued with racist thoughts and beliefs. Definitions contaminated with silent racism, then, will necessarily produce racist actions, including when those actions are deliberate. The definition of the situation consists of the total of all recognized information from one's point of view (Ball 1972). Individuals both rely on the information they have in devising their definitions *and* interpret the information through their particular point of view. As data from this study illustrate, the white point of view is consistently represented by misconceptions, negative emotions, and white assumptions regarding race matters. Because one's definition of the situation is precisely what is regarded (by the actor) as relevant in determining behavior, individuals without awareness of their own silent racism cannot see that any behavior following from it, deliberate or otherwise, will be racist.

Symbolic interactionism is helpful in illustrating that what people think (that is, their definitions) determines what they do intentionally. This line of thinking is useful when well-meaning white people take action purposefully that inadvertently produces racist effects. For example, in Thomas and Thomas's preceding statement, "examination" and "deliberation" as well as "self-determined act of behavior" all imply that people choose their behavior based on their thoughts and images. Consider Karen's patronizing attitude toward her black friend in the ice cream parlor. Karen believed that Belle could not negotiate ordering her own ice cream, a paternalistic assumption. This belief is why Karen ordered Belle's ice cream for her. Karen's deliberate act suggested that Belle was her inferior. Belle sensed Karen's patronizing attitude and rebuffed it. It does not matter that Karen did not intend, or even know, that the effect of her act would be racist.

If a patronizing incident similar to the one above occurred in the workplace, it would be problematic for Belle, who might be seen as difficult or even a troublemaker by her white coworkers if she rebuffed what they would likely see as a generous gesture. The only other response for Belle—not reacting to a coworker's patronizing attitude—would produce stress of a different sort. She would then be putting up with white people's everyday racism, a type of stress that may account for why turnover is greater in more diverse work groups (O'Reilly, Caldwell, and Barnett 1989; Wagner, Pheffer, and O'Reilly 1984).

The role of silent racism in the minds of well-meaning white people produces institutional racism in two ways: through racist practice that is taken routinely without thought, and through everyday racism, which is action that is intended even though the racist effects it causes may not be intended or even known to the actor. Because silent racism is protected by the oppositional categories of racism, changing how we think about racism is an important goal. Another reason to change the oppositional categories is the passivity of some well-meaning white people. Some of the passivity is a result of the "not racist" category, indicating that evidence for eliminating the categories is mounting.

Passivity and the Production of Institutional Racism

A central question must be answered in this section on the production of institutional racism: is passivity in the presence of everyday racism and racist practice, itself, racist practice? I turn to social network theory for insight into this question. Network analysts avoid explaining individuals' motives for behavior, relying solely on action and its effects (Wellman 1983). In explaining social phenomena, network analysts therefore ignore both attitude—a central component of macrosociologists—and human agency—an underlying assumption of many microsociologists. Network analysts instead focus on the "social distribution of possibilities: the unequal availability of resources such as information, wealth, and influence as well as the structures through which people may have access to these resources" (Wellman 1977: 163). This makes network theory especially compatible with Bourdieu's theory of practice and the concept of racist practice. Social network theory also ignores categorical variables such as race and class, focusing solely on relational data such as number of social ties and strength of ties (Wellman 1983). This relational method allows network analysts to describe structure in terms of its inhabitants' connectivity rather than in terms of group attitudes or other normative characteristics.

A modeling approach demonstrates that theories of social structure should not only consider what actors do but also what they do *not* do. "Social causation is a process" that entails action and/or inaction (Whitmeyer 1994: 156). Because neither action nor inaction can be performed by a structure, human actors—or groups of actors—are a necessary component of the model. This means that in order for institutional racism to cause racial inequality, individuals' action (everyday racism and racist practice) and inaction (passivity) will be involved in the process. Passivity, then, is a significant feature in the production of institutional racism. Patterns develop through the action and inaction of actors, producing a given effect, called structure; therefore, an individual actor's performance is not the focus of the modeling approach. Patterns within an organization are what count.

There are three components of the network model: action, inaction, and effect. *Action* refers to what people do, *inaction* refers to what people do not do, and *effect* refers to the outcome of the other two components of the model. Regarding the production of institutional racism, action is the everyday racism and racist practice that results from silent racism in the habitus; inaction is the passivity found in well-meaning whites, those who are either detached from race matters, who experience apprehension about being racist, or who are confused about race issues; and the effect of these—everyday racism, racist practice, and passivity—within a given social system is indirect

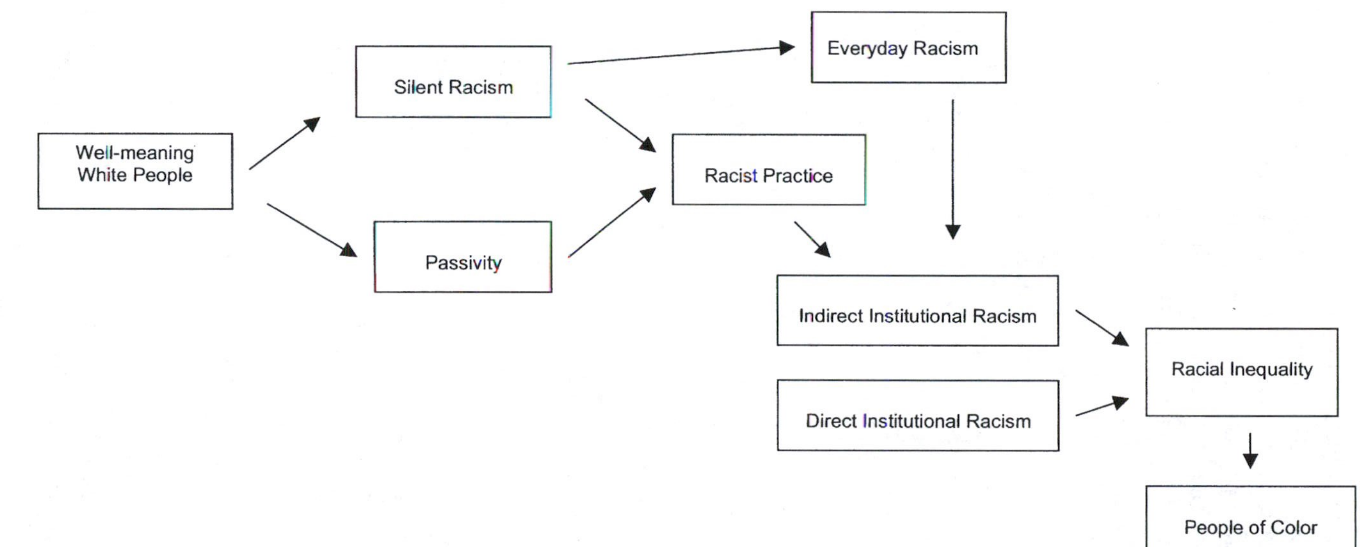

Figure 4.1 Map of Production of Institutional Racism

institutional racism. See Figure 4.1 for a map of the production of institutional racism by well-meaning whites.

If passivity, or inaction, matters, then it produces some effect. Social network theory answers the question posed earlier in the affirmative: passivity in the presence of everyday racism and racist practice is, itself, racist practice. If we recall the literature on the bystander role, we will remember that passive bystanders have a significant effect on the people involved in an incident of wrongdoing, especially on the transgressor, who is empowered (Staub 2003). In the case of institutional racism, passivity, then, has an empowering effect on others' racism, and this effect alone qualifies it as racist practice. Passivity, whether it is caused by detachment from race matters or from the latent effects of the "not racist" category, is a noteworthy component in the production of institutional racism.

Conclusion

In this chapter, I have offered a theory that explains how well-meaning white people—in contrast to overt racists and to color-blind racists—perpetuate racism. Silent racism and the racist practice and everyday racism that follow from it are forces behind much of the institutional racism that perpetuates the racial divide. Furthermore, the passivity of well-meaning white people encourages institutional racism. In addition to direct institutional racism produced intentionally by whites who harbor ill will toward blacks, indirect racism performed daily by well-meaning white people who intend no harm deserves theoretical attention. As it stands, most sociological race theory ignores this less obvious form of racism in favor of "a phenomenon anchored in whites' rational defense of their collective ... advantages" (Bonilla-Silva 2003: 193). Racist practice, everyday racism, and passivity are significant and should not be ignored or misinterpreted as a defense of white privilege. This is the racism of racial progressives—the neoliberals and new abolitionists—who are the putative allies of blacks and other people of color today, just as abolitionists and antisegregationists were their allies in the past.

The existence of the "not racist" category produces in the minds of well-meaning white people the illusion that they bear no responsibility for institutional racism or for racial inequality. Yet, silent racism cannot be isolated from the racist practice and everyday racism of white people who produce indirect institutional racism daily, regardless of their recognition of it or their intention to do so. In this way, the illusion that most white people are "not racist" virtually ensures the perpetuation of institutional racism. Although silent racism by definition is not spoken aloud, it would be a mistake to assume that it is of little importance or that the behavior following from it is not racist. Passivity by white people is also important in maintaining the process of institutional racism. It not only colludes with institutional racism, allowing it to operate without interruption, but also encourages it.

Most white people believe that race is no longer a problem in the United States (Blauner 1994), that racism disappeared when slavery ended and legal segregation was abolished. To the contrary, the ravages of slavery persisted throughout the Jim Crow era,[4] and racial inequality supported in the past by law continues to this day. Nevertheless, some conservative writers (e.g., Thernstrom and Thernstrom 1997) argue that racism has declined precipitously since the mid-1960s, a claim that has a strong hold on the white American psyche. But the conservative claim ignores subtle forms of racism, focusing instead on overt racism. Given that the oppositional categories "racist/not racist" uphold this false claim, racial conservatives have a stake in keeping the categories as they are. Nevertheless, the truth that everyone is somewhat racist and that the silent racism hidden by the "not racist" category perpetuates the racial divide—a truth that most blacks already know—could cause a cultural/political shift if recognition of the truth occurs at the "less racist" end of the racism continuum. It is not imperative or probable that all whites would recognize the truth of these ideas. Neither would all whites consider that they might be racist. However, if racial progressives—the least likely whites to be racist—recognize their own racism and act on that acknowledgment, the category "not racist" would not hold.

I point out in the next chapter that race awareness should receive at least as much attention from race theorists as white people's racism. Whites, including those who are well meaning, are woefully ignorant of race matters. Many well-meaning white people know little of the history of racism in the United States, and most are not aware of institutional racism. Fewer still are aware that their own silent racism shapes what they do, often without their knowing, and that racist practice, silent and everyday racism, and passivity hold the racial formation in place.

Notes

1. It is interesting to note that Turner and Singleton claim that the working class is less likely to hold progressive beliefs regarding racism, a claim that is contradicted by Bonilla-Silva's finding that working-class females are the most likely whites to hold antiracist beliefs. This disjunction may be the result of gender difference rather than class difference. Turner and Singleton's claim is based on Bonacich's study (1972), which was done in the early 1970s and was based primarily on working-class men, not women.

2. Practice being outside an actor's awareness is related to Hall's (1959) observation that what people learn informally has an impact on action even if the impact is not in the person's awareness.

3. In many cases, the plaintiff must prove intent to discriminate through a burden-shifting formula: one, the plaintiff's case must show that a discriminatory action occurred; two, the employer must articulate a nondiscriminatory reason for the action taken; and three, the plaintiff must prove that the employer's stated reason is fabricated in order to hide discrimination.

4. I encourage you to visit the Jim Crow Museum on-line at www.Ferris.edu/jimcrow/ for an informative glimpse into many artifacts from the era of segregation.

Chapter Five

Race Awareness Matters

IN THIS CHAPTER I ILLUSTRATE how race awareness affects what people do and do not do. Arguing that well-meaning white people should be more concerned about their level of race awareness than about whether they are racist may sound shocking unless you remember the primary finding of this study: all white people are somewhat racist. The shift from focusing on whether one is racist to focusing on one's race awareness is useful because race awareness in well-meaning white people is instrumental in lessening institutional racism in the post–civil rights era.

Race awareness entails understanding three facets of racism. First, race awareness requires knowledge of the racism that has occurred throughout U.S. history, including the cultural practices and beliefs that supported slavery and segregation (see Feagin 2001). Second, race awareness requires recognition of whites' advantage over blacks in today's racial formation (see Bonilla-Silva 2003 and Wellman 1993). Called *white privilege,* the advantage includes the effects of institutional racism that disadvantage blacks (therefore advantaging whites) despite passage of antidiscrimination laws intended to prevent it. And third, race awareness requires insight concerning one's own silent racism—the images and assumptions about black Americans in one's own mind and the actions that proceed from them (Trepagnier 2001).

Other authors have constructed concepts similar to silent racism that indicate a relationship to race awareness. For example, *unconscious racism* refers to white people's irrational racist thoughts, which are at odds with the American values of fairness and equality. Unconscious racism is said to be learned and then repressed by all white Americans (Ross 1990). Similarly, *dysconscious racism* refers to distorted thinking characterized by a tacit agreement with white norms and the privileges they engender (King 1991). Both concepts are thought to keep whites from recognizing the advantages they receive from the racial status quo. Although use of the word *unconscious* is not altogether uncommon in the sociological literature, I avoid it because of the implication that what is unconscious is inaccessible except through some sort of theraputic intervention.[1] I prefer to stress that silent racism, which is learned informally, though outside of people's awareness is not in their unconscious as defined by Freud (Hall 1959). Racism is accessible, just as one's bad manners or inappropriate language is assessible, particularly if someone else points it out.

Race awareness concerns individuals' mindfulness of race matters, including their own racism.[2] Very high race awareness implies critical self-reflexivity regarding race matters; that is, the tendency to consider one's own behavior in terms of race and racism. Social reflexivity, a concept derived from self-reflexivity, implies that one is critically aware, not only of the effects of one's personal behavior but also of the effects of the collective actions of one's social group (Trepagnier 1993). Social reflexivity, then, includes the sense that dominant group members treat black Americans, as a group, unfairly. This outlook may or may not be accompanied by an explicit understanding that race inequality is tied to social structures.

Developing race awareness entails listening to people who have knowledge about racism (Frye 1983)—primarily black Americans and other people of color. Relationships with black acquaintances and friends are especially helpful if they are based on trust and if conversations about race occur. Developing race awareness also requires obtaining correct information. White people often lack historical facts about racism, facts that are available for people who want them.

The Race Awareness Continuum

The comparisons in this chapter illustrate the importance of race awareness in well-meaning white people. It is important to keep in mind that the analyses do not concern participants' level of racism but, rather, their level of race awareness, which is also depicted by a continuum.

Although there is a relationship between one's level of race awareness and one's level of racism, the two differ significantly. The racism continuum, as discussed in Chapter 2, depicts racism characterized as more racist (race hatred characterized by blatant, overt racism), moderately racist (color-blind racism), and less racist (silent racism that produces racist practice and everyday racism). The race awareness continuum, in comparison, indicates people's understanding of racism in terms of historical, societal, and personal significance.

Based on responses and interaction in the focus groups, I have identified participants on the race awareness continuum at the following points: *very high* race awareness (three participants), *high* race awareness (six participants), *moderate* race awareness (six participants), *low* race awareness (four participants), and *very low* race awareness (six participants).[3] See Appendix C for a list of the participants in order of their race awareness. Figure 5.1 is the race awareness continuum.

The analyses in this chapter are arranged into three sections, each of which compares two focus group participants from different points on the race awareness continuum. The first analysis compares participants at opposite poles of the continuum—Ruth, who has "very high" race awareness, is compared to Janice, who has "very low" race awareness relative to other participants in the study. The second and third analyses move to the midpoint on the continuum, comparing participants with "moderate" race awareness to each end of the continuum. More specifically, Elaine, who has "moderate" race awareness, is compared to Martha, who has "very high" race awareness; and Molly, who has "moderate" race awareness, is compared to Joan, who has "very low" race awareness. Each of the three comparisons offers interesting insights into why race awareness in well-meaning white people is important.

Very High and Very Low Race Awareness (Ruth and Janice)

Ruth and Janice differ qualitatively in terms of race awareness: Ruth has very high race awareness whereas Janice's race awareness is very low. Yet, despite their differences regarding race awareness, Ruth,

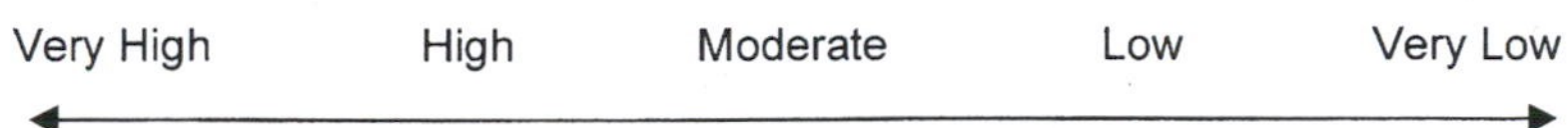

Figure 5.1 Race Awareness Continuum

age forty-seven, and Janice, age thirty-nine, have many similarities in terms of their biographies. Both participants were born on the West Coast and have lived there most of their lives. Both were raised in "mainstream" religions that they have since rejected. Ruth and Janice also both consider themselves feminists, although their definitions of feminism differ dramatically. Ruth views feminism as "dealing with equality at all levels, including issues such as affirmative action, sexual harassment, and diversity in the curricula." Janice defines feminism in very general terms as being "woman-centered" and includes no mention of social justice issues either for women specifically or for any other group. Figure 5.2 illustrates Ruth and Janice in relation to the race awareness continuum.

Ruth's very high race awareness stands in stark contrast to Janice's very low race awareness. Janice is characterized by an inclination to defend white people's social position in relation to other groups, with no consideration of historical differences such as slavery and segregation. Janice's color blindness presuppposes a level playing field between blacks and whites. Furthermore, people with very low race awareness such as Janice do not perceive race and racism as important issues.

A defining difference between Ruth and Janice concerns their divergent attitudes regarding *whiteness* as a concept. Although Ruth and Janice took part in different focus groups, I have constructed a "metadialogue" about whiteness between these two very different participants. Ruth's and Janice's relative stances regarding how they respond to others' racism are also compared.

The conversation about whiteness begins with Janice, who spoke openly of her misgivings about the idea in a post–focus group interview, which Janice requested instead of writing in a journal. The incident concerns Janice's upset about Charlotte using the phrase "so white." Janice said, in her post–focus group interview, "Those are the kinds of things that really bug me. I've always thought, 'But what does that mean to say something like *so white*?' It's always said

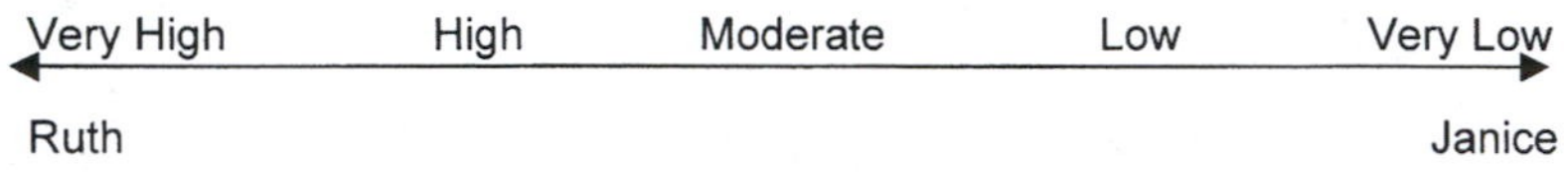

Very High	High	Moderate	Low	Very Low
Ruth				Janice

Figure 5.2 Ruth and Janice on the Race Awareness Continuum

with a certain tone; it's definitely a negative thing. And yet I thought [that] if anyone said, 'Oh, that is so black!' they would be the first to jump in and say, 'Oh, that's racist.' I felt offended by that phrase." Janice reasoned that if "so black" is deemed racist by liberals, then "so white" is also racist. Lacking in Janice's analysis is recognition of the concept of white privilege, the idea that whites have advantages that blacks do not have. The negative tone that Janice correctly interprets in Charlotte's use of the phrase "so white" derives from Charlotte's view that white people are overadvantaged in comparison to blacks. However, Janice does not acknowledge the overadvantage of whites, so she interpreted the phrase "so white" as personally demeaning to white people.

Ruth would disagree with Janice that "so white" is racist in the same way that "so black" is. Ruth, a teacher at a local community college, stated in her focus group that the privileging of white over black is built into the English language:

> One of the most astounding exercises I got caught up in came out of a study that was in a textbook where they were talking about using different colors of football jerseys, black and white, and having people assess the amount of violence that the players engaged in. The players in black [jerseys] are always perceived as being much more aggressive. This led to getting out a huge dictionary and looking at the two terms "black" and "white." And when you read the definitions, which I now make my classes do, it just hits you right between the eyes that you can't use those two words without being prejudicial because it's in the language. And that's why referring to African Americans as "black" is truly demeaning. Because you're saying they're on the dark side, they're on the sinister side, and those are definitions by Webster. So all of a sudden [it] was a real eye-opener for me. When you talk about implied racism, that's where I think it is. It's in the language.

Ruth says that *black* is intrinsically racist and therefore must always imply racism whenever it is used. I understand Ruth's point that negative meanings are attached to *black* and related terms. However, her analysis does not consider the "black is beautiful" movement and the fact that many black Americans prefer the term *black* over *African American.*

Janice, in turn, would disagree with Ruth that the meanings attached to *white* and *black* have any relevance in terms of human beings.

She argued in her focus group that using skin color, including black, as a marker has no negative connotations. Janice said:

> I lived in Mexico for three years—and there everybody talks about skin color. Here [in the U.S.] we don't constantly talk about skin color, but people there [do]—they've got all these words for different shades of people's skin. You use it in the course of describing someone. But here you might stop and think before you said, "Oh, it was a black woman." Just in terms of description, it's just sort of a given, it's a matter of course, it's a matter of describing someone, because everybody has, basically, the majority have black hair and maybe black eyes, but there are these fine shades of skin color. I got a lot of comparison too, being from the United States and obviously my [blond] coloring. Down there, it would just come up because I was the one that was different.

In claiming that skin color has no negative connotation in Mexico, Janice seems to imply that it therefore has no negative connotation in the United States. Yet, can we make that assumption? Ruth would say no, offering herself as evidence that using color as a marker is indeed sometimes racist. As mentioned in Chapter 3, Ruth referred to the issue when I asked if anyone in her focus group would share about how they have carried out subtle forms of racism:

> Oh, I do [that]. This friend of mine teaches Race and Ethnic Studies and so we go 'round and 'round with this all the time. Our position really is that you can't grow up in this society without being racist, and I'll catch myself saying—well, I have this really bright student in my class except, before, I'd say to her, "A really bright black student in my class," or "A really bright Chicano in my class," or something of that sort, and she'd turn around and say, "Why did you say that? Isn't he just a student?" So I have caught myself where I have felt that I really needed to acknowledge that, by Jove, I had a bright black student in my class who had a lot to add to the course and stuff of that sort. And so I've really begun to watch those instances. Now I may stop myself from saying it, but I still have the mental voice that's noting that it was a black student.

Ruth's point is that it can be racist to use color as a marker if, in doing so, there is an unstated assumption about that person. In this case, the fact of the student's blackness gave the statement meaning.[4]

The preceding conversation about whiteness demonstrates a fundamental difference in the perspectives of Janice and Ruth in regard to race issues. We can infer that Janice would not perceive racism in cases where Ruth undoubtedly would. Janice and Ruth's differences extend to other themes that arise in the data as well. Ruth was the first person in her group to acknowledge her own racism; Janice, by contrast, could not remember ever having been racist. This was clear when I asked participants in her focus group if they could remember a time when they had been racist in the past. Janice replied,

> Well, uh, I don't know; I've been trying to draw parallels because more of my experiences come from interacting with Mexicans, Mexican Americans, Latinos, and on a larger scale. One thing that I was thinking of a few minutes ago was what you [Anita—a group member] were saying about identifying parallels, like being a lesbian. For me, growing up, I really saw a parallel in the class issue, and I definitely was aware of being, sort of, you know, on the wrong end of the class scale. I can remember as a kid seeing those parallels and I think I was aware of racism because of what I felt—the classism that I felt.

Janice seems to deflect the question about remembering a time she was racist by exploring the issue of class discrimination instead. Her shift to class issues is not evidence of racism; rather, it is evidence that Janice may be unaware of any racist tendencies in herself. While it is important to say that Janice's lack of awareness is not a sign of racism, neither does it imply that she has never been racist.

Despite the differences, there is one similarity between Janice and Ruth that bears mentioning. Both have had, or currently have, a close relationship with a black American. Janice mentioned in her post–focus group interview that she has had an eighteen-year friendship with a black woman. They have traveled together several times and were in touch during the time of the focus group and the interview. Ruth also mentioned relationships with black women over the years. Nevertheless, this similarity does not seem to affect the marked difference in race awareness between the two women. It could be that the difference results from whether the black-white relationships involve conversations about race. Ruth shared in her group about a conversation that she had with black women at a conference about race. There is no evidence that Janice has had such conversations.

Janice and Ruth are not exact replicas of the other participants at the ends of the race awareness continuum. However, differences between them are emblematic of differences between participants at opposite poles of the race awareness continuum. Like Ruth, other participants in this study who have very high race awareness have a keen sense of their own racism, however subtle it may be. Participants who have very low race awareness, by contrast, do not see that they have any relation to racial inequality, nor do they sense that they are in any way racist, although some within this group have "good intentions" regarding race matters.

Moderate and Very High Race Awareness (Elaine and Martha)

The second comparison explores differences between Elaine, at the midpoint on the continuum, and Martha, who has very high race awareness. Their placement on the continuum indicates that they both have some degree of awareness, even though Elaine differs from Martha in important ways. In terms of background and personal characteristics, the two do not differ significantly. Elaine is thirty years old; Martha is thirty-two. Both were born in California and have lived most of their lives there. Both women are in graduate school, Elaine in sociology, Martha in educational psychology. Elaine comes from a "nonspecific, nonpracticing" Protestant family, and Martha was raised a Christian Scientist; neither participant is involved in religion today. These participants' definitions of feminism differ noticeably. Elaine has a distinctively sociological definition of feminism: "Fighting the systems which propagate inequalites like the economy, education, marriage laws, and cultural issues." Martha's definition of feminism is less precise. Martha is wary of what she considers the divisiveness caused by the women's movement, and she believes in equality for everyone. She said that she sees herself as a humanist rather than a feminist. Figure 5.3 illustrates Martha and Elaine in relation to the race awareness continuum.

The most fundamental similarity between Elaine and Martha concerns their corresponding views regarding race difference and their sense of race awareness. Elaine expressed this when telling the group about an

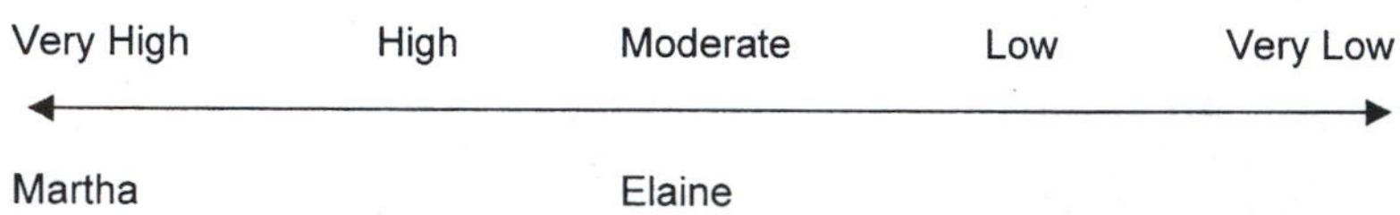

Figure 5.3 Martha and Elaine on the Race Awareness Continuum

experience she had in high school with a black student. Elaine said, "I had these really strange experiences with this [black] guy in my algebra class in high school. He was really angry, and he would—I don't know what I did—I was passing papers back. He would turn around and scream, 'I'm tired of your people oppressing my people for four hundred years.' And I was ... oh man, you know? I felt bad but I also felt, I don't know why I had set him off, he would have said it to anyone." I asked if she had any further encounters with the student. Elaine replied:

> Yes, I told him that we [her family] haven't even been here that long—we're pretty fresh off the boat. I'm sorry, we got here way after slavery. [I used] some of those huge defenses like, "that's not my family"—trying to distance myself from it. At that time I was fourteen or fifteen and [I thought] I'm not implicated in that because to me then, the only implication could have been historical through some sort of lineage—that my grandparents would have had to have been slaveholders or something. He [the student] was such an unlikeable person, but still, it sort of resonated with me and that's been one of the experiences that I've had different interpretations of as my attitudes have changed. At one point it was, "Screw you," and then after that it was, "Maybe he's right, well, I *should* feel bad," moving through that to "Well, I'm not sure." I know I was scared—I was terrified.

I asked Elaine what she would say to him now, and she answered, "Now I would ask him what he meant by 'my people' and sort of 'fess up to, you know, talk about institutional racism and white people historically. But at the same time, I didn't know what to say." Elaine openly gives us a sense of how scared she was and of her defensive posture at the time the incident occurred. More important, she reveals how her thinking has progressed, from originally distancing herself from racism to considering her own privileged position in relation to racial inequality.

After high school Elaine attended a "very white college where racism was talked about in the abstract." Like most white people who hear of white privilege at all, Elaine learned about it as a theoretical concept. Martha is an exception; she shared the following story of how she learned about white privilege:

> I guess it just hit me. A [black] friend—we were going to a faraway basketball game and it involved staying in a hotel. The whole family was going, so we had her mom, [her] brother and sister, and me. When we pulled up to a hotel I sort of assumed that the mother would make the

> arrangements for the hotel room because it was her family and I was just along as a guest. But it was more or less unspoken on their part; they were surprised that I wasn't getting out of the car right away. They had to explain it me. They said, "Look, you would get a better room, so why don't you go make the arrangements?" I thought, oh, wow, talk about privilege! I'm assuming [there is none] and they just reminded me. Because they live with it every day. And it was a good experience for me to spend a lot of time and realize what it's like every day—every day. I even had nightmares—I thought, "What would it be like, every single moment of every day, being reminded that you're not good enough—for no particular reason." ... I can actually think of several other times too, and it just didn't feel good to have that kind of assumed power—and I realize I'm benefitting from it constantly.

Martha's firsthand experience of white privilege resulted from having it pointed out to her by black traveling companions who were surprised at her lack of awareness concerning her own race privilege. Whereas Elaine's awareness results from the *information* she has been told about "white privilege," Martha's awareness is experiential and therefore deeper.

Both of these participants are aware of their own racist tendencies. Elaine's apprehension about race difference and her inclination to avoid relationships with blacks as a result were shared openly by her (see Chapter 3). Martha also shared an example of having been racist (see Chapter 2), referring to an incident that had occurred recently in a conversation with a student from Uganda in which Martha implied that the exchange student differed in a positive way from black Americans. Martha was not only immediately aware that she had been racist but also tried to figure out a way to repair any harm her statement may have caused. Martha's example of racism differs from Elaine's in that it occurred recently whereas Elaine's occurred many years ago. Elaine knows that she holds back in this area and would like to stop doing so. She stated:

> At the beginning of your question you asked, "Where do you hold back?" And that made me think, just in terms of the kinds of relationships that I seek, that I do tend to stick very close to home and socialize with people that are like me.... It's comfortable, it's easy, the knowns outweigh the unknowns. And I think working against racism includes that fear of offending someone or fear of saying or doing the wrong thing and not being aware of it—like doing antiracist work in relationships

> because you don't have to do that if you're hanging out with people like you. So it's almost backwards in terms of being oversensitive. It's not like, "Oh, I don't want to be friends with you because you're black and you're strange, you're different," but "I don't want to be friends with you because you're black [and] because I realize that I really can't understand you or we have a lot of different things and I want to respect that"; I'm afraid I'm going to fall short of that, or maybe I'm going to subawarely or unawarely do something [like] I'm gonna make a mistake, and I don't want to have to worry about that.

Elaine's response illustrates her avoidance of involvement with blacks. Her concern about making a mistake is at the heart of her difference from Martha, who seems able to laugh at herself—"I didn't know whether to apologize to her or just sort of take my foot out of my mouth and go on"—despite her concern over making a racist comment. Martha is more deeply concerned about the race issue itself than about her own feelings. Her interest is evident in the following story. The incident occurred immediately after the 1992 Los Angeles uprising—the disturbance precipitated by the acquittal of the police officers who beat Rodney King, a black man:

> I was at a warehouse shopping area where people from certain [minority] communities would come to do their shopping, and I had the radio on and heard [about the acquittal]. This was right around 4:00, right when things were getting serious, and I just fell apart. I was still parking my car and [I] started sobbing and the car next to me had some people in it—there was a black family who'd come to shop. I thought, "I'm crying; everybody is going to see that I'm a wreck." So as I was getting out of the car several of the people—there was eye contact—and I said, "I just heard on the radio and I don't know what to do." I just fell apart in front of them and was saying, "I'm a teacher and I just don't know what to do. What can we do?" And they didn't know what to do with me. [laughing] But they got sympathetic, I guess, and they said, "Keep teaching, just keep teaching. And thank you." They said "thank you." I still cry when I think about it.

This illuminates the difference between one participant whose focus is inward, and another whose focus is outward. Elaine's distress about her own relationship to race matters, especially in the area of personal relations, keeps her attention focused inwardly to a degree. Martha has little distress in that area, and therefore her attention is focused in a more outward direction, on what she can do to make a difference in terms of race issues. Martha's ability to think more clearly about race matters—that is, her high race awareness—allows her to be actively antiracist.

Moderate and Very Low Race Awareness (Molly and Joan)

The final comparison considers differences between Molly, characterized by moderate race awareness, and Joan, who has very low race awareness. Although apparent, differences between Molly and Joan are not consistent. That is, one difference suggests that Molly is more aware than Joan, whereas another suggests the opposite.

Molly is a little over sixty years old, and Joan is in her mid-forties. Molly was born in California and has lived there most of her life. Joan was born in Michigan, moved to Oregon as a young child, and then lived in California beginning in her mid-thirties. Molly was raised Protestant; Joan had no religious affiliation growing up. Molly is a widow, following a twenty-five-year marriage, and has several grown daughters. Joan has never been married. Both women consider themselves to be feminists whose definitions vary somewhat, but not qualitatively. Molly cited "equality and choices for women" as her criteria for feminism, whereas Joan sees feminism as educating people about "mythologies that keep women and other groups down." Figure 5.4 depicts Molly and Joan in relation to the race awareness continuum.

Molly, who has moderate race awareness, stated that without the input she received from her daughters, she would not have the informed view of black Americans she has today. She said in response to a question about "holding back" in terms of being actively antiracist: "We need to be able to get to know [blacks] socially, and see that . . . they aren't the way they're portrayed on many of the television shows." I asked Molly how she thinks white women can get to know blacks. At first she replied, "I'll tell you right now . . . trying to get something

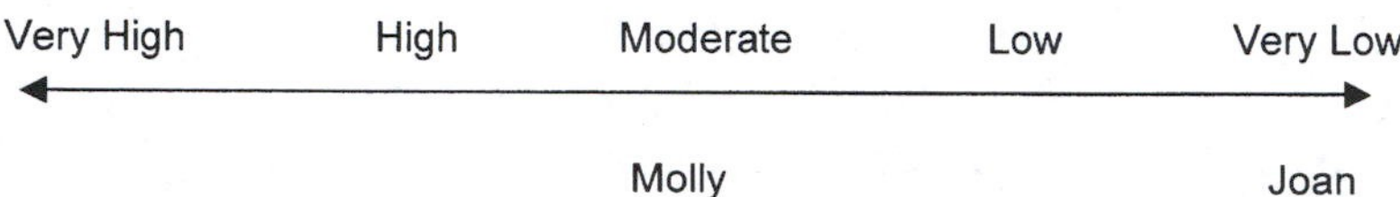

Figure 5.4 Molly and Joan on the Race Awareness Continuum

other than white women in the [League of Women Voters] is very, very difficult. We have one black member, and that's it. It's hard. How do you [get to know black women]?" Molly was frustrated that her political organization cannot attract black members, yet she seemed to lack information about why black women are not interested in her group. She did not mention the organization's agenda and its relevance for black women.

Despite Molly's seemingly tenuous connection to race and race issues, she was the first to answer when I asked participants what they do when a racist comment or joke is expressed around them. Molly responded emphatically, "I don't take it anymore. I simply don't take it anymore. If somebody tells an off-color ethnic joke I just say, 'I don't want to hear that. I don't like to hear jokes like that anymore.'" I asked Molly what kind of reaction she usually gets, and she said, "Well, sometimes they're sort of embarrassed, and sometimes they're almost angry, as though 'What's the matter with you?' But I don't see any reason to have to listen to it." Molly was neither hesitant nor tentative in her answer to the question, and her definitive response to racism around her suggests an active antiracist stance.

Joan, in comparison, has a very low race awareness. She spoke of a time in San Francisco in which she had experienced an intense fear of black men (described in Chapter 2). Her fear in itself does not characterize her as having low race awareness; however, Joan's insistence that the fear was not in any way irrational or racist does indicate an evasion of race as an issue.

Joan's unawareness is also evident in her response to the question, "What do you do if someone around you makes a racist comment?" She said,

> Well, I have a couple of family members that somehow got stuck about three generations back, and my brother, who is forty-something and does yard work which he calls landscaping, but when he's in a bad mood he calls it a slang term—he calls it "nigger-work." I don't talk with him very much, and that's one reason why. But when that first came up I was so shocked, I didn't respond. And, too, I have certain family dynamics where I've learned to shut up. In an office situation or something I'd probably correct someone or say, "Where did you get stuck?" In that situation [above] it was just so shocking because this person is my blood relative. I was shocked right into silence, I guess. Not so much by choice. Maybe next time—not that there will be one,

> but I would say, "Well, get with it!" And I don't know if he really feels that way, it's just like, it doesn't matter. [He should] leave that language alone; it's not his to toss around.

Joan's shift from telling about an actual past experience in her family—where she felt unable to interrupt the racism—to speculating about a hypothetical office situation are both indications of a passive antiracist stance. Although Joan clearly has good intentions, no antiracist action is evident in what she said.

Why Race Awareness Matters

The comparisons in this chapter offer implications for several lines of reasoning. The first is that race awareness increases as information about race issues and conversations with blacks about racism increase. White people—that is, well-meaning white people, not all white people—who have high or very high race awareness know that they are at times racist; it follows, then, that they would be less likely to defend against being racist, or that they would be colorblind. The three aspects of high race awarenes are, first, an understanding of the history of racism; second, an awareness of institutional racism and white privilege; and third, an awareness of one's own racism. High race awareness diminishes the need for defenses against being—or appearing to be—racist. Defenses protect the illusion that one is *not* racist, an illusion that is not present in those who have high race awareness. Even data from participants who have moderate race awareness support this view. Therefore, instead of striving to maintain a "not racist" image, increasing race awareness is a more constructive goal for well-meaning white people.

The comparisons in this chapter also imply that except for well-meaning white people with very high race awareness, like Martha and Ruth, apprehension about making racist mistakes is more likely in whites who have some degree of race awareness than those who have little race awareness. This point is counterintuitive until it is thought through. Well-meaning white people who have a moderate level of race awareness due to information about racism—like Elaine—understand that they benefit from the racial formation in the United States; in addition, they also realize that they are racist to a degree. Thus, information important to developing race awareness can also generate apprehension in well-meaning white people who believe that they should be "not racist." Furthermore, participants at the low end of the race awareness continuum, like Janice (and Sharon, mentioned elsewhere), who are *not* aware of their relationship to race or race issues and are *not* aware of their own racism, feel little personal accountability for the racial status quo or their own racism. The dissociation from race issues promotes a sense of indifference in whites that reinforces the belief that they are not implicated in race matters, including racial inequality.

This chapter highlights another interesting pattern in the data: participants who identify themselves as feminists do not necessarily have high race awareness. I assumed that self-described feminists would be more likely than other women to join the study because white women interested in ending sexism—the fundamental tenet of feminism—could be expected to have similar views about lessening racism. Overall, twenty of the twenty-five participants define themselves as feminists, and three of the five women who are ambivalent about feminism have very low race awareness. Furthermore, the most highly race-aware participant in the study—Martha—does not consider herself a feminist; however, she does see herself as a humanist. This finding could also be related to different definitions of the word *feminism* or to negative connotations about the word that became popularized by conservative talk show hosts like Rush Limbaugh.

Although people who have a moderate level of race awareness due to increased information about race issues are more apprehensive than people who have low race awareness, people who have very high race awareness are not apprehensive about their own racism even though they recognize it. What sets people with high race awareness apart appears to be their relationships with blacks and their conversations about race in those relationships. Both Martha and Ruth mentioned such conversations: Martha related how her black friends had to tell her to sign for the motel room, and Ruth mentioned the black women at a conference who were being ignored (see earlier in this chapter and Chapter 6, respectively). Participants who have a good deal of information about race matters but little interaction in terms of race issues with blacks are more likely to feel apprehensive about the possibility of "messing up," particularly if their attention is focused on themselves.

Having conversations about race with black friends or acquaintances appears to also increase the likelihood of lessening silent racism as stereotypical views of black men and women are replaced with insights gleaned from everyday interactions with black individuals. This idea, called the *contact hypothesis,* has been demonstrated in various studies.

The contact hypothesis—the view that interaction between members of two social groups promotes positive attitudes—was first introduced in the pre–civil rights era by Gordon Allport (1954). Since that time the theory has received mixed reviews (Sigelman and Welch 1993), resurfacing in the 1990s with renewed promise (Sigelman and Welch 1993; Smith 1994). The one consistent finding is that black/white interaction between equals is associated with positive attitudes about blacks among whites, although not always with positive attitudes about whites among blacks (Smith 1994). What is not clear is whether the positive attitudes among whites were caused by the interaction or were what precipitated interaction in the first place (Sigelman and Welch 1993). Data in this study corroborate three conditions of the contact hypothesis: first, the black/white contact must include conversations about race; second, the black/white contact must be between people that have equal rank—that is, it should be between friends or colleagues; and third, the black/white contact must involve a well-meaning white person who is open to having a close tie with a minority.

The symbolic interactionist concept of role-taking may be a critical element in why close ties with blacks, as well as conversations with blacks about race, increase whites' race awareness. George Herbert Mead saw the mind as a social entity—a process that becomes evident in interaction with others (Manis and Meltzer 1972). One of the primary concepts involved in this process is role-taking: seeing from the point of view of others (Charon 1998). Taking the role of the other serves two functions, a reflexive function and an empathic one. Both are important to this discussion. Reflexive role-taking refers to people seeing their own position in relation to the other. In black/white conversations about racism, white people may recognize that their own past behavior has at times been racist. Empathic role-taking refers to seeing the other's position and having an emotional response. Both forms of role-taking entail face-to-face interaction, which is why black/white contact is essential to understanding more about racism and about one's role in it. It appears that unequal relations obstruct role-taking for the person in the dominant role (Forte 1998), which helps explain why stereotyping is more common for people in dominant positions than those in subordinated ones, particularly in terms of empathy. Friendships, whether formed at work or socially, should be egalitarian if race awareness is to be increased.

Most of the studies on the contact hypothesis measure positive attitudes of whites—and sometimes blacks—using surveys. However, qualitative studies of how race awareness develops through close contact are needed. Neither race awareness nor conversations about race is included in the studies on the contact hypothesis. Nevertheless, the theory is compelling and merits consideration.

Whether having close relationships with persons of color increases race awareness or having high race awareness increases the likelihood of having close relationships with persons of color cannot be discerned definitively by the data collected here. However, each participant in the study who has high race awareness also has a close relationship with one or more persons of color, and racism is discussed in the relationship(s). Furthermore, the one participant—Janice—who had a close relationship with a person of color but did not have high race awareness indicated that race and racism were not discussed in the relationship. Therefore, close relationships with people of color do not guarantee that race awareness will increase. However, when conversations about race are part of the relationship, high race awareness is likely to develop. Out of all the participants in this study, Janice did not mention her eighteen-year friendship with a black woman when asked about cross-racial friendships in her focus group. Later, in her post–focus group interview, she said that she had not thought of referring to her longtime black friend during the focus group because "I don't think [having a black friend] is how I'm dealing with racism—that's not the way I frame it." For Janice, thinking of her friend as a "black friend" itself seems offensive, an example of racial etiquette that cannot acknowledge race. Ruth, Martha, and Lisa (mentioned in Chapter 6), the three participants who have very high race awareness, all have relationships with blacks and engage in discussion about race issues in their relationships.

Conclusion

Data indicate that low and moderate race awareness are related to passivity, which not only condones others' racist practice but also encourages it. When institutional racism occurs in the presence of well-meaning white people who have low or even moderate race awareness, racist practice and everyday racism are protected and promoted by their passivity.

The relationship between race awareness and racism warrants further discussion as well as further study. Nevertheless, based on the data in this study and current race theory, we can tentatively state the following: First, well-meaning white people who have high race awareness are less likely to perform racist practice and less everyday racism than those with low race awareness. Second, well-meaning white people with high race awareness are more likely to interrupt others' racist practice and everyday racism than those with low race awareness. Therefore, high race awareness in well-meaning white people would, it appears, decrease institutional racism that is caused unintentionally.

Race awareness in well-meaning white people—including racial progressives—is both sorely lacking and a critical piece of the racism puzzle. And yet, white racial progessives along with black and other minority racial progressives, if they were not so segregated and beset with misunderstanding, could shift the racial status quo by shifting how they think about racism. This is the project presented in the next chapter.

Notes

1. The idea that racism requires treatment is held by Alvin Poussaint (2001), who argues that extreme racism is a mental illness that should be treated professionally.

2. Well-meaning whites with high race awareness should not be confused with the concept of "race-conscious whites," those white people who harbor fears about the white race disappearing (Swain 2002: 317).

3. It should be noted that even the least race-aware participant in this study is likely to have more race awareness than some people in the general population. This presumption is based on the fact that all of the participants care about racism and made a decision to participate in the study.

4. Ruth's point here is similar to the point I make in Chapter 3 about when using *black* is racist. However, I disagree with Ruth's point earlier that *black* is necessarily always racist because of its negative connotation in the English language.

Chapter Six

Antiracist Practice

In Chapter 5 we considered three sets of focus group participants in terms of their relative levels of race awareness. The principal finding in the chapter was that people's race awareness is closely related to their passivity regarding racism. In Chapter 4, Bourdieu's ideas on practice—what people do without thinking—were helpful in illustrating the role of well-meaning white people in the production of institutional racism. I devised the term *racist practice* in reference to what whites do unintentionally that produces negative effects for people of color. Racist practice, along with everyday racism and passivity, are fundamental to much of the institutional racism that causes racial inequality. In this chapter we consider the question, If their race awareness were increased, could well-meaning white people's practice lessen institutional racism instead of producing it? To answer this question in the affirmative, we must assume two things: first, that an increase in race awareness would transform the white habitus; and second, that the transformed habitus would produce a different kind of practice: *antiracist practice,* the subject of this chapter.

Practice and Social Change

If the habitus can be "transformed" depending on circumstances operating in the social field (Jenkins 1992: 82), then race awareness may transform the white habitus. However, less clear is the ultimate effect the presumed change in the habitus would have upon organizations where institutional racism is produced. An irony in Bourdieu's theory of practice suggests keeping one's claims modest: "Major social change does not for the most part come about as an *intended* consequence of action. Change is largely a by-product, an *un*intended consequence of action, however rational the action may have been" (Ortner 1994: 401, emphasis in the original). According to Bourdieu, individuals' intention to change structure is not instrumental to social change. Rather, what people do unintentionally—without thinking—matters most. If change in institutional racism results from a change in the white habitus of well-meaning white people, we cannot say with certainty what the change will be.

Antiracism as practice requires changing the white habitus so that the "set of dispositions to act in certain ways" (Waters 1994: 200) is less ignorant of race matters. This implies that an increase in race awareness will not only increase the purposeful acts of well-meaning white people that challenge and interrupt racism but will also transform the white habitus, changing *racist practice* into *antiracist practice.* And if an increase in race awareness mitigates everyday racism and lessens the passivity of well-meaning whites, then it will also produce antiracist practice. Well-meaning white people will notice that they react differently in situations, choosing not to perform everyday racism when, in the past, they might have performed it. They will also be very aware of becoming more active when exposed to others' everyday racism by interrupting it. However, the increase in antiracist practice, which by definition is unnoticed, will not be obvious to the actor. Ironically, the change that is less obvious to the actor will be the more important change in lessening institutional racism.

Antiracism: What It Is and Why It Matters

Antiracism refers to taking a committed stand against racism, a stand that translates into action that interrupts racism in all its forms, whether personal or institutional, blatant or routine, intended or unintended. Antiracism is active by definition—the opposite of passivity, which colludes with racism. If one claims to be antiracist but takes no action against racism, the claim is false.

Much of the literature on antiracism is focused primarily on people in organizations that have sprung up around the country, including Race Traitors (Ignatiev and Garvey 1996), New Abolitionists (Winant 2004), People's Institute for Survival and Beyond, and Anti-Racist Action (O'Brien 2002), and on people who do antiracist work as professionals or volunteers (see Feagin and Vera 2002; George 2004; O'Brien 2002). Unfortunately, this creates a false impression that people who are *not* involved in organized antiracism are not truly antiracist, which is not the case (O'Brien 2001). With the exception of one participant, none of the women who took part in this study has ever been involved in organized antiracist work (that exception is Lucy, who is an antiracism workshop leader). Nevertheless, several of the participants live antiracism in their personal lives. When I speak of antiracism, I am referring to individuals' personal behavior, not to the collective action of members in antiracist organizations.

Personal antiracism means more than simply taking an abstract stand against racism; it entails acting on the commitment. All well-meaning white people are in favor of ending or lessening racism in an abstract sense. However, saying one is "against racism" and acting against racism are very different things. An implicit assumption at the outset of this study was that the participants would be concerned about racism—they would be well-meaning white women. It is not surprising, therefore, that all of the participants expressed an explicit desire to lessen racism. This includes Vanessa and Katie, both of whom also expressed blatant misinformation and racist ideas in their respective focus groups. Nevertheless, although the participants in this study would like to see racism end, many do not think in terms of *doing* anything that would lessen racism, and only a few demonstrated antiracism, such as interrupting racist comments and challenging misinformation about race matters.

Being Antiracist

I question the utility of identifying people as "antiracists." I take my cue from hooks (1984), who endorses feminism and yet eschews identifying herself as "a feminist." Hooks argues that saying people are feminists converts what they do into who they are (hooks 1984). She sees herself as a black woman who embraces feminist ideals, working to achieve feminist goals. Similarly, saying someone is "an antiracist" implies that antiracism says everything about them; it unnecessarily sets them apart from people who are not (yet) antiracist.

Antiracism is not hard to detect in people. I observed it in the focus groups when a participant interacted with another group member by questioning a racist statement and offering an alternative viewpoint. Antiracism also appeared in some of the stories participants told about interrupting racism in their families, or with friends and coworkers.

An example mentioned in the discussion of synergism is a good indication of antiracism. Ruth interrupted Kelly, who had said, "I think a lot of prejudice is really classism. That's my strong feeling; any prejudices I have are towards lower income people, whether they're white or black or whatever. . . . I think a lot of prejudice is about class, it just gets down to income." Ruth's interruption was gentle, and yet she clearly let Kelly and the others in the group know that class issues do not override race issues. Here is a full account of Ruth's experience at the teachers' conference:

> I agree with you [Kelly], although there are some instances that come to my mind—I was at a conference a few years ago and I was going to a breakout session and we were dealing with racism. [A] few of the African American women there—I really appreciated one [who said], "You just do not know how we live with this twenty-four hours a day, seven days a week. All of us are wearing our name tags, we're all conference people, we're all dressed in suits, there's 300 of us in this hotel," and she said, "yet, pay attention when we are in the restaurant—we have to absolutely demand service. And we get service last." And we were at one of the posh hotels in Los Angeles. And she was correct because they had been ignored. They had not gotten the water when they asked the busperson for water. And it dawned on me, yeah, you can be a professional, and yet that person of color is confronted with a different world. And it was very clear to her that we might be bleeding-heart liberals and be very empathetic, but we have no idea how much they're confronted with all the time.

The importance of the exchange between Kelly and Ruth, for the purposes of this chapter, is neither synergism nor the specific information that Ruth brought to the discussion. Rather, the fact that Ruth entered into the interaction with Kelly, instead of just letting what Kelly said stand, is important. By countering Kelly's point that class is more important than race, Ruth demonstrated her commitment to lessen racism by correcting misinformation. Ruth's commitment is grounded in her everyday interactions, and her antiracism seems to have had an effect on Kelly, who later reconsidered her point, saying, "When I think about it, my first reaction when you [indicating Ruth] started talking about that seminar was, 'God, do I have any prejudices?' And as I thought about it, so many of my prejudices are about what I've seen on television."

Kelly progressed from questioning whether she is prejudiced to acknowledging that she is and relating it to stereotypes she has seen on television. Whether Ruth's intervention had a lasting impact on Kelly is hard to tell. However, it is clear that, for a moment, Kelly questioned her own racism because of Ruth's decision to speak up. The incident demonstrates that interrupting others' racism can make a difference. Unfortunately, exhibiting antiracism does not always result in people changing; however, this should not be an excuse to remain passive in the face of racism.

Martha's antiracism, like Ruth's, was evident in her interactions with those in her focus group (see Chapter 5). Martha consistently interacted with the other participants—giving information and interrupting racism. I commented on Martha's involvement in the following exchange:

> **BT:** What does it mean to you to be antiracist?
>
> **Martha:** It means that I would want to make people aware of the racism that exists, including when it exists in me, and try to help people recognize one another's view.
>
> **BT:** So you see yourself as a teacher in a very large sense. That's good, yes. And I've noticed that you interrupt misconceptions when they come up.
>
> **Martha:** I can try. I don't want to sound like some saint because I realize I'm still making mistakes.
>
> **BT:** But to me part of being a saint is realizing [your mistakes]. If I ever met somebody who thought they didn't make a mistake, that would be the last person I would call a saint.

Martha referred to an "epiphany" she had that changed how she thinks about racism. She said, "My teaching experience was in a high school that was inner city and a mix of students, and I heard awful things—I substituted during my free periods. One other teacher said, 'Watch out for those *N-word* in the corridor.' And I just didn't want to hear it—I mean, how can you talk about students that way? How can you talk about people that way?" I asked Martha how she had responded to the teacher, to which she replied,

> We were in the hall and we were surrounded by students—how could I say anything? I realized that here was a man that I couldn't change. I did tell him later that I was not comfortable with that kind of language, but he was so hardened—I couldn't change him. Anyway, it was four years of teaching before I had [the following] epiphany. I was walking down the halls, and crowds of people were going by every which way and for some reason, I remember [having] a thought about racism. Suddenly it just hit me, and I don't even know how to give it words, but suddenly it hit me how weird it felt that anyone could think of people just in terms of their color. And the main difference was that I had students in my classes that I had grown to know and love. And I was really enjoying our particular girls' basketball team at that time, which was mostly black, and I just got comfortable with people. And I realized that perhaps that's what I needed to do with everybody, you know, Latino people and everybody.

Martha's "epiphany" was like a religious awakening—she even refers to it with a biblical term. Martha shifted from seeing black Americans in a stereotypical way to seeing them as individuals, a shift that only occurs through interaction in relationships. In other words, moving from knowing about blacks to having a personal experience with blacks comes in relationships with blacks and other people of color. Martha's shift in consciousness likely resulted from her numerous relationships with black acquaintances and friends.

Lucy shared in depth when I asked her focus group if anyone was antiracist. She said without hesitation:

> Me? I'm antiracist. I never used that [word] before [but] to me it means being active, and it means doing the personal work, and healing. It means working on my internalized oppression; the places where I am stuck, where I feel disempowered because I feel like the more I'm there, then the harder it is for me to embrace other people and shift to see where they are coming from without having my buttons pushed. Like when I work with a black man and I feel like he's oppressing me and he's feeling

> like I'm oppressing him. The more I'm clear about what my shit is, the easier I can work with him.... But also, it is for me about making systemic change in whatever way that means. Like, in training about changing the organizations so they're not so exclusive. Maybe that'll mean with laws, so in some way that's bigger than just changing myself, even though I think that's the start, and really important. I've met too many people of color who say, "You know, I don't really give a shit if you like me or not, just make sure I get a job, and just respect me."

Lucy's description of her antiracism is comprehensive even though she had never heard the word before. She starts by looking at her own racism but does not stop there. For her, introspection is merely the starting point in preparation for more active work. I asked Lucy what she does when someone around her makes a racist comment or tells a racist joke. She said, "I try to talk about it, like I go, 'Oh yeah, what's that about? [In the case of a joke,] tell me the funny parts,' or 'let's talk about it.' And get in some education sometimes. If I really care about the person, then I do that more. I almost always address it, and I try to be light." Not only does Lucy interrupt the racism around her, but she interrupts it with humor when possible. This is an indication that she has either had a lot of experience interrupting racism or has given it a great deal of thought.

Molly demonstrated that she is antiracist when I asked participants in her focus group what they do when a racist comment or joke is expressed around them. Molly responded emphatically, "I don't take it anymore. I simply don't take it anymore. If somebody tells an off-color ethnic joke I just say, 'I don't want to hear that. I don't like to hear jokes like that anymore.'" I asked Molly what kind of reaction she usually gets and she said, "Well, sometimes they're sort of embarrassed, and sometimes they're almost angry, as though 'What's the matter with you?' But I don't see any reason to have to listen to it."

Molly, Lucy, and Martha are clearly antiracist; however, if people say that they are antiracist but take no action against racism, the claim is unjustified. For example, when asked, "What do you do when someone tells a racist joke or makes a racist comment in your presence?" abstract statements about what participants *would* do, in contrast to statements about what they actually have done in such a case, are evidence of passivity; that is, they indicate an *intention* to interrupt racism but no evidence of ever having interrupted it. When the intention to interrupt racism remains abstract, it serves merely to soothe one's conscience.

Karen illustrates good intentions that stop short of an antiracist commitment. Although she had never heard of the word *antiracism,* Karen assumed that it implies an active stand against racism. She was candid when I asked her directly if she is antiracist. Karen answered, "That's interesting. I kind of related to that word [antiracism] although I've never thought about it. Kind of, yeah. I don't know whether I'd say yes. I would prefer to say yes, but I don't feel like I could claim that word. But I do try in personal situations." Karen *wants* to identify with antiracism yet feels she cannot claim the word for herself. She openly acknowledges that, although she has good intentions, she is not commited to active antiracism. Karen's comments are closely related to the litany of examples of passivity presented in Chapter 3.

Becoming Antiracist

I have argued that having close relationships with black friends and acquaintances in which conversations about race occur is a necessary condition of race awareness and that race awareness and racism have an inverse relationship. By implication then, race awareness is correlated with antiracism. Other avenues suggested in the literature for increasing race awareness include being involved in other progressive causes, gaining an understanding of racism through the writing and music of black writers and musicians, and relating racism to other forms of oppression experienced personally, called *overlapping approximations* (O'Brien 2001).

None of the participants in this study mentioned being involved in progressive causes; however, several of them talked about the importance of their cross-racial friendships. Some also mentioned getting correct information about racism by reading the work of black authors. A few also said that their understanding of racism was deepened by comparing it to their own experience as lesbians (an example of overlapping approximations). These and other strategies are discussed below.

Cross-Racial Friendships. Friendships between blacks and whites are a critical part of raising whites' race awareness, primarily because white people, no matter how well meaning or progressive, cannot understand race matters without input from outside the white habitus. Whites are not good judges of whether they are "race-neutral" in their decisions regarding issues concerning race or people of color (Flagg 1997: 222). The *transparency phenomenon* refers to the idea that white people do not think of themselves as raced; that is, white has no meaning except or unless counterposed against black or ethnic difference, such as when a white person is in a situation where almost everyone else is a person of color. Only then does race come to the foreground for whites, much as oxygen is noticed only when in short supply.

The idea that race is transparent for whites and is therefore hidden helps explain why racist acts are often done unintentionally. Decision-making that is perceived as race-neutral by the white decision maker is often actually race-specific. White people should adopt a "skeptical" stance in regard to their ability to be race-neutral (Flagg 1997: 222). This view supports the idea that white people would do well to get the perspective from a person of color in terms of race matters.

Martha explicitly suggested the importance of making friends with blacks. Her suggestion occurred in an interaction with Katie, who said, "I hold back in seeking out relationships with black people. . . . I think they don't want to be friends with me . . . and I don't know where to find them." Martha encouraged Katie when she said, "Just be you and be happy to be you and enjoy them [blacks] for being them. They have the same doubts as you. [You will] find them on campus—at the library, in line getting food. Aren't they in class? It's just easier to be with people you know will accept you than to reach out and take a chance. You have to be willing to take a chance." For Martha, making friends with blacks is no harder than making friends with whites because she sees blacks more clearly than most white people do. Although Martha did not explain the value of having black friendships, I am convinced that her high race awareness is a result of the many people of color in her life.

Lisa also sees the importance of having black friends, even though she revealed that in the past, she expected a negative response from them. She described meeting Diane, who is now a good friend. Lisa said, "I just said 'hello.' I had no idea who she was. And her son was there too. . . . She said 'hello' back, and we started to talk . . . and I was amazed [when] she said, 'Well, would you like to go to the movies?' [I was so shocked,] I swear I said, 'You want to go to the movies with *me*?'" When I asked Lisa to fill in what occurred between their exchange of hellos and Diane's invitation to go to the movies, she said, "After I said 'hello,' instead of acting like, 'Well, nice to meet you, see you later,' I started to talk about, you know, 'My name is Lisa, my son's in school, where does your son go? Where do you live? ...' Just trying to really stay connected and [be] open. Show her that I was willing to pursue it. I was just floored when she suggested going to the movies because I realized ... that I expected black women to hate me." After that, Lisa made friends with black women as easily as she did white women.

Lisa talked about meeting Val at a laundromat. She said, "An [incident occurred] after I had done some black studies work. I met Val [who] had just acted in 'Spell #7' by Notaze Shange, [who is] a black feminist writer and dramatist, a poet. I knew 'Spell #7,' so I started to talk to her about Shange and other writers. And she looked at me completely differently." Lisa's reference to how Val looked at her "completely differently" refers to the surprise on Val's face that a white woman would know who Notaze Shange is and could converse about her work.

Clearly, talking about racism in her relationships with black friends has been important for Lisa. I realize that black women teaching white women about race issues is problematic in that it shifts the burden for knowledge acquisition away from white women. Nevertheless, despite black women's exasperation over having to teach white women about their racism, some blacks feel that talking with whites about the issues of difference and racism is not a bad idea (e.g., hooks 1989). Lisa receives information about Diane's personal experience as a black woman that helps her in thinking about racism, including her own part in it. Without dialogue across race and ethnic boundaries, the white perspective is likely to remain constricted. Lisa shared about an incident that helped her realize how little she knew about race. She said:

> I remember one particular incident when I was with Diane, and we were in this store, and she was saying, "Boy, that little girl is so lucky. If only I could have worn a bow in my hair when I was little." ... And I was thinking, "Boy, when I was little, I hated bows!" Bows were the last thing I wanted—my mother was putting bows on me and I was like, "Get out of here with your bows, I want to climb trees." ... This whole thing of being able to be seen as pretty, being able to be seen as a lady ... [Diane thought] she could never be seen as a pretty little girl. But when she first said it, I was thinking of it as a white feminist [would]

> ... and I said to her, "But why would you want to do that?" ... Things she would say would trigger all the ignorance I had about her lived experience growing up black, just mowing right over it with my own agenda, my own perceptions about what should happen. And because I wasn't sensitive, I was so invested in [the issue] politically, I wasn't really giving myself a chance to see what I was doing.

I asked Lisa if she and Diane talked about it, if she told Diane about the thoughts she shared with the group. Lisa said, "Oh, we argued all the way home.... She asked what it was like growing up beautiful, and I went into this big spiel about my childhood, about being put on a pedestal and being objectified, and about being molested and not being seen for who I am but [being] owned. But to her it was something else. So I had to listen to what it was for her, and it was really painful—it was very hard to do." Lisa exemplifies the importance of humility, an essential characteristic of whites who want to learn about racism from black friends and associates (O'Brien 2001).

Reaching across the color line, as Lisa did, is a model for all of us. When Lisa first approached Diane, a black woman she had never seen before, she did not know what to expect. Nevertheless, she deliberately struck up a conversation, not out of habit but as a conscious decision to reach out. She was surprised when the conversation led to a friendship that has presumably been mutually satisfying. However, without conversations about race, Lisa's cross-racial friendship would have been nice but would not have produced the understanding that helps bridge the gap between black and white. Lisa's race awareness comes from many sources, but the understanding she gains in her relationships with Diane and Val has a large impact.

Friendships between whites and blacks would not only benefit whites by increasing their understanding of race matters but would also produce the strong black-white ties in largely white organizational networks that would increase the informal support that is now lacking (Wellman and Wortley 1990).

Getting Correct Information. Getting correct information is also important in increasing race awareness. Jean demonstrated this when she told about how hard it was to repudiate the early training in racism she received in her family, much of it justified by religious tenets. For Jean, getting correct information originally occurred in her undergraduate coursework. She said, "I took psychology and world religions ... and that made me start thinking of things differently. It took me about five years to actually extract myself from that [childhood] belief system. It was real difficult." Jean says that the classes she took "made [her] start thinking of things differently." This indicates that the content of the courses, the information itself, served to stimulate her questioning of the racism she learned as a child in her family. Judging from the courses Jean mentions—psychology and world religions—she was not seeking information about race issues per se. Nevertheless, her own thinking was changed by the new information as she began to question the beliefs of her family.

Early in her undergraduate career, Lisa, much like Jean, did not seek out courses in race relations. In explaining why obtaining new information was a crucial step in the development of a more aware race consciousness for her, Lisa said, "I think reading is what I'm doing more than anything else because there's so much I don't know, and it interests me. [Learning about racism] is what I found when I [took] women's studies—[I was] not necessarily looking for it." Lisa's comment that she learned about racism in women's studies courses although she was "not necessarily looking for it" indicates that she was not purposefully seeking correct information about race. Nevertheless, her interest in race and racism was piqued in her coursework, and she now actively seeks more information in her reading.

Joan mentioned that the lack of information about black culture made it especially difficult to write a scene she was working on for her comic strip. Joan said, "It's an entirely black scene, and I had a really hard time writing it. Dialogue, interaction, anything, because I don't have much information. I feel really stupid. I mean, I feel culturally deprived. I have this huge curiosity and respect as far as culture and as far as family structure goes, and how powerful I think the women have to be in order to exist. But I don't have interaction, and I feel deprived." Although Joan's phrase "I feel deprived" implies victimhood in the sense that responsibility for her deprivation lies with someone else, the more important point to notice is her sense of wanting to know more and not knowing where to go for good information. It appears that Joan has not considered the possibility that having black friends in her life would be an excellent source of the information she needs.

For some participants, getting information means reading—Violet, Anne, Corrine, and Katie all mentioned that they were reading works by people of color, especially women, in order to increase their understanding of racism. However, of all the women who are seeking to gain information about race, only Lisa—who gains that information in her close black-white friendships—has "very high" race awareness. Jean, Violet, and Anne have "high" race awareness, Corrine has "moderate" race awareness, and Katie has "very low" race awareness.

Overlapping Approximations. For some of the participants in the study, noticing similarities between racism and other forms of oppression, forms that they have experienced firsthand, were helpful in learning about racism. Using overlapping approximations or analogies can be effective in trying to understand the ordeal of others facing discrimination. However, the use of analogies is somewhat problematic in that the one doing the analyzing may fail to consider ways in which the oppressions also differ. Being female or even seeing one's self as having feminist ideals does not appear to translate into empathy for racial minorities; many white feminist scholars who know a lot about sexist oppression have demonstrated unaware racism in their writings. However, being a lesbian does seem to create empathy for others. Two participants in the study—both lesbians—compared their experiences of gay oppression with racism.

Karen feels that her experience of being discriminated against as a lesbian has helped her to understand her high school friend's experience of racism. Karen shared her feelings about a recent conversation with Belle when she said, "I have [gay oppression and racism] related. My friend Belle [was] my closest high school friend, and I feel like I can now talk to her much more openly about racism since I feel like I'm justified to talk about it. I [can] say [to myself], 'This is like when I . . . ' and try to relate [her experience to] the situations [in my own life]."

Karen's relating her own oppression as a lesbian to racism not only helps her to better understand racism but also helps her feel more comfortable in raising the issue with her black friend. Although the respective oppressions differ, Karen's experience of being oppressed as a lesbian gives her a way to think about racism that she had not considered before. Her comment that she now feels "justified to talk about it" indicates that before she made the connection, Karen could not speak about racism.

Anita is also a lesbian and, like Karen, feels she can better understand racism because of her own experience of gay discrimination.

She stated in reference to conversations with her black coworker and friend in Chicago: "We drew a lot of parallels between [us].... She was surprised at things that she thought I wouldn't understand, but I was drawing from my experience of being a lesbian, and not from anything else." Anita's comment that her friend was "surprised at things she thought I wouldn't understand" is evidence that this strategy has merit. In other words, her friend realized—to her surprise—that Anita had some understanding about racism.

Sometimes analogies between oppressions produce insights about being a perpetrator of oppression as well. Marilyn Frye, a feminist philosopher, drew parallels between herself and a black feminist who accused her of being racist at a meeting. She said that the black woman "seemed crazy" to her at first (Frye 1983: 112). She then noticed that she had been in the position of "seeming crazy" to others. She states that when she had accused them of discriminating against her because she is a lesbian, she was in the same position as the black woman at the meeting. "I know [that feeling] from both sides; I have been thought crazy by others too righteous, too timid and too defended to grasp the enormity of our difference" (p. 112). This parallel goes deeper than the experiences described by the focus group participants. Rather than merely noticing analogies between the oppressions—as was the case with Karen and Anita—Frye also saw that in the case of race, she was "too righteous, too timid and too defended" to hear what the black woman was saying.

Self-Reflection. Self-reflection, or introspection, is generally prompted by something, whether it be someone who interrupts another's racism or from getting information that contradicts a preconceived notion about race. Several participants mentioned self-reflection as a strategy for lessening self-acknowledged racism. Elaine described self-reflection when she said, "[I] try to understand myself [and] keep in mind taken-for-granted things that we're all carrying around, and trying to locate those. And not step on someone's toes by insulting behaviors [like] projecting my own experiences onto other people. So [I am] trying to locate myself as [a] white middle-class woman with a particular history while getting a better handle on what other people bring to an interaction."

Elaine's reference to "keeping in mind taken-for-granted things that we're all carrying" suggests that she knows that she has incorporated racist notions into her own perspective, and that she must first locate them in order to eradicate them. Elaine also expresses a desire to avoid the ethnocentric tendency within feminism that presumes all women's experience is similar to one's own by not "projecting my own experiences onto other people." This is an important insight; many black feminists have voiced the complaint that white feminists within the women's movement regularly project their (white) views onto women of color in the movement (Frye 1983; Smith 1982). Minnie Bruce Pratt (1984) captures this idea when she speaks of her own ethnocentrism as having a "constricted eye, an eye that has only let in what I have been taught to see" (p. 17).

Like Elaine, Lisa presumes her own racism. She said, "I have to keep asking myself how I'm racist, and I have to keep questioning how the racism that's in me is coming out in my everyday living. Because I know it is, and I know that there are more ways that I'm not aware of." As in Elaine's case, Lisa's assumption that she is somewhat racist is prudent because the denial of being racist decreases the probability of learning about her own racism.

Charlotte illustrated this point when she told about the effect of a class she attended in college that was designed to educate students about racism. Charlotte said, "By the end [I] was able to say, 'I am totally racist at the same time that I'm antiracist,' and I'm going to struggle between those two things. That's going to be my spectrum instead of, 'I've never had a racist thought and nor has anybody else that I know.'" Charlotte's ability to embrace both the racist and antiracist aspects of her experience indicates her openness to learning about her own racism. White people who do not see themselves as racist are not likely to discover the ways they perpetuate racist practice and everyday racism. Regardless of how well-meaning they are, only if people presume that they are racist are they likely to discover their role in producing racism through self-reflection.

Self-reflection for Jean includes dealing specifically with the racism that she learned as a young child. Jean said, "Having racism in my family when I was young, it was something that I had to take an active stand against, actively try to overcome in myself. And that's where I am with it—trying to find all the places it's hiding [in me], and learn[ing] more about it, and about myself and how it works in me." Jean feels that she is especially susceptible to being racist due to the racist legacy in her family. Her comment "I had to take an *active* stand against [racism]" underscores the importance of white people not remaining passive in relation to racism.

Introspection would also be prompted by changing the "racist/not racist" categories to a racism continuum, which—as I have argued—would encourage progressive whites to ask, "How am I racist?"

White Identity Issues. Exploring white identity issues is a controversial topic, both in the literature and among participants. Some theorists express concern about focusing on white identity issues divorced of a concern for racism (Andersen 2003; Frankenberg 1993). The recognition of white privilege and one's implication in the racial formation, important aspects of an antiracist consciousness, are critical; however, spending time on how one feels about being white seems unnecessary. For example, white people working on feelings of being "ripped off" because they don't have "any culture"—ideas expressed by Joan—seems unproductive in terms of lessening racism.

Discussions that occur in all-white groups are especially seen as problematic. Lucy, who leads antiracism workshops, brought up an interesting issue in terms of white people working on their own racism. Lucy said:

> I've done workshops with all white people, and workshops with [white people and] people of color, and I think it's much more effective to do mixed groups.... But I also see that, in those workshops, a lot of it gets taken up with white people saying, "I don't have any culture, I feel ripped off." Not that that's not important, but I think that white people have so much more work to do on this than people of color, because people of color are dealing with it every day. And if white people don't get together and just blow off some of this, then no one's going to want us in their group working on racism with them.

Lucy points out that for some white people, a common first response to doing work in an antiracism workshop is to feel a sense of loss about their own lack of a racial identity.

Penny shared a comment from a friend regarding Penny's participation in this study. She said, "When I told a friend that I was coming to this [focus group], she said, 'You know, it's just another one of those white women get together and talk about racism [things]. How many years are we going to do that?'" The insinuation is that white women talking about racism cannot possibly produce meaningful results. And, at first glance, this sentiment appears to be accurate—what difference could it make to black women how white women feel about themselves? White women who "feel ripped-off" are likely to have a low level of race awareness; but will focusing on their own heritage increase race awareness? Loretta addressed this point:

> At a reading in San Francisco, a poet was talking about the need for white people ... to become grounded in their own identity before do[ing] antiracism work. She said, "Figure out who you are, so that you're not going around trying to be everybody else." Unless I know who I am, saying the right things and having the right people in my social group is still coming from the wrong place and is like trying to be this politically correct person instead of figuring out, "Who am I?"

Loretta also acknowledged the danger of "all-white" groups by comparing them to groups of men working on sexism. Loretta said, "I want men to educate themselves, and I want them to be allies in doing the work, [but] I get terrified with men's groups. I can understand people of color feeling the same way about whites around racism. It feels like it has the potential to be really positive, and also really dangerous."

The danger that Loretta alludes to is that men's groups will reinforce stereotypes that degrade women, or agree about behaviors that are hurtful to women. The danger in the case of white women working together on their racism is the possibility that someone might begin to think, for example, that a statement like Vanessa's about IQ and racial difference has merit, or that Katie's question about black Americans going "back" to Africa might be a viable solution to the problem of racism in the United States. Whether or not these dangers outweigh the value of "all-white" group-work is unclear.

A Model Antiracism Workshop

The model antiracism workshop sketched here may be useful for well-meaning white people who wish to raise their race awareness and limit silent racism.[1] It is important to keep in mind that antiracism workshops are not a substitute for close relationships with people of color in terms of increasing race awareness. Nor are they a solution for decreasing racism, including institutional racism. Nevertheless, workshops that deal with racism on all levels can be an important first step, especially for well-meaning whites who want to increase their race awareness but do not know what steps to take.

If you cannot find an antiracism workshop to attend, I suggest that you make a commitment to become the workshop leader that is needed in your area. The resources listed in Appendix D will give you helpful background knowledge. If you are white, conversations with people of color will help clarify your thinking. If you are a member of a church or other organization that may offer the facilities, equipment, and even the support (including participants), that will be a plus.

For whites, becoming antiracist is like moving "from the safe circle into the wilderness" (Williams 1991: 129). Whites should expect to feel uncomfortable and even "crazy" (Frye 1983) as the understanding of things they came to know in childhood is challenged by new knowledge. Despite the discomfort for many, the antiracism journey can be a satisfying one in that it will not only deepen racial understanding but also enrich life experiences. The goal of antiracism workshops is to increase race awareness, which is expected to result in increasing intentional antiracist acts as well as increase antiracist practice.

Content of a Model Workshop

A good antiracism workshop must address all three prongs of race awareness: knowledge of the history of racism, recognition of institutional racism, and insight concerning one's own racism.

Historical Racism. American values that stress individualism, personal responsibility, and a strong work ethic predict a future-oriented perspective (Perry 2002). This viewpoint obscures the importance of the past, including the relevance of slavery and segregation. This perspective prompts whites to see not only their own past as unrelated to the present but also that of other groups, including blacks. The history of racism in this country is essential in an antiracism workshop since most people, especially whites, have very little knowledge of it (Kailin 2002) and understanding racism today requires understanding racism of the past.

Books, films, and music that tell the story of racism should be part of the workshop. A list of some of the resources available appears in Appendix D. Along with the historical facts of slavery and the Jim Crow era, models of black and white antiracists should also be included. Stories from the lives of black men and women such as Frederick Douglass, Harriett Tubman, Sarah Grimke, and Fannie Lou Hamer, to mention just a very few, whet the appetite for more. Anecdotes like the one in Chapter 1 about the postman William Moore are more interesting than dry facts about the past. Important historical facts will ultimately be revealed as the stories unfold, and the models of antiracism are an inspiration for people to become antiracist (Kailin 2002).

Institutional Racism. Institutional racism is the prong of race awareness that is the most difficult to impart to whites but not to blacks and other people of color, most of whom have experienced the effects of institutional racism. Whites, in contrast, generally think individualistally, due in part to a strong belief in the myth of individualism. We have been told that the pioneers who settled this country were rugged individualists who never needed a hand from anyone. The truth is that the early settlers were highly dependent on each other and on the government (Coontz 1992). The white focus on self-reliance predisposes people to see themselves as disconnected from others and from the racial formation. Sharon's belief that race has nothing to do with her life is a prime example. She has no sense of the white privilege she enjoys daily. Teaching antiracism requires shifting participants' individualist lens to a sociological one that includes correct information.

Using C. Wright Mills's (1959) idea of the *sociological imagination* can be useful, and it can be adapted to race matters. Mills pointed out that a sociological imagination allows people to see how their daily experiences are inextricably tied to both history and society. In terms of race, the everyday lives of both blacks and whites in the United States are tied to the historical legacy of slavery and Jim Crow as well as to the racial status quo, which places blacks at a disadvatage in terms of the material and nonmaterial resources of society (Bell 1992; Hacker 1992). If blacks are at a disadvantage because of institutional racism, then whites have an overadvantage. Developing a sociological imagination takes time and may result more from discussions with people of color rather than from information about institutional racism or white privilege.

Another reason whites have difficulty in recognizing institutional racism is because of their location in the dominant group. Feminist standpoint theory explains this in terms of gender when it argues that women's particular position on the margin of society—in relation to the central position of men—affords women a clearer conception of gender issues (Harding 1991). It is assumed that the location of centrality itself produces a distorted perspective. Similarly, black feminists and other feminists of color argue that because of their unique position in society in relation to white women, they have experience and insights that are not available to white women and white feminists (Collins 1986; Moraga and Anzaldúa 1983). Most people would agree that men and women view gender issues differently; feminists would say that women have insights about gender that men do not have. The same is true regarding race: blacks and other people of color have insights about racism that white people do not have given their position in society.

The PBS program called *A Class Divided* records teacher Jane Elliott's brown eyed/blue eyed exercise, which is helpful in getting participants to see how racism operates in group behavior. Although the classroom exercise was originally done in 1968—the day after Martin Luther King Jr. was killed—the program (available as a videotape; see Appendix D) is timeless as it captures a teacher's commitment to do something about racism and her courage to attempt a classroom exercise that her colleagues and the students' parents thought was objectionable.[2] Elliott divided her third grade class into two groups based upon the color of the students' eyes—brown or blue. She then gave one of the groups privileges denied to the other group. Later, the privileges were switched to the other group so that all of the students could experience both the emotional impact of being discriminated against and of being privileged.

Personal Racism. The white habitus causes limitations in what white people see, and this limitation necessarily results in ignorance. Ignorance can only be overcome by people acknowledging that there are things they do not know, things of which they are unaware (Pratt 1984). The historical and institutional content of the workshop will encourage people to think about their own ignorance and the ways that ignorance might have been hurtful to people of color or might have caused negative material effects for them. The most helpful tool in the discovery process may be writing in journals. Discovering one's personal racism is the most painful part of an antiracism workshop, and emotions are likely to surface. However, admitting to one's racism is important in lessening the denial that well-meaning white people are sometimes racist.

The goal of the workshop is for participants to take a stand against racism. At some point in the workshop, participants can and should be encouraged to interrupt racism as part of their personal stand against racism. If the workshop spans a period of weeks or months, participants sharing about their experience of interrupting racism can be useful in encouraging others as well as giving support to those who share about the experience. Interrupting racism is not easy at first, particularly when one is embedded in the group where racism occus. Loyalty to the group and its members will likely make interrupting racism difficult. It takes courage for most white people to interrupt racism, and the risk of offending people may feel like too high a price to pay. America's unspoken rule is that white people ignore everyday racism even when it is noticed. Breaching that rule can upset others; interrupting racism implies that the person being interrupted is racist, and being labeled "racist" is tantamount to being labeled "deviant." Despite this, as people's race awareness increases, and after they have done it a time or two, interrupting racism gets easier. People with very high race awareness interrupt racism with ease. Neither Martha nor Ruth seemed nervous when they interrupted other participants' racism in this study. They both have a commitment to antiracism, not to placating others' purposeful racist acts or racist practice for fear of reprisals. For people with high race awareness, interrupting racism becomes second nature—they do it without thinking. For them, interrupting racism is antiracist practice.

Nevertheless, for most whites, being an active bystander takes courage (Staub 2003). Therefore, in addition to race awareness, racial progressives need a firm commitment to antiracism. That commitment requires the moral courage to be autonomous and take a stand against racism. Confidence in the value of racial equality is a key factor in building moral courage regarding racism. Clarity about racism and one's stand against it are also important in recognizing when racism is taking place and knowing one's part in the situation—with hope, that of an active bystander. And finally, the support of others who hold antiracist values is important in sustaining an antiracist stand (O'Brien 2001).

White people speaking out against racism can be the targets of racist bigots today much as they were in the past. For example, Jane Elliott's children were harassed and her parents' business lost customers because she refused to end her brown eyes/blue eyes exercise.

However, regardless of how others will react, antiracist action, including interrupting racism, is the right thing to do. Not to interrupt racism implies agreement with it.

Mechanics of a Model Workshop

Although the content of a workshop is the most important part to consider, how to carry out a workshop and who will participate in it are also important. Equally important are decisions about how the information will be presented and exercises for the participants to take part in during the workshop as well as after it. If possible, the workshop should extend over a period of weeks or months. Otherwise, information and insights are easily forgotten.

Preparation. Including a mix of participants in terms of racial and ethnic identity provides the most useful discussions in a workshop; this can be difficult for the people of color who are tired of hearing ignorant statements from whites, but their presence is valuable and they benefit as well (Kailin 2002). It is helpful to advise participants to be tolerant of each others' location on the race awareness continuum. If possible, two workshop leaders who differ in racial identity is ideal. Workshops that have both a person of color and a white person as facilitators provide a measure of safety in an environment that may feel intimidating for some participants. In addition, every participant should freely choose to be at the workshop. Resistance in workshops, a major difficulty with the diversity programs attended by employees of formal organizations, occurs largely because people are forced to be in the training. This often creates a caustic environment for everyone, participants and facilitators alike. Antiracism cannot be forced on anyone: becoming antiracist is a choice.

Getting Started. Participants should get to know each other at the first meeting, so name tags and introductions are helpful. If the group is not too large, all of the participants should tell a little about themselves to the group. Why they came to the workshop could be included in the introduction. This can be accomplished in small groups if needed in order to save time. Participants should be given a preview of what to expect. This may calm some fears. Keep in mind that the participants care about racism and did not choose to become racist. They are part of the solution, not the problem.

Ground rules for the discussions are an important part of processing the information presented in the workshop. People are not accustomed to talking about race in groups where both minorities and whites are present, and they are likely to feel unsure about doing so. Having participants develop their own set of ground rules can be empowering; however, facilitators should feel comfortable to add rules if they feel something important has been omitted. Ground rules often center on respecting others' right to their point of view, not dominating the discussion, listening to understand, maintaining confidentiality, and not using language such as the N-word, even when talking about others using it (Kailin 2002).

Discussion Groups. Discussion groups should be structured around questions that prompt participants to explore their experiences of race matters (Kailin 2002). Discussion of any videos shown also helps participants in the workshop process the information and get closure on it. The question, "Have you ever done anything that you *now* consider racist?" may be useful in this regard. Depending on the total number of workshop participants, I suggest using both small groups (of four to five participants) and large groups (of about twenty participants) for small and large discussions. Everyone should be encouraged to share in the small groups; however, only volunteers should be expected to share in the large groups. Paired-sharing between two participants should also be included in the format.

Encourage participants to continue the conversations they take part in during the workshop at home, at work, and with friends. They are especially encouraged to engage in conversations about race with the people of color in their lives or that they encounter.

Journals. Keeping a journal is also suggested for participants, and sharing what has been written in the discussions is particularly helpful (Kailin 2002). Some time during the workshop can be designated for journaling, but participants will benefit from writing between sessions as well. The following list of "prompts" is expected to encourage introspection. A handout with suggestions for writing is helpful for some participants. Directions should indicate that participants complete the following "stems," writing as much as they wish about each one.

The goal is for participants not only to discover their silent racism but also to realize how much they care about racism:

- If I think about becoming more race aware, I feel ______________________________.
- If I pay more attention to how I relate to blacks/whites, I might notice that ______________.
- The scary thing about becoming more race aware is ______________________________.
- If I become more aware of my own racism, I might ______________________________.
- If I take responsibility for what I learned about blacks/whites, I will ___________________.
- If I took the next step in becoming race aware, I would ______________________________.
- If I were more courageous regarding race matters, I would ______________________________.
- If I were committed to lessening racism, I would ______________________________.
- What is good about becoming race aware is that ______________________________.
- If I were to stay fully engaged in race awareness, I might ______________________________.
- What is hard about staying fully engaged regarding race matters is that __________________.

Request that participants take approximately twenty minutes a day to write in their journals. Each stem should be answered six to eight times.

In addition to the resources listed in Appendix D, information can be found on the Web by searching for "antiracism workshops."

Conclusion

I argued in Chapter 4 that intentional acts of racism are not what hold institutional racism in place. Rather, it is the unintentional action—racist practice—of whites, including well-meaning whites, that produces much of the institutional racism in place today. This chapter on antiracism makes a similar claim: intentional antiracism is important, but antiracism that is not intended—antiracist practice—is what may balance the scales of racial justice. Taking an antiracist stand is a deliberate undertaking; nevertheless, antiracist practice, which is not intentional, will also result when race awareness is increased.

Malcolm X (1965) said, "The well-meaning white people ... [have] to combat, actively and directly, the racism in other white people" (p. 375). Combatting racism takes many forms. Be creative (Wise 2002). I cannot tell you what antiracism will look like for you, although I can say it will not collude with racism and will therefore be "subversive" (Thompson 2001: xv). Teaching and learning about race is antiracist practice; writing a letter to the editor of the local newspaper when an issue regarding race is in the news is antiracist practice; and interrupting the racism in your families, workplaces, and schools is antiracist practice. Antiracists notice racism and point it out to others; only the methods used to point it out vary. Antiracism that becomes a "way of life" (Thompson 2001: xxvii) is the goal, for only then will it be antiracist practice.

Keep in mind that practice refers to what people do that either reinforces or changes social institutions. And, racism within organizations is "increasingly covert," couched in terminology that cannot be explicitly tied to racism (Bonilla-Silva 1997: 476). Antiracist practice that is unintended becomes critical in such circumstances if social change is to occur because change occurs as a latent, unintended effect. If no perpetrator is evident, interrupting racism explicitly and intentionally is less of an option. However, if what we do without thinking matters, as Bourdieu convincingly argues, then race awareness is a critical factor in lessening racism, particularly institutional racism.

Practice theorists generally assume that change in a social system will be undertaken by the subordinate group that perceives itself as disadvantaged, not the dominant group that benefits from the system. However, the allies of those in the subordinate group—well-meaning white people—can and should increase their race awareness, which will prepare them to both intentionally and unintentionally further the cause of racial equality.

Thinking differently regarding any issue—a mindshift—is essential if people expect to do things differently in a given area. Rolf Smith (2002) asserts that a mindshift takes people *off* autopilot; I argue that if well-meaning white people increase their race awareness and think differently about their relationship to racism, the white habitus will be transformed. At that point, what people do without thinking will be antiracist practice. And, changing racist practice to antiracist practice will be a social phenomenon, not a personal one. This is not to imply that what individuals do is not part of the process. Reading and thinking about the ideas in this book is an individual endeavor. Friendships and conversations about race are personal matters. However, the shift that will make a difference in the racial status quo will occur only when these ideas permeate the less racist end of the racism continuum—those well-meaning whites—not all whites, but progressive whites open to thinking differently about racism.

Notes

1. Many of the ideas for the antiracism workshop presented here are based on the book *Antiracist Education: From Theory to Practice* (2002), by Julie Kailin.

2. Elliott stated in a talk given in 2004 at Texas State University–San Marcos that her parents' store in the all-white town in Iowa where she lived was boycotted as a result of her exercise.

Chapter Seven

Silent Racism at Work

I HAVE ARGUED IN PREVIOUS CHAPTERS that the silent racism of well-meaning white people produces harm in the lives of African Americans and other people of color. The harm, whether intended or not, is often brought about through decisions that have consequences for others. This claim is supported when we consider that young African Americans are overrepresented in two U.S. systems whose mission is to serve all children: special education and child welfare.[1] Called racial disproportionality, the overrepresentation of black youth in these systems when compared with their number in the population undoubtedly has multiple causes; however, studies in both areas show that racial bias accounts for some of the overrepresentation (Harry, Klingner, and Sturges 2002; Johnson et al. 2007). I have also argued previously that increasing race awareness lessens the likelihood that silent racism will result in racist practice or in everyday racism. This claim is borne out by the decrease in racial disproportionality in the child welfare system in Texas.

This chapter is divided into two very different sections, both dealing with racial disproportionality. I begin with brief overviews of the systems mentioned above, where black children do not fare as well as white ones: special education and child welfare. I then shift from a general discussion of racial disproportionality to an in-depth portrayal of achievement in dealing with it. Texas Child Protective Services (CPS) has put in place an array of strategies designed to reduce disproportionality for the most vulnerable kids in Texas, including strategies intended to increase race awareness. The successful strategies have come to be known to child welfare agencies in other states as well as to educational professionals as the *Texas Model.* Practical implications from both the research and the successful Texas program are presented at the end of the chapter.

Racial Disproportionality and Children

Recognition of disproportionality in special education and child welfare is evidenced by the fact that federal mandates intended to address the problem have been passed in both of the systems. Although the cause of disproportionality is complicated, the studies outlined in this chapter indicate that disproportionality unmistakably relates to silent racism and racial passivity.

Special Education

Although difficult to compare, state data regarding relative levels of disproportionality indicate that, in the United States, minority children, especially African American children, are overrepresented in special education classes (K–12). National data show that black children are almost three times as likely to be placed in special education as white children (Losen and Orfield 2002). The problem is compounded by a shortage of teachers qualified to work with children with disabilities (Bullock and Gable 2004). The Individuals with Disabilities Education Act (IDEA) passed by Congress in 1975 intended to ensure that children with disabilities receive an education that equals the public education guaranteed to all children. Since then, IDEA has been amended several times (in 1997, 2002, and 2004) to include provisions requiring that states monitor racial disproportionality and take measures to remedy it.

Most children with disabilities enter school undiagnosed (Losen and Orfield 2002). This means that placement in special education is prompted by "social decision making" within the school system (Harry et al. 2002: 72). Teachers in the regular classroom initiate 90 percent of the referrals for special education services (Harry and Klingner 2006), and the primary disabilities cited for the referral include mental retardation and behavioral disturbance. Both of these disabilities are difficult to measure with objective tests (Harry et al. 2002), which means that decisions to refer students for special education classes are largely based on teachers' judgments. Race is central to the process, given that teachers are often white and students being referred for removal from the regular classroom to special education are predominantly black. The question is: How exactly does race play into the problem?

A recent study revealed that teachers often presume that poverty causes the disabilities in question (Skiba et al. 2006). However, we know that a stronger relationship exists between race and special education than between poverty and special education (Parrish and Hikido 1998). And, although poverty may have an indirect impact on disproportionality primarily because of its association with malnutrition, gender differences within the African American group—males are significantly represented at higher rates than females—confound the direct link between poverty and disproportionality (Skiba et al. 2006). Moreover, overrepresentation of African American students does not occur regarding medical disabilities such as blindness or deafness (Losen and Orfield 2002). Whereas black students have the same likelihood as white students of being referred for a medical disability, they are almost three times as likely (2.88) as white students to be referred for mental retardation or emotional disturbance (Parrish 2002).

Terms such as "more outspoken," "louder," and "disrespectful," offered by teachers about "problem students" in the Skiba study (2006: 1437), and a negative impression of African American families, often depicted as "dysfunctional" in the Harry study (2002: 78), are part of the context within which teachers make decisions about retardation and behavioral disturbance of black children. Researchers have referred to these students as having a particular behavioral style (see Hosp and Hosp 2002). The pejorative terms represent the stereotypical images of silent racism that play a part in the decision-making process. This does not mean that white teachers are intentionally racist or wish to harm their black students. Rather, it means that white teachers, not unlike white people generally, carry negative images and assumptions (silent racism) that bear on their decisions.

Child Welfare

A similar problem of racial disproportionality is evident in the child welfare system. In 1974 the Child Abuse Prevention and Treatment Act (CAPTA) was passed by Congress in order to provide funds to states for the protection of children in the system. CAPTA has been amended numerous times, and in 1992 provisions were included to address "culturally sensitive procedures" within the system (Child Welfare Information Gateway 2003). Racial disproportionality rates in the national data indicate that black families[2] are more than twice as likely as white ones to be involved with the child welfare system, and the rates in some states are even more striking. For example, in Illinois, 19 percent of the population of children is black but 46 percent of children in the welfare system are black (Rolock and Testa 2005), indicating that black children are almost three times more likely than white children to be in foster care. In Minnesota the proportion of black children in the child welfare system is *six times* the number in the population of Minnesota (Johnson et al. 2007).

At first glance, it does not seem entirely surprising that black children as a group are more likely than white ones to enter the child welfare system given that African Americans experience the primary risk factor for child abuse—poverty—at a higher rate than whites. Black families also experience other risk factors—single parent families, unemployment, and four or more children in the family (Sedlak and Schultz 2005)—at higher rates than white families, which contributes to the expectation that black children will be overrepresented in the system. However, the concern over racial disproportionality arises when the actual rates of child abuse are considered. Black children as a group, despite being at higher risk than white children as a group, are not abused more than white children (Derezotes and Poertner 2005). Protection mechanisms, such as close extended family members (Allen and Farley 1986), resilience (Hill 1998), and flexibility (Hill et al. 1993) are possible rationales for this finding. So, why do African American children disproportionately end up in the child welfare system?

Overreporting of African American children has been seen as a possible reason for racial disproportionality in child welfare (Morton 1999). Entry into the child welfare system starts with a phone call either from a concerned relative, a friend, or an acquaintance, or from someone in a professional capacity mandated by law to report suspected child maltreatment (primarily doctors, nurses, and teachers). National Incidence Studies undertaken in 1980, 1986, and 1993 report that screeners are more likely to bring black children into the child welfare system than they are to bring in white children (Derezotes and Poertner 2005). Decision making within this system, like other systems that serve children, requires careful analysis. The Racial Equity Scorecard, developed by the Alliance on Racial Equity and spearheaded by the Annie E. Casey Foundation, offers a useful method of measuring and tracking racial disproportionality at key decision points (Deretozes et al. 2008).

A nationwide qualitative study (Chibnall and Dutch 2003) includes interviews at child welfare agencies in eight states (California, Georgia, Illinois, Michigan, Minnesota, North Carolina, Texas, and Virginia) exploring agency workers' perceptions of disproportionality. Like the teachers in Skiba's study, social workers pointed to poverty as the primary cause (Chibnall and Dutch 2003). Interestingly, black participants raised racial bias in their white colleagues as an additional problem. More specifically, black caseworkers said that white caseworkers have very little context for understanding cultural differences, including disciplinary practices within the African American community.

It is reasonable to expect that professionals reporting suspected child abuse, as well as decision makers in the child welfare system, hold the same negative stereotypes and assumptions as the U.S. population generally. For example, the fact that a child is more likely to be removed from the home if the father is black than if the father is white could be related to the fear of black men, a prominent finding in the silent racism study (Trepagnier 2001). Unless there are race awareness trainings within the child welfare system, there is no reason to think that white caseworkers would have higher race awareness than the participants in the study of silent racism.

Racial disproportionality is clearly a problem in all three of these systems, and it occurs in every state. People across the nation are working to lessen the problem, many with a great deal of success. The story below is about the commitment, hard work, and progress in Texas CPS as the agency battles racial disproportionality. I detail the successful strategies implemented since 2004 regarding the policies and practices of CPS with the explicit goal of lessening racial disproportionality.

The Texas Model: A Case Study

By definition, a case study entails the close examination of a special situation or bounded system; the *case* in this study is Texas CPS. An *instrumental* case study seeks to explore a particular circumstance regarding a given case (Stake 1995). The following case study focuses on the issue of racial disproportionality in Texas CPS. Specifically I examine the vision and strategies that have begun to reduce the level of disproportionality in the child welfare system in the Lone Star state. As a member of the Texas Statewide Disproportionality Task Force, I am both an insider and an outsider in relation to CPS: I met most of the people who inform this research before the study began, either at task force meetings or the State Annual Disproportionality Conference, yet I am not involved in the day-to-day operations of CPS, so my observations occur largely through the eyes of a spectator.

I first heard of racial disproportionality from Russell Skiba of Indiana University, who heads the Equity Project and whose work on disproportionality in special education and school discipline is recognized nationally. Through talking with Skiba and by reading his work, I came to see that disproportionality is—to some extent—the outcome of thousands of small decisions fueled by silent racism and left standing by racial passivity. In other words, racial disproportionality is silent racism at work; it happens at the everyday level where well-meaning white people—similar to the participants described throughout this book—live their professional lives.

In November 2008 I attended the State Annual Disproportionality Conference, where directors, disproportionality specialists, staff, and stakeholders from each region came together in Austin to share ideas. I was moved by the enthusiasm and dedication of the entire group as participants reported on projects in their respective regions. I decided then to conduct a case study of the work being done by the people in the room. Initial interviews for the study were conducted electronically and, in some cases, by phone. I also met in person with key informants and relied on reports and other information from CPS and Casey Family Programs (hereafter Casey). Finally, as a member of the task force, I had access to reports on progress in reducing disproportionality across the state and heard from fellow task force members quarterly about events addressing the problem in each of the eleven regions.

Almost exactly a year before the decision to carry out this study, my partnership with CPS in Austin began. I received an e-mail from Sheila Sturgis Craig, the disproportionality manager for Texas CPS, who said that Deputy Commissioner of Family and Protective Services Joyce James wanted to meet with me. (At the time, James was assistant commissioner of CPS.)

My first trip to CPS was on a crisp day in November 2007. I arrived a little early at the six-story building where the CPS offices are located in Austin just north of downtown. Sturgis Craig, a native of New Orleans who moved to Texas in the aftermath of Hurricane Katrina, welcomed me warmly and thanked me for driving up from San Marcos where I live. We entered a small conference room and were joined by James, CPS Director of Field Colleen McCall, and a CPS researcher. James expressed her enthusiasm about the ideas in *Silent Racism* and we talked about the connection between silent racism and racial disproportionality. I was struck by her fervor regarding the issue—what she calls "the work"—a first impression that has been borne out time and time again over the last two years. Eventually, the deputy commissioner said that she wanted me "at the table." She also invited me to participate in the next Undoing Racism training set for the following spring. As the meeting came to a close, James mentioned that she was composing a task force and encouraged me to become a member. The following May, I participated in an Undoing Racism workshop, and in July I received a formal invitation to serve on the Statewide Disproportionality Task Force, an invitation I accepted without hesitation.

Texas is the second most populous state in the United States and has one of the youngest populations in the country, with just over 28 percent under eighteen years of age compared with the national average of 25 percent under eighteen (U.S. Census 2000). Given these statistics, it is not surprising that Texas has one of the largest foster care populations in the nation, and that the state shows evidence of racial disproportionality. Despite these facts, Texas CPS, in partnership with Casey, is in the forefront of such institutions nationally in addressing the problem. Texas has become a model for starting with data in identifying and tracking disproportionality in the system and in developing strategies that, while strengthening all of the families in the system, are effectively lessening disproportionality.

The progress in Texas has not gone unnoticed by child welfare agencies in other states. As disproportionality manager for the state, Sturgis Craig has received inquiries from nine states and Washington, D.C., about the Texas Model.[3] She said that other systems as well, such as juvenile justice, secondary and postsecondary education, faith-based agencies, and community organizations have asked for "technical assistance on the Texas Model for addressing disproportionality."

Reducing Racial Disproportionality

Deputy Commissioner James grew up in Port Arthur, Texas, when it was a boomtown, before the oil and gas industry along the Upper Gulf Coast began its decline. She had returned to her hometown as a young social worker for CPS and eventually became the regional director of CPS in the Beaumont/Port Arthur region. For years, she had noticed the high number of black children served by the system, well before the term *racial disproportionality* was known in Texas. In 1996, James collaborated with area universities—Stephen F. Austin State University in Nacogdoches and Lamar University in Beaumont—to study the inordinate number of African American children in the CPS system in her region. The data showed that African American children were indeed overrepresented in the child welfare system in the Beaumont and Port Arthur area—they were reported twice as often as the white children (Belanger 2002). In addition, the poverty and unemployment rates were also found to be high, especially for black families.

With the support of county and city officials in Port Arthur as well as community organizations, the faith-based community, and many other interested parties, James created Project HOPE (Helping Our People Excel), a community center located in Port Arthur. The goal was to offer the families of African American youth one-stop services that would keep them out of the child welfare system. In reference to her work in Beaumont/Port Arthur, James said in 2007: "The commitment level among the staff and our partners was very high, and we were on our way to building new practice models for addressing disproportionality in Child Protective Services. I was so excited because the target site was the community I grew up in—a community that once thrived. I so wanted to be a part of a revitalizing effort for families in this area" (Casey Family Programs and Texas Child Protective Services 2007).

The services offered by Project HOPE are part of a four-stage model called the Community Engagement Model. Each part of the model is intended to address disproportionality in some way. The stages are community awareness and engagement, community leadership, community organization, and community accountability. This model has been integral in identifying and lessening those obstacles that keep African American parents and their children from reaching their goals. In doing so, it greatly improved the life chances of many of the young people involved. Project HOPE remains an important center in Port Arthur and is currently a model for centers opening in other regions in the state (Arlington/Dallas, Austin, and Houston). After Hurricane Rita devastated much of Port Arthur in 2005, Project HOPE remained standing, a symbol of refuge for families that lost everything to the storm.

In April 2004 when she was named assistant commissioner of Texas CPS, James took her fearless dedication to lessening disproportionality in her home region to the state level. Her passion for the work was met in Austin with enthusiasm and commitment by Carolyne Rodriguez, senior director for Texas Strategic Consulting of Casey Family Programs. Casey is a Seattle-based nonprofit organization founded in 1966 by Jim Casey, the same Jim Casey who in 1907 at age nineteen founded the delivery service that eventually became United Parcel Service (UPS), also based in Seattle. The Casey mission is to provide, improve, and ultimately eliminate the need for foster care by supporting families whose children are placed in it. The foundation carries out its objectives by providing direct service to families nationally and by collaborating with county and state agencies, promoting advancements in both policy and practice strategies.

At Deputy Commissioner James's suggestion, Rodriguez and leadership teams and staff from both Casey and CPS added disproportionality to the Texas State Strategy (TSS). The measures TSS set into motion would reduce the rate of racial disproportionality, touching not only the children and families they are committed to serve but also countless community members throughout Texas. James said, "CPS must be committed to working differently with families to change outcomes and help families be more successful. We have built this relationship with Casey on a shared vision and commitment to examine and address disproportionality, racism, and cultural insensitivity in Texas' child welfare system" (Casey Family Programs and Texas Child Protective Services 2007). The vision referred to by James is succinct: "Children First: Protected and Connected." The values supporting the vision are five:

Respect for culture
Inclusiveness of families, youth, and community
Integrity in decision making
Compassion for all
Commitment to reducing disproportionality

The vision of Texas CPS and the core values outlined above set the tone for mutual understanding that is a guide for everyone working to reduce disproportionality in the Texas child welfare system. I first met Carolyne Rodriguez at the Undoing Racism training I attended in May 2008. She greeted me as I entered the large room and introduced me to others taking the training. I noticed that she seemed to know everyone, but I did not realize at the time what an essential role she and Casey play in the work at CPS. Rodriguez, a native Texan, was born to a World War II veteran and his new bride from Britain. She worked for CPS for thirteen years before leaving to obtain her Master's of Social Work and joining Casey in 1984, so her partnership with the agency and with James is natural. Rodriguez said the following in reference to the shared mission forged by the TSS workgroup: "Courageous work is being done by CPS leaders and managers to ensure that internal culture change within CPS involves all staff. It is imperative that there is clarity for all staff about how every aspect of their work connects to a compelling vision and set of values that demonstrate commitment to family-centered practice throughout every stage of CPS service" (Casey Family Programs and Texas Child Protective Services 2007).

Data-Driven Planning

Gathering and analyzing data has been the cornerstone for decreasing racial disproportionality in Texas starting with James's work in Port Arthur and Beaumont. Statewide statistics in 2003–2004 indicated that, although there was no racial difference in terms of abuse, black children in Texas were twice as likely to be reported to the system as white or Hispanic children. Additionally, once a case file was opened (only about 25 percent of them are), black children were 2.5 times more likely to be removed from the home than white or Hispanic children. As the new assistant commissioner, James was determined that these troubling statistics would not be allowed to stand.

The ongoing tracking of outcomes in each of the eleven Texas regions includes racial/ethnic categories in the collection of data as well as in implementing programs that target special concerns in a large and diverse state. Linking outcomes to changes in policies and procedures also includes indicators such as age and gender of children, size of caseload, source of referrals, types of abuse/neglect, and other variables. Findings based on these data were used in the early planning stages to develop strategies that would increase conversations about race and disproportionality among service providers, a cornerstone of the Texas Model.

The vision and values—with the new emphasis on disproportionality—were established and the data were clear. James met with her regional directors across the state with a pioneering message that stressed the importance of "owning" the situation in their regions. Her message was, and remains, clear: "This is *our* system and *our* data. We have contributed to racial disproportionality, and now it is *our* responsibility to get rid of it." James believes that the best way to generate leaders is to give them authority, and her message to regional directors, disproportionality specialists, and other leaders throughout the state—people she calls "passionate champions"—is to "always raise the bar, seeking new practice models. We must leave families better off after they have been touched by CPS than they were before they met us."

And then in June 2004, three months after James arrived in Austin as assistant commissioner, Governor Rick Perry declared that an overhaul of CPS was needed. The timing could not have been better. Armed with data demonstrating that disproportionality existed throughout the state and the vision intended to lessen it, James, along with the first disproportionality specialist she appointed, Debra Green, and Karen Hilton of Health and Human Services (HHSC) worked with a team of staff from both agencies to develop the reform package that, once approved by the executive commissioner for HHSC, could change everything.

Legislative Support

Senate Bill 6—passed by the 79th Texas Legislature and signed by Governor Rick Perry in 2005—mandates the strategies discussed below, giving them statutory authority. Without this support from the top of state government, the vision so carefully crafted by the TSS workgroup may well have remained just that: a vision. Instead, Senate Bill 6 rendered the vision a reality. Sheila Sturgis Craig, my first connection to Texas CPS, said the following about the bill's importance to the work of lessening disproportionality:

> I began my career in Texas immediately after the rollout of Senate Bill 6 of the 79th Legislature. I was amazed that a state as large as Texas (and as conservative) would take on such a huge undertaking. Texas is at the forefront in identifying disproportionality for African American and American Indian children—the two groups disproportionately represented in the system—through data and research. The findings became the basis and catalyst for more culturally competent leadership, staff development, and training. (Casey Family Programs and Texas Child Protective Services 2007)

There is not room here to cover every plank of the bill or to give a detailed description of every policy and strategy that has contributed to the lessening of disproportionality in the Texas child welfare system. Nevertheless, below I portray the programs that have been central to the changes taking place in Texas, roughly using Senate Bill 6 as an organizational framework.

Cultural Competency Training

As mandated by Senate Bill 6, Texas CPS must offer cultural competency training to staff members who provide services to families and children. The in-house training, Knowing Who You Are, is a cultural competency program developed by Casey Family Programs and delivered by the Professional Development Division of the Texas Department of Family and Protective Services. In addition, the Undoing Racism training offers an effective antiracism analysis. Both of these training programs, central to addressing racial bias in decision making, are discussed in depth below.

Knowing Who You Are

The primary goal of the Knowing Who You Are (KWYA) curriculum is to inform caseworkers and caregivers about race and ethnicity questions likely to emerge in the lives of children in the care of foster families different from themselves. This three-part curriculum begins with a short video, includes an online tutorial, and culminates in a two-day event with a trained facilitator. Watching the video and participating in an online tutorial are prerequisites for the face-to-face seminar.

The KWYA training prepares families for courageous conversations about identity issues in the lives of the children of color in their care. It is based on the assumption that anyone providing care and support for children from a different racial and cultural background must "arrive at some level of understanding and awareness regarding their own individual racial and ethnic identity" (Casey Family Programs 2005: 13). The twenty-four-minute video focuses on open dialogue in a group of alumni foster youth, caseworkers, and parents (both foster parents and birth parents) sharing their thinking and feelings about race and ethnicity, a topic inherently difficult to talk about especially when talking across racial and ethnic boundaries. KWYA facilitators are trained to lead discussions after the video screening that help viewers process concerns brought to the surface by the video.

The online session is self-paced and delves more deeply into issues children in foster care are likely to confront, including racism and white privilege. This part of the KWYA curriculum challenges the beliefs of many who take part in it, especially well-meaning white people who may not have ever thought deeply about race matters. This part of the curriculum encourages self-reflection, which is supported by the privacy of an online program, and allows participants to think about their own racial/ethnic identity as well as the biases and stereotypes (that is, silent racism) embedded in their own perspectives. The third component of the KWYA curriculum is a two-day event led by a trained facilitator. A safe environment ensures that participants can acquire the needed information and skills that will increase the likelihood that their day-to-day encounters with people of different cultural and racial backgrounds will be positive.

KWYA, which began as cultural competence training for incoming (newly hired) caseworkers, has been expanded in Texas CPS to include incoming investigators as well. In addition, ongoing caseworkers and investigators are encouraged to take the training; the ultimate goal is that every administrator and staff member at CPS will take part in the training. Casey reports that in 2008 there were 100 KWYA trainers in the United States, and that 70 of the 100 were in Texas. These statistics are testament to the seriousness of James and other administrators who are committed to increasing race awareness in all personnel at Texas CPS.

Undoing Racism

The Undoing Racism training is presented by the People's Institute for Survival and Beyond, headquartered in New Orleans. Delivered by veteran community organizers, this training is based on the idea that racism in U.S. society began in slavery, was sustained throughout the Jim Crow era, and continues today as institutional racism. The goal of the training—to "undo" the causes of racism rather than to simply treat its symptoms—is achieved by producing antiracism leaders. The philosophy of the training is based on the following core principles:

- antiracism leaders must understand the history of racism in the United States as well as the role of power in its perpetuation, including the power of gatekeepers;
- antiracism leaders must maintain accountability to their constituents and to other antiracism leaders within their system; and
- antiracism leaders must recognize that racial oppression includes both internalized racial inferiority and internalized racial superiority, and that racial equality requires undoing both of these aspects of racial oppression.

Members of the People's Institute believe that racism has been consciously and systematically erected in U.S. society and that individuals have the responsibility to dismantle the legacy of racism where they live. The multiracial team "challenges participants to analyze the structures of power and privilege that hinder racial equity and prepares them to be effective organizers for social justice" (Casey Family

Programs and Texas Child Protective Services 2007). Outcomes of the training include understanding the following processes, among others: How institutional racism relates to participants' work; how institutions penalize communities of color, ensuring that some people remain poor; how the historical racial classifications in the United States continue to harm people; and how community organizing and coalition building can lessen racism.

Since the two-and-a-half day trainings became part of the cultural competency mandate in 2005, more than 2,000 people in Texas associated with CPS have participated in 79 trainings held across the state. Participants include CPS administrators and staff, task force members, community partners and stakeholders, parents, and foster care alumni youth. To date, feedback from participants indicates that the training can be "life changing" and helps people see through "a different lens." Sturgis Craig said the following about the response of most participants: "Individuals report that the training helped them to see the systemic issues that create barriers for families and children impacted by the child welfare system. The training has been the catalyst for a cultural shift which in turn has helped to transform Texas Child Welfare." One CPS employee, Linda Wright, had a profound response to the training.

I met Wright, the disproportionality specialist in the Arlington/Dallas region, at the Undoing Racism training I attended in May 2008. Wright moved to Texas from Michigan in the 1980s to attend college. She became an intern with CPS before she graduated, and eventually she became a regional director. I asked her to tell me the story of how she ended up in the position she now holds. Her response is testimony to the importance of the Undoing Racism training.

> We began looking at the disproportionate representation of African American children in our system [while I was still regional director]. I had a great struggle with this when I learned we were making the connection with racism. Although I knew racism existed, I did not see the connection or correlation with disproportionality and did not see myself as contributing to disproportionality. Our agency provided Undoing Racism workshops, and my first attendance with my team was a disaster. I did not agree with most of what was presented and had serious considerations about quitting my job knowing that I could not provide leadership for something I did not believe in. After much painful struggle and research I somehow connected and understood

> the whole concept of institutional racism and how we all contribute in various ways and how it is self-perpetuating in our institutions. After that epiphany, doing antiracist work was really all I wanted to do. I was able to do it in my [regional director] role but not sufficient to my satisfaction. I retired March 31, 2008, with plans to do volunteer work with our local YWCA, which is committed to eliminating racism. Two months after retirement I learned of the state disproportionality specialist position, and I applied and was selected for the position. (Linda Wright, e-mail to author)

Wright told me that she made a commitment in her region to be at any Undoing Racism training that someone from her staff attended. She has participated in at least twenty trainings, including many across the state. Her struggle with the truth about racism and her willingness to share it has been both a comfort and an inspiration to many, especially to well-meaning white people like herself whose race awareness before the training was low.

The Undoing Racism training is followed a few weeks later by a debriefing where people who have attended one of the trainings are invited to meet with the trainers to talk about outcomes and questions related to the training. Crucial conversations about race among CPS staff members have been the result, and several spinoffs of the debriefings have come about as well. Sturgis Craig described three informal offshoots of the more formal debriefing at our last task force meeting. *Talk Backs* are a continuation of the dialog that occurred at the most recent Undoing Racism debriefing. Staff members have the opportunity to talk about issues raised either in the training or in the debriefing. *Shop Talk* is based on the idea of a (black) barbershop and the talk that goes on there. Staff members discuss language use and raise questions about which terms are offensive and which ones are not. The third spinoff is the *Liberated Zone,* which is a space where caseworkers and managers can converse about race matters without fear of reprisals. The assumption that it is acceptable to make a mistake (say something that may be racially insensitive) creates a safe space to discuss issues and questions that likely would not be mentioned otherwise. These strategies emerged spontaneously among CPS staff across Texas as a result of participating in the Undoing Racism training and the debriefing that follows it. They are increasing race awareness in ongoing conversations about race, and they are evidence that people want to talk about race and racism but need a safe space in order to do so. It is also evidence that racial passivity is lessened as race awareness increases. Well-meaning white people throughout CPS are talking about race matters. This shift is significant and would not have occurred without the trainings sponsored by CPS.

Collaborative Partnerships

Another strategy, also mandated by Senate Bill 6, requires Texas CPS to develop collaborative partnerships with community groups, agencies, faith-based organizations, and other organizations in order to provide services that are culturally sensitive. Yet, involving stakeholders and other community members was already instrumental in Texas CPS before Senate Bill 6 was signed in June 2005. In fall 2004 Herschel Smith, president of the Harris County Leadership Council, and a number of unhappy parents whose children had been removed by CPS were picketing the CPS office in Houston with complaints about the system's treatment of African American families. Smith invited Randy Joiner, CPS director of the Houston Region, to a town hall meeting. The letter of invitation began with these words, "Our African-American families have been torn apart by CPS. Our people will be expressing our grief publicly and collectively and we would like for you to join us." Joiner called James for guidance, and she instructed him to accept the invitation and add two guests. She and Audrey Deckinga, who has since moved into the position of assistant commissioner of CPS, would travel from Austin to Houston and attend the town hall meeting with him.

Northside Missionary Baptist Church was packed that night; police officers, Court Appointed Special Advocates (CASA) for abused and neglected children, clergy, legislators, and CPS clients filled the hall. Many of the families told their stories, and Smith asked James to respond. She acknowledged that the system needed improvement, and told the audience about the work already being done. She asked Smith publicly if he would join an advisory committee and contribute to the work.

That night, CPS and the Houston community forged a partnership that is ongoing. Smith currently serves on the Houston Disproportionality Advisory Committee as well as on the State Disproportionality Task Force; his voice is highly valued at both the regional and state levels. In a 2007 interview with Rodriguez, Smith praised the work of Casey and CPS in their efforts to lessen racial disproportionality in Texas. In his words:

> Personally, being on the Houston Disproportionality Advisory Committee, seeing what other agencies do, and learning more about policies and procedures, I have learned to see that this [disproportionality] is a systemic problem. It has moved me to "another level"—I do more homework, educate myself, building understanding and deepening my understanding of policies and constraints [of the CPS system].... Both sides need to listen. Formerly, I didn't feel heard; now, they [CPS] are hearing me out. There is open dialogue! (Herschel Smith, e-mail to author; Casey Family Programs and Texas Child Protective Services 2007)

Disproportionality Advisory Committees

All eleven regions in Texas have Disproportionality Advisory Committees like the one to which Smith refers. Members of the regional committees are community leaders and CPS staff, including the disproportionality specialist. Data on regional disproportionality are shared with partners and stakeholders, with the same message James sends to her leaders within CPS: This is *our* system, and these are *our* data; we must do the right thing for our children.

Using the community engagement model first developed by James and her partners when she was director of the Beaumont/Port Arthur region, the goal of the committees is to increase awareness in the community by sharing the data regarding disproportionality in their region and encouraging conversations about how to deal with the problem at the local level. Stories are encouraged at the meetings from people in the area who receive services from CPS (or who have received services in the past). Committee members become "informed advocates" and are invited to participate in the Undoing Racism training. The focus on community organizing and coalition building, core principles of the Undoing Racism philosophy, empowers committee members to own the changes needed in their region to lessen disproportionality.

Sherry Gomez, director of the San Antonio Region, is a native Texan who is in her twenty-fourth year with CPS and "can't imagine doing anything else." Gomez told me about a few of the activities in her region that involve community engagement. For example, "we hold 'hair-a-thons' where African American or biracial children in foster care get their hair done, and caregivers are taught proper ethnic hair and skin care by stylists. We also held an ethnic hair and skin-care product drive to collect items to disperse to children coming into foster care." In addition, Gomez mentioned an outreach project called Mission Engage that invites churches to partner with CPS in various ways. For example, a church might be asked to "sponsor a hair-a-thon by donating refreshments for the event or hair care products that the youth can take with them."

Collaborative partnerships throughout Texas, including the regional advisory committees, are essential to the grassroots organizing needed to support vulnerable families *before* losing their children. These committees in Arlington/Dallas, Houston, and Austin have laid the groundwork for pilot programs modeled after the original Project HOPE in Port Arthur.

State Disproportionality Task Force

The task force James mentioned to me at our first meeting is composed of forty-five members, including some of the advisory committee members and community stakeholders from across the state. Other members include administrators and staff from CPS, Casey, and other state child- and family-serving agencies; faculty from universities, community colleges, and school districts; and court officials from juvenile and family courts. And, importantly, members include alumni of foster care as well as parents who have experienced the child welfare system, including biological parents whose children have been removed, foster parents, and adoptive parents. The task force meets quarterly and is cosponsored by Texas CPS and Casey. Members are also invited to attend the annual conference on disproportionality. The term of service is two to three years, except for standing members of the task force.

The task force is a working group with four ad hoc committees—staff support/learning, community support/learning, public policy development, and best practices. Leadership responsibilities include guiding, informing, and sharing ideas for lessening racial disproportionality in Texas as the work moves forward. Another outcome of task force participation is the cross-systems partnerships that are forged and that are explicit in the task force charter. Judge Oscar Gabaldón Jr.—a task force member—and his work in El Paso exemplifies the critical partnership between child welfare and the judicial system.

Gabaldón, born in El Paso as a U.S. citizen, spent his early childhood in Ciudad Juarez, Chihuahua, Mexico, a metaphor for his appreciation today of both Mexican and American cultures. Before marrying and attending law school in Houston, the young Oscar spent a number of years in the seminary studying to be a priest. Today he is associate judge for the Texas Family Court and presides over the El Paso County Child Protection Court. His is a model court, which means it is part of the Model Courts Project, of which the purpose is to speed up decisions regarding children who have been removed from their families so they can either be reunited with their birth families or become available for adoption as soon as possible.[4] Gabaldón said the following about his work:

> My overall cultural awareness and sensitivity have heightened in light of the realities and challenges involved in my work with disproportionality in the foster care system. I have become more cognizant of the fact that it is absolutely crucial that I be a judge that is respectful and appreciative of everyone's ethnic, racial, and cultural background in order to more successfully fulfill my judicial responsibilities in the administration of justice. As judges, it is our non-negotiable moral and ethical duty to consistently work at growing in our level of cultural competency in order that we may better serve the needs of those coming to our courts.

Gabaldón's dedication to families and high ethical standards are evident in the cross-systems partnership between his model court and child welfare agencies, including CPS, in the El Paso region. Together they formed the Teen Initiative, a support system designed to supply services to youth aged sixteen to twenty-five aging out of foster care. At the Preparation and Resources for Independence with Determination and Excellence (PRIDE) Center, El Paso foster youth and alumni receive housing referrals, job opportunities, life skills training, and access to a computer lab as well as voicemail and mailboxes. The collaborative effort draws from area agencies and colleges, local churches, and many other organizations, but the best part is that the foster youth themselves participated in planning the center. This group effort gives the young people ownership of the PRIDE center and reflects the importance of collaborative partnerships—in James's spirit of having a diverse group of people "at the table."

Disproportionality Prevention Policies

Although key policies that address system improvement regarding racial disparities in Texas were central to the Texas State Strategy well before Senate Bill 6 was codified, the bill requires that Texas CPS develop and implement strategies intended to reduce racial disproportionality. Rodriguez, James, and their team consulted with community partners, alumni foster youth, and birth parents as they considered best practices throughout the nation. The goal was to develop policy in Texas based on the values listed earlier—respect for all cultures; inclusiveness of families, youth, and the community; integrity in decision making; compassion for all; and a commitment to reduce disproportionality—with an eye on what is working in child welfare systems in other states. The result was Kinship Care, which has become the cornerstone of inclusive CPS services in Texas, and it exemplifies the CPS vision: Keep children protected *and* connected.

Kinship Care

If removal of children from the home is deemed necessary because of confirmed abuse or neglect, where the children should go in the immediate future is a pressing decision. A family-focused approach, Kinship Care emerged from the assumption that children are best served if they are related to those who will care for them, whether extended family or "fictive kin" (Ebaugh 2000: 189). The term fictive kin first emerged in anthropology and generally refers to a relationship based not on biological ties but on close (long-term) friendship or religious ties. In Texas CPS, Family Group Decision Making is founded in the Kinship Care principle of inclusion.

Family Group Decision Making

The assumption that families want the best for their children and therefore should help make decisions about them underpins Family Group Decision Making (FGDM). This strategy brings in families and other advocates whenever decisions about children are made. FGDM entails two processes: Family Group Conferences and Family Team Meetings.

Texas CPS not only invites families to participate in Family Group Conferences but also encourages them to name the time and place as well as who will attend the meeting. Families are encouraged to invite people who care about their children and whom their children know and trust. Decisions informed by birth family members, extended family members, and close family friends will be decisions that serve the children best. Originally, FGDM only became available to families after a child was removed from the home; today, Family Team Meetings are available to the family from the first contact with CPS, which reduces the number of placements in foster care and allows for family reunification to occur more quickly if a child is removed.

Sturgis Craig, who served as state kinship specialist before becoming state disproportionality manager, told me the following:

> As a result of these [Kinship Care] and other efforts, reductions in disproportionality are seen in five of the six counties [regions] where the disproportionality work began. More children are placed with kin and more are served in their own homes, which means that fewer children are being removed. What is more amazing is that these reductions are also seen across racial and ethnic lines.

Philip Ikomi is originally from Koko, a port city in Nigeria. Today, he is a researcher at Prairie View A&M University and a member of the Texas Statewide Disproportionality Task Force. Ikomi reported at the task force meeting in June 2009 that the percentage of children reunified with their families almost doubled, from 4.5 percent in 2005 to over 9 percent in 2008. Because African American children are disproportionately represented in the data, a reduction of this sort impacts black families at a higher rate than other families, thus producing a decrease in disproportionality. Programs like FGDM support all children at the same time they reduce disproportionality, thus bearing out James's claim that "if we raise the bar for our most vulnerable children, we raise it for all of our children."

The Texas Model

Texas is clearly reducing racial disproportionality in the child welfare system. In addition to more children being reunified with their families, removals of all children in Texas have decreased since the work on disproportionality began. And even though more African American children in Texas continue to be removed relative to their numbers in the population than other children, the disproportionality rate is lower than it was when the work began in 1996. For example, between 2005 and 2008 the rate of removal of white children in Texas decreased from 6.1 percent to 5.1 percent, one percentage point. For the same period, the rate of removal of black children decreased from 7.8 percent to 6.2 percent, a 2.5 percent decrease. These statistics should put to rest any fears that focusing on reducing racial disproportionality would somehow give preferential treatment to African American children over white children, a concern raised by some. Clearly, all children are benefiting from the efforts to reduce disproportionality.

No one believes that racial disproportionality in the child welfare system or in special education is the result of intentional racism. Rather, the racial bias involved is the result of silent racism and racial passivity, the same as that described throughout the early chapters of this book. Moreover, the decrease in racial disproportionality in Texas CPS is in part because of an increase in race awareness resulting from the Undoing Racism and Knowing Who You Are trainings as well as the conversations about race taking place in CPS offices in the eleven regions in Texas.

The changes in Texas continue to require hard work and committed leadership. Producing change in a large bureaucracy is never easy, and producing change that involves race matters may be the hardest of all. And yet, change is occurring in Texas CPS. Evidence of the change is that in the very difficult economic climate, the success of Texas CPS in reducing racial disproportionality generated additional support from the 2009 Texas legislature.

The strategies that make up the Texas Model have been tested and can be replicated by passionate champions in child welfare systems in other states as well as adapted by special education programs. Many of the strategies can also be used outside of the systems discussed here; workplaces and organizations generally would benefit from increased race awareness, partnerships with people in other systems, and policies of inclusion. And of course, critical to the enterprise are committed conversations about race.

Notes

1. Other systems produce racial disproportionality as well, such as the justice system and health care.

2. In some parts of the United States the overrepresentation of Native American children is even greater than that of African American children (see Derezotes et al. 2008 for details).

3. The states asking about the Texas Model, in addition to Washington, D.C., were Arizona, Colorado, Iowa, Kentucky, Louisiana, Minnesota, New York, North Carolina, and Washington.

4. Thirty of the fifty U.S. states have at least one model court; and because Judge Gabaldón has recently mentored the Austin jurisdiction in becoming one, Texas is now the sixth state to have two model courts. The six states with two model courts are California, Louisiana, Nevada, New York, Ohio, and Texas.

Chapter Eight

Epilogue

AMERICAN RACIAL CULTURE HAS HISTORICALLY been predicated on blackness counterposed against whiteness (Lipsitz 1998). Whiteness in the form of domination was achieved deliberately and consciously during slavery and segregation. Since then, these racist structures have been transformed into a new, less obvious structure we know as institutional racism, with remnants of the racist ideology continuing today. Whites assume the white legacy without question and often without notice. However, the mindlessness of whites surrounding the legacy of whiteness in no way diminishes its impact. Because racism continues to permeate U.S. structures and ideology, understanding the racial history of this country and how racism operates systemically is imperative to understanding individuals' relation to the racial status quo.

Bearing in mind the institutional support of racism historically and recognizing that no matter how well-meaning white people may *feel*, the assumption that they have not been influenced by the historical legacy concerning race is shortsighted. Slavery lasted 300 years in the United States (including its preunion years as British colonies) and was characterized by legalized acts of terror and brutality against blacks. Slaves were branded like cattle; they were regularly beaten, sometimes tortured, and occasionally dismembered; resistance on the part of slaves was punished harshly by hanging and, in some instances, by burning at the stake for females (Giddings 1984). In Louisiana, five slaves accused of revolting against their owners were killed, decapitated, and their heads put on poles as an example to other slaves. All of these practices were legal and sanctioned by religious beliefs of the time. The ideology that grew out of such practices was that blacks were uncivilized and evil; that blackness was a curse from God; that "black beastiality" must be controlled, requiring slavery; and that blacks were "ill-suited for freedom" (Turner and Singleton 1978: 1005).

For one hundred years following the Civil War, the United States legally enforced segregation accompanied by frequent lynching and other brutality, especially in the South. Dominant beliefs continued to disparage blacks; the racial ideology held that blacks were inferior to whites; that they were not taking advantage of their freedom from slavery and the equal opportunity that Reconstruction gave them; that they were lazy, had criminal tendencies, and wanted to rape white women; and that they should be kept separated from whites (Turner and Singleton 1978: 1006).

Legal segregation was weakened with the U.S. Supreme Court decision *Brown v. Board of Education* in 1954 and ended with the Civil Rights Act in 1964. However, just as slavery was transformed into segregation, segregation has been transformed into institutional racism; unofficial segregation continues today in terms of education, justice, and healthcare. Moreover, although the racist ideology has changed, it has not been eliminated. The ideology in place in the post–civil rights era is that blacks' inability to succeed in American society is due to their own lack of motivation (Bonilla-Silva 2003; Feagin 2001). Opponents cast government policies that level the playing field as "reverse racism," a color-blind view that denies both the effect of structures (slavery, segregation, and institutional racism) on blacks and the effect of racial ideology on whites. Institutional racism and the racist ideology operate to the advantage of whites and the disadvantage of blacks, and they operate in tandem. To ignore either is to distort how racism is produced.

The role of well-meaning whites in the production of institutional racism is hidden by the way white Americans think about racism. The oppositional categories of racism obscure how institutional racism is produced because they effectively imply that "racists" are the problem and "nonracists" have nothing to do with racism. Nothing could be further from the truth. The data in this study demonstrate that the term *nonracist* is a misnomer because all whites are somewhat racist.

Changing the racial status quo in the United States today requires a shift in the minds of well-meaning white people away from the notion that they are not racist and toward the idea that they are part of the problem. This claim includes people who are antiracist—that is, who are working to lessen racism. They do not differ qualitatively from other whites any more than people who are overtly racist. Rethinking racism as suggested throughout this book requires a shift away from whether or not well-meaning white people are racist—we are all somewhat racist—and toward people's level of awareness regarding race issues. This would achieve two important goals. First, the focus on awareness would motivate well-meaning white people to increase their awareness of race issues; and second, the focus away from whether or not people are racist would decrease the emphasis currently placed on people's intentions, illuminating instead the *effects* of racist behavior—regardless of what is intended—because those effects are what perpetuate the racial divide.

I have offered three grounds for why the "racist" and "not racist" categories should be replaced by a racism continuum. First, I have shown that the racism categories are meaningless given that silent racism exists in white people generally, including those least likely to be racist. Second, I have demonstrated that silent racism upholds institutional racism in that many decisions made daily that discriminate against people of color are shaped by silent racism. Third, I have illustrated that the racism categories are problematic because the "not racist" category itself produces a latent effect—passivity, which reinforces institutional racism.

I have further argued that the shift from oppositional categories to a racism continuum will increase race awareness in well-meaning white people (although perhaps not all of them). However, even if the targeted group is small, it could matter. Small contingents of racially progressive whites in concert with progressive blacks have mattered in the past in dismantling the racist structures of slavery and segregation.

The shift from a categorical modern form of thought to a more fluid postmodern approach characterized by the continuum is consistent with a pragmatic tradition that encourages self-reflection. There is irony in an awareness of one's unawareness that will accompany the shift from oppositional categories regarding racism to a continuum. Well-meaning white people who have a high level of race awareness sense that their knowledge of race matters is partial and distorted, and that they harbor racist stereotypes and assumptions that are likely to influence their behavior. Race-aware white people are open—not defensive—in terms of receiving information about their own racism. They know they will occasionally make mistakes and do not feel compelled to avoid or deny them. Instead, they expect to learn from their mistakes, painful though that might be. Race-aware white people are engaged with race matters because they know that race is a central factor in their own lives, a point that is hidden by the way most people, well-meaning or not, think about racism.

Oppositional categories were useful in the 1960s when the civil rights movement was on the rise and overt racism was rampant in the United States. At that time the category "not racist" was meaningful in that white people who saw themselves as "not racist" took a stand for change regarding the racial formation. Today, the "not racist" category all too often represents a passive endorsement of the racial status quo with no commitment to changing it. The construction of oppositional categories regarding racism that was functional before the civil rights movement has outgrown its usefulness. Even worse, today the outmoded construction is causing more harm than good.

Some individuals believe that white people, well meaning or not, giving up white privilege is not "rational" and therefore is not likely to occur. Cornel West expressed this view when he said in a lecture I attended that white people would give up race privilege *only* if they viewed the United States as a sinking ship and everyone on board would drown unless a solution were found.[1] I maintain, in contrast to West, that some well-meaning white people would care about race matters if they recognized the important role they play in perpetuating the racial status quo. The rethinking of racism proposed here would precipitate that realization.

I acknowledge that this is a "sympathetic" reading of well-meaning white people. However, doing the right thing was the rationale of those whites who assisted in the Underground Railroad, the whites who marched with Dr. Martin Luther King Jr., and whites like Morris Dees of the Southern Poverty Law Center and Senator Bill Bradley, both of whom work determinedly to lessen racism today. Rather than holding on to white privilege—the putatively rational choice—some well-meaning white people would take a stand against the everyday racism surrounding them if a shift occurred in their race awareness.

The racism continuum exposes what many well-meaning white people already suppose to be the case: that they are indeed racist to a degree. For some, confirmation of their own reality will be a welcomed relief. For others, eliminating the "not racist" category will present a dilemma forcing them to consider—perhaps for the first time—whether they are as "well-meaning" as they presume.

Language, according to Bourdieu, is "fair game for sociologists" (quoted in Jenkins 1992: 153), although it is not often explored as a site for social change. This project to change the language well-meaning white people use to think and communicate about racism is such an attempt. If the ideas in this book were widely accepted by racially progressive whites and blacks, I believe, the categories would be discarded and a continuum of racism would replace them. This change in language would set off the other changes described throughout this book, epitomized by these precepts:

- Replacing the "racist" and "not racist" categories with a racism continuum exposes silent racism that has been hidden, shifting how well-meaning white people think about racism. This shift will:
    - indirectly increase race awareness in well-meaning white people. This will:
        - decrease everyday racism, racist practice, and passivity;
        - increase antiracist practice; and
        - decrease institutional racism.

Who are the well-meaning white people who will adopt these ideas? They are the *early adopters* and *early majority* who will recognize the truth and the usefulness of the ideas.[2] They correspond to the progressive white people during America's slavery period who rejected the dominant belief that blacks were inferior and recognized that slavery was wrong and should be stopped. They correspond to the progressive white people during segregation that stood with blacks against unfair voting practices and fought against segregation. They are the white people who would *not* be threatened by the change—whites who are already the most aware of racism, including their own.

The findings in this study suggest areas for future research. One area is studying whites who are highly race aware and would perhaps confirm my claim that close relationships with people of color are essential to increasing race awareness. Other factors that increase race awareness may also emerge. Conversations between blacks and whites offer another avenue for study, one that I am undertaking with one of my colleagues. We hope to discover the areas where such conversations get "stuck" as well as where they lead to valuable information about silent racism. Studying blacks who are in close relationships with whites may also yield interesting results about the race awareness of the whites in the relationships. And finally, studying well-meaning white men or exploring racism against other groups may also prove useful.

Doing the Right Thing

Antiracism—a natural outgrowth of race awareness—is a moral stand. Antiracist white people should challenge racism because it is the right thing to do. In June 2003 the U.S. Supreme Court upheld affirmative action, a policy that came out of the civil rights movement of the 1960s intended to remedy past wrongs. Justice Sandra Day O'Connor, the swing vote on the case, suggested that the need for affirmative action should be alleviated within the next twenty-five years. If that challenge is to be met, a major shift in the racial status quo must occur. It is past time that progressive whites stand up and be counted. It is past time that we do the right thing.

Notes

1. West made this comment in a lecture in 1994 at the University of California at Santa Barbara.

2. Taken from the Everitt Rogers model of innovation adoption curve, which consists of five categories: innovators, early adopters, early majority, late majority, and laggards.

Appendix A: Methodological Concerns

THIS APPENDIX IS DESIGNED AS SUPPORT for studying racism from the inside out; that is, exploring racism from the viewpoint of the white persons performing it. This approach requires that participants talk openly about a topic most people rarely discuss in a personal way: racism. In order to achieve this goal, I set up eight focus groups in which twenty-five well-meaning white women living on the West Coast talked openly about racism. This appendix offers the thinking that went into setting up the study, including methodological questions that needed to be answered.

I

The research question in this study was, "How do well-meaning white people who care about the issue think and feel about racism?" The soundness of the study required first considering whether the project should employ qualitative or quantitative methods. Other choices also required consideration, such as whether to limit participation in the study to one social category or to open the study to anyone interested in participating. Another factor concerned whether to limit the topic to racism aimed at black Americans or to include racism targeting other minority groups as well.

Quantitative research methods are identified with random samples, hypothesis testing, and statistical procedures (Babbie 2001). The quantitative approach is a good way to collect data from large numbers of people and is often used to portray features of a given population; identify opinions; and measure, explain, or predict group behavior. As early as the 1930s, national opinion polls were used to gauge whites' attitudes toward blacks by many survey research centers, such as the National Opinion Research Center (NORC) and General Social Survey (GSS).

Qualitative research methods, in comparison, are identified with nonrandom samples, firsthand observation, and inductive reasoning (Strauss and Corbin 1991). The qualitative approach offers an in-depth portrayal of people's beliefs and feelings and provides insight into people's motivations and meanings. So, although survey research continues to be used in studies of white attitudes, exploring racism from the inside out entails using qualitative research methods that allow the researcher to probe beyond the surface.

Because this study was not intended to measure racism or discrimination but to explore how well-meaning white people construct their definition of racism, in-depth interviews—an earmark of the qualitative approach (Denzin and Lincoln 1994)—were appropriate. In-depth interviews allow researchers to delve into the issue being studied with the participants. The goal was to understand well-meaning white people, including myself, who sometimes have racist thoughts and at times may express them despite the best efforts to not do so. This study allowed participants to express their racist thoughts and feelings. Moreover, the questions I asked were intended to explore participants' early lessons regarding racism and what they consider to be racist.

Discussing racism and the meanings attached to it relies on attaining data that can be analyzed with a "sympathetic" ear (Cooley 1916: 17); however, having a sympathetic ear does not imply approval of the racism expressed by participants. To the contrary, the analysis in this study is penetrating and decisive, at times at odds with a given participant's point of view. Having a sympathetic ear means understanding the person whose racism is being portrayed; it does not mean accepting the racism expressed. The use of probing questions, a common practice of qualitative researchers, allows for detailed exploration of what participants intended in their responses. Probes such as "Tell me more about that," or "What exactly do you mean?" were used consistently in the discussions. These opportunities were essential for encouraging participants to elaborate their views, thus offering details that enriched the findings.

II

Validity has a variety of meanings methodologically, three of which are pertinent to this study. Two forms of validity are borrowed from quantitative research: internal validity, which refers to whether researchers are measuring what they intend to measure; and external validity, which generally refers to reliability. The third form of validity, catalytic validity (Lather 1991), emerged from within qualitative research and refers to whether a research project had an impact on (hence, was a catalyst for) participants in such a way that it changed their behavior or perspective regarding the topic. Catalytic validity is discussed further when a brief analysis of the journals provided by participants is presented at the end of this appendix.

Internal validity is considered a strength of qualitative methods and a weak aspect of quantitative research, especially studies relying on surveys. This means a concept must be operationalized so that the categorical answers to survey questions will reflect the concept accurately. If a question or set of questions intended to measure a concept (e.g., racism) measures something else instead, the survey is said to be lacking internal validity. In qualitative research, internal validity is a strength rather than a weakness because researchers have the opportunity to observe when participants misinterpret a question and can make sure the concept discussed is the one being explored. The presentation of participants' words in almost all of the chapters of this book offers readers evidence of internal validity. Although a reader may disagree with my interpretation of a given statement regarding whether it is racist, the grounds for my interpretation are clear and comport with sociological race theory. In other words, disagreement about the analysis is not likely to be a matter of whether the research has internal validity but a matter of disagreement with the tenets of sociological race theory presented.

Generally speaking, reliability refers to whether a study can be replicated; that is, would another researcher doing a similar study come to similar conclusions? Some qualitative researchers question the idea that any research project could be truly replicated (Holstein and Gubruim 1997); others argue that replication is not a useful goal for qualitative researchers (Hughes and Sharock 1997; Marshall and Rossman 1999). Many researchers focus on issues they deem more appropriate to qualitative research; for example, words like *trustworthiness* (Glaser and Strauss 1967) and *dependability* (Lincoln and Guba 1985) are used instead of *reliability* (see Ritchie and Lewis 2003). Regardless of which words are used, the underlying issue concerns this question: Would another researcher doing a similar study come to similar conclusions? Readers need assurance that a given study is not simply a "quirk" of the particular sample chosen (Ritchie and Lewis 2003). Two strategies for offering this reassurance—and increasing reliability—are building transparency into the study (Seale 1999) and offering sufficient evidence for the claims made (Ritchie and Lewis 2003).

Other researchers can reproduce good qualitative research if the original study is transparent—that is, if its methods are presented in detail (Berg 2004). Some authors point out that a researcher who has a similar approach as the original researcher, who seeks participants from a similar population as the study in question, and who asks similar questions about participants' experiences regarding a given topic can expect to have similar results (Strauss and Corbin 1990). I am confident that a similar study of well-meaning white women who see themselves and are seen by others as not racist, performed by a symbolic interactionist with a sociological view of racism, would uncover evidence of racism in the participants. Furthermore, transparency is apparent in this study in the form of field notes, which are included in the analysis whenever an issue concerning the data requires clarification. Moreover, there is a strong correspondence between the data presented and the analysis thereof. Any disjunction between the findings of this study and those of a similar study would result from a different view regarding what constitutes racism.

Concerning whether the findings can be generalized, the research design did not consist of a random sample, and therefore statistical generalization cannot be assumed. Nevertheless, although qualitative data are limited in offering theoretical certainty of a given claim, they offer evidence that the claim has merit (Orum, Feagin, and Sjoberg 1991). The value of qualitative research, and more specifically of case studies, is that it offers evidence that supports theory development (Black and Champion 1976). Nevertheless, in order to generalize from qualitative data, the theorist must downplay specificity, focusing on similarity across cases (Burawoy 1991). For example, even though participants expressed different kinds of negative images about blacks, the fact that they virtually all expressed or acknowledged negative images is noteworthy.

Although generalizability is limited statistically, the findings here can be used to suggest that racism, because it is evident in the participants in this study, is likely to be evident in other well-meaning people. Studies show that women are less racist than men generally (Burnham, Connors, and Leonard 1969), so it can be postulated that if racism is found in well-meaning white women, it is likely to be found in well-meaning white men. The second argument has less merit but should not be discounted. Because the sample in this study has a relatively high level of education, some studies support the claim that its participants should be expected to be *less* racist than well-meaning white people with less education, not more racist. Bonilla-Silva's (2003) findings do not support this claim, although other studies show that a higher level of education indicates a lower level of racism (Burnham 1969; Campbell 1971; Schuman, Steeh, and Bobo 1985).[1] Theoretically, then, if racism is evident in a sample that is expected to be less racist than the population from which it is drawn, we may assume theoretically that racism would be evident in the population generally.

Early in the emergence of the social sciences, research methods followed the lead of the natural sciences. This step was seen as necessary in gaining recognition and prestige both within and outside the academy. Objectivity along with quantification was viewed as an essential component of good research. More recently, the possibility of researchers being entirely objective has come under close scrutiny (see Guba and Lincoln 1998). Moreover, theoretical frameworks generally have been recognized as being value-laden instead of value-free.

I acknowledge that I am not dispassionate about the topic of racism; from the beginning, my "bias" was clear. The flier advertising the study was titled "Women Against Racism," a population in which I include myself. However, I would argue that my explicit bias against racism (in the flier) strengthened the study rather than weakened it in that individuals joined the study precisely because they saw an opportunity to contribute to lessening racism. This was the population I sought; I did not want participants who would defend against being racist or vent their anger regarding what they regard as reverse discrimination. Rather, I wanted participants willing to talk about their understanding of racism, including their memories about it and their participation in it. This strategy was not foolproof in that some participants did not recognize their own racism.

In terms of the presentation of findings, I do not attempt to restrain my bias against racism and my wish to lessen it. I follow the view that acknowledging one's perspective increases, rather than decreases, objectivity because self-disclosure alerts readers to an author's point of view, allowing readers to take it into account in their assessment of the study (Harding 1991).

My approach toward the issue of racism is critical of the status quo; it also clearly seeks change. In this broad sense, then, a critical approach in undertaking this research project is evident. The critical approach implies (and I acknowledge explicitly) that this research is an attempt to change social arrangements regarding race; the project itself is therefore political.

Cornel West (1988) urges social change as a methodological strategy when he suggests that critical researchers document evidence of resistance against racial domination in people's daily lives. Judith Rollins's (1985) research exposes domination in the lives of black domestic workers in the South. Rollins not only interviewed workers but also posed as one when collecting data for her study. Her personal interactions with the white female employers she worked for gave her firsthand experience of the white domination she sought to expose. Rollins, a black researcher, explored domination from the position of subordination; she observed and interacted with white female employers as they performed dominance. Like Rollins's work, this study also seeks social change in the area of racism; however, in contrast to her study, this research engages white women explicitly and directly regarding how they view racism.

III

Once the decision to use qualitative methods was made, additional issues about the interviews were addressed: how to conduct them, who should be in them, how limited the topic of discussion should be. In addition, I needed to consider the issue of how much information about myself should be included in the project.

Using focus groups as an interview vehicle enhanced this study in several ways. Focus groups are often utilized to gain insights into participants' unconscious motivations and commonsense explanations (Calder 1977). In addition, interaction among group members in focus groups produces a wider range of information and insight than is available from the cumulative data of individual interviews (Churchill 1988). This bandwagon effect occurs when a comment from one respondent triggers a response from others within the group (Churchill 1988). The bandwagon effect occurred often in the focus groups and was marked by a participant prefacing her remarks with a comment like, "When (so and so) was talking, it reminded me of the time." An example of this occurred in the second focus group when, after one participant told about an experience in her family, another group member shared a similar story about the close relationship of her grandparents with a black couple who had worked for them. The second participant's memory was clearly prompted by the first participant's account.

A sense of solidarity occurred in some of the groups, especially in one group that planned to meet again after participating in the study. The unity I perceived in this group appeared to result from empathy expressed among the participants, such as head-nodding and affirmative comments like, "Yeah, me too." This type of bonding did not occur in all of the groups. For example, in focus group number four, very little bonding seemed to occur, as evidenced by the field notes: "I think the women were so different in their awareness of racism, either in themselves or as an issue, that the discussion was not especially illuminating. It was more like three separate interviews, except for one interaction about what is and is not political." Although the discussion in this group seemed to lack cohesiveness, there is evidence that the participants were fully engaged in the study. All of the participants returned their journals, one of them writing eleven pages regarding her insights about racism since being in the group.

Although I have stressed the unity experienced in the groups, I do not mean to imply that the groups did not also experience difference of opinion. Many participants at times were not hesitant to question others' statements or to disagree with another's point of view. A criticism of using the focus group format in studying sociological issues is the possibility that participants may alter their responses to agree with other group members (Zeller 1993). Although I do not think this was a serious problem, it may have occurred in focus group number four, as documented in the field notes: "It seems that one participant may have been influenced by others' answers. For example, Karen agreed with the answer given by the person speaking before her on several occasions, even when their answers were unusual for the women in the study as a whole."

IV

Implementing the study entailed not only planning the discussion groups but also utilizing the data once they were collected. In an attempt to appeal to women who are concerned about racism, fliers entitled "Women Against Racism" were distributed in women's political organizations, book stores, lesbian centers, and university women's centers at several California campuses. Snowball sampling was also employed; that is, participants were asked to tell others about the study and invite them to join it. Several women joined the study on the recommendation of a friend who had participated.

After all the groups met, I made two paper copies of the transcripts to be used for sorting, organizing, and indexing processes. The transcripts were literally cut into pieces and sorted into groups. The first working transcript was grouped into folders according to participant. I used the participant folders to determine patterns among the women in the study, such as number of relationships with blacks, level of information about racism, and level of awareness of one's own racism. This information, while not directly pertinent to the construction of the concept of silent racism, was useful in developing the argument that race awareness is imperative in taking an active stand against racism, an important theoretical as well as practical finding.

The second transcript was cut up and the pieces grouped in folders according to theme, such as family lessons about black Americans, domestic workers, misinformation, liberal racism, emotions, and racist beliefs, to name a few. As interpretation of the data in the theme folders progressed, the themes themselves became more focused, eventually producing the concept of silent racism.

I wrote field notes after each focus group documenting my impressions of the group and of each participant. My notes also include a general description of the discussion as well as thoughts on how the group members interacted. Field notes were written as soon as possible after the group met and, along with information from the background sheets, eventually became the basis for a summary of each group. The summaries helped me stay in touch with the context and tone of each focus group as I began the interpretation process.

Each of the participants was given a blue book and two requests. First, they were asked to give me feedback about the group—what they thought went well and what they thought could have gone better.

Second, they were asked to keep a record of any thoughts or insights about racism or race relations that occurred to them in the weeks following the discussions. They were asked to mail the journals to me three weeks after their focus group met. Ultimately, 75 percent of the participants returned their journals.

V

Interesting differences are apparent when comparisons are made between this study and other qualitative studies of racism that focus on white participants. Here I draw comparisons among the studies of David Wellman (1977), Ruth Frankenberg (1993), and Eduardo Bonilla-Silva (2003). The comparisons focus primarily on differing samples and what Gubruim and Holstein (1997) call "method talk" (p. i).

Of the studies mentioned here, this project most closely resembles that of Frankenberg, both in terms of sample and type of interview questions used. Regarding samples, Frankenberg and I limit our studies to white women, though Frankenberg's sample spans the political continuum and my sample consists of liberal and progressive white women. Wellman and Bonilla-Silva include both white men and women in their samples and, like Frankenberg, their samples are more representative of the U.S. population in that they include self-described conservatives whereas my sample does not. In terms of interview questions, Frankenberg and I borrow more liberally from ethnography, asking about participants' experiences and encouraging introspection regarding their "private thoughts and feelings" (Gubrium and Holstein 1997). Wellman and Bonilla-Silva, in contrast, ask questions about racial policies such as school busing, affirmative action, and reparations that prompt rational explanations.[2]

Even though this study and Frankenberg's are similar in several ways, the two studies differ as well. For example, Frankenberg asked her wide range of participants about their experience of race as they construct a white identity. Her data led to an analysis of white women's identity formation in terms of racial issues. She states that her respondents embrace three paradigms concerning race matters: essentialism, color blindness/power evasiveness, and race cognizance.[3]

Not only was my sample more narrowly defined, but I also focused more narrowly on the participants' experiences regarding racism. In this way, I focused more on explicit forms of antiblack racism, not on whiteness or white identity issues. Despite these methodological and theoretical differences, the studies are similar in approach, given that introspection was encouraged. Frankenberg and I focus on differing sides of the same racial coin: whiteness and silent racism. The racism I found is more likely to appear in liberal and progressive white people who are in favor of policies intended to level the racial playing field. The most racially progressive women in Frankenberg's study, those who are race cognizant, also may have racist thoughts (silent racism) that are acted upon occasionally without thinking.

The ideas surrounding the exposure of silent racism are complementary to the Wellman and Bonilla-Silva theories discussed above even though they differ in some ways from each of them. First, Wellman's study made clear the important concept of white privilege: the idea that whites sense an advantage over minority groups and fear losing the advantage. The concept of silent racism focuses on another—different—aspect of racism, one that is not motivated by maintaining, and does not defend, white advantage. Silent racism and color-blind racism are very similar in that both forms of racism derive from a racial ideology that privileges whites, and both are hidden. However, silent racism does not "defend the contemporary racial order" (Bonilla-Silva 2003: 25) as does color-blind racism. Silent racism also validates Omi and Winants's theory of racial formation as well as Feagin's concept of systemic racism.

VI

Studying racism from the inside out has proven to be a fruitful goal. The approach was multidimensional, borrowed largely from traditional qualitative research but stamped with a feminist consciousness and a critical edge. The group format used throughout the study not only produced interaction among the group members, as expected, but also provided the opportunity for participants to interrupt others' racism, a significant contribution to understanding the importance of race awareness.

Notes

1. There are two alternate views: First, Jackman and Muha (1984) argue that higher education may enable the expression of racist ideas in nonracist language; and second, Sears (2003) argues that, regarding symbolic racism, higher education may support a correlation between one's intolerance and one's political point of view.

2. A number of contentious questions were used in the Wellman study that may have influenced the data. Two examples are: (1) "There are a lot of different words that people use to refer to the Negro group. How many can you think of?" And, (2) "Do you think black men prefer white women?" Both of these questions were likely to lead respondents to answers that would appear racist by most standards. By the same token, several of Bonilla-Silva's questions were problematic: A leading question was, "Many whites explain the status of blacks in this country as a result of blacks lacking motivation, not having the proper work ethic, or being lazy. What do you think?" A question that would produce speculation in most whites was, "Why do blacks fare worse than whites?" The participant's answer was couched in phrases like, "I don't know" and "It might be," more a function of low race awareness than "cultural racism" (p. 41).

3. Specifically, Frankenberg's (1993) categories consist of essentialism, using biological explanations for race inequality, much like early race theorists used physical differences between blacks and whites to demonstrate the inferiority of blacks. Color/power evasiveness is characterized by resistance to race or power differences among groups, with a consequent denial of white privilege. People in the race cognizant category, Frankenberg's third category, acknowledge race differences, with particular emphasis in terms of race privilege bestowed on white Americans through institutional racism.

Appendix B: Biographies of the Participants

The following biographical sketches are based on data taken from the background information forms completed at the time the focus groups met in 1992/1993.

Focus Group 1

Corrine was twenty-five years old. She was born in Colorado, where she lived most of her life. She attended college in Colorado Springs and was a graduate student at the University of California at the time of the study. Corrine was raised Catholic but is no longer practicing. In the extra space on the information sheet, Corrine added that the town she grew up in, her high school, and her alma mater in Colorado were mostly white.

Heather was twenty-three. She was born in Santa Fe, New Mexico. She lived most of her life in Los Alamos, New Mexico. She received a BA degree at the University of California and worked as a school health assistant at an elementary school in California when she participated in the study. She was raised by Christian parents and is now agnostic. Heather added that she is bilingual.

Kelly was forty-one at the time of the study. She was born in Massachusetts, where she lived for twenty-one years, including several years at a liberal arts college. She then moved to New York where she lived for six years, completing an MBA at New York University. Kelly moved to southern California and subsequently to central California, where she has resided with her husband for thirteen years. Kelly was raised Catholic and stated that she is now "possibly agnostic."

Ruth was forty-seven. She was born in a small town in California and has lived most of her life there. Ruth holds a master's degree in psychology and taught at a community college in central California when the study was conducted. She was raised in the Catholic faith, which she rejected at age eighteen.

Focus Group 2

Julie was twenty-three. She was born in Maryland but has lived most of her life in central California. She said she hopes to return to college, but was a full-time mother to her two children when she took part in the study. Julie had worked in the service industry, specifically at hotels, delicatessens, and athletic clubs. She was raised Unitarian but was not a churchgoer at the time of the study.

Katie was twenty-two. She was from Lake Charles, Louisiana, where she lived until she moved to central California to attend college. In addition to her studies, she was coproducing an independent feature film when the study took place. Katie attended Catholic schools as a child but was raised in a Methodist family. She added that in high school she participated in a group of black and white students who met regularly to explore topics such as abortion and substance abuse.

Martha was thirty-four years old. She was born and had lived most of her life in southern California. She attended the University of California in northern California for a year, returning to southern California to complete her undergraduate degree. Martha has worked at various jobs including legal assistant, property manager, and teacher. She was in graduate school in educational psychology when the study took place. Martha was raised a Christian Scientist but wrote "currently agnostic" on the background form. Martha added that she races outrigger canoes, loves writing, and keeps binoculars in her car for bird watching.

Focus Group 3

Alyssa, the youngest participant, was eighteen at the time of the study. She was born in Fort Worth, Texas, and lived there ten years, at which point her family moved to southern California. She was in college in central California when she took part in the study. While in high school, Alyssa worked as a culinary hostess for Disneyland. She was raised Methodist and continues to have a strong Christian faith.

Anne was twenty-five. She was born in California but had lived most of her life in New York City. She did her undergraduate work in Connecticut and returned to California for a graduate degree in sociology. Anne was raised in a Protestant family but was not practicing any religion at the time of the study.

Molly was sixty-eight. She was born in California and, except for seventeen years in Germany and three years in Montreal, has always lived there. She went to college in Berkeley and has since worked as a secretary and as a receptionist in addition to raising several daughters. Molly was raised Protestant and is a widow.

Focus Group 4

Lisa was forty-one years old. She was born in central California and was attending college when the study took place. Before returning to school, Lisa worked as a communications technician at Pacific Bell, where she was one of the first women allowed into that job. She was raised Mormon but stated on the background form that she is a Dianic witch. She was married for twelve years and has a child.

Karen was twenty-eight. She was born in Phoenix, Arizona, but lived primarily in Texas until she moved to California to attend college. She worked for a county in California as a cartographer (map maker) when she participated in the study. She had no religious background and was not affiliated with a church at the time of the study.

Sharon was sixty-eight years old. Born and raised in New York, she moved to California with her husband when she was in her mid-thirties. She retired several years before the time of the study, having been employed as an office worker for many years. She was an active member and officer of the League of Women Voters, where she heard about the study. Sharon was raised Jewish but did not consider herself to be a practicing Jew at the time of the study. She is divorced and the mother of three grown children and three grandchildren.

Focus Group 5

Jean was age forty-one. She was born in Oklahoma but has lived most of her life in southern and northern California and has attended colleges in both regions. Jean has worked in the clerical field, both for a company and as a small business owner, making and selling jewelry. Jean was raised in a fundamentalist Christian home. Having rejected that religion, she said she has studied Buddhism and New Age Paganism. Jean married at age eighteen and divorced at age thirty-five. She has a son (age twenty) and a daughter (age seventeen).

Lucy was twenty-eight. She was born in San Francisco and has lived in northern California all of her life, including her college years. She has worked in food service and as an "on call" staff person for a community center. She has led multiculturalism workshops. Lucy was raised in an agnostic family and was seeking spirituality akin to that practiced by Native Americans when the study took place.

Vanessa, the oldest member of the study, was seventy-six. She was born in California and has lived all of her life in that state. She holds a master's degree in psychology and had worked in a nursery school as well as in parent and adult education prior to retirement. She continues to practice the Quaker religion in which she grew up. Vanessa has been in her second marriage for twenty years, after a thirty-three-year marriage to her first husband, who died. Vanessa's great-grandfather was an ardent worker in the Underground Railroad.

Focus Group 6

Loretta, age twenty-nine, was born in St. Louis, Missouri, and lived there until she left for college in New Hampshire. She remained in the Northeast until her recent move to northern California. Loretta has worked as a counselor in the areas of substance abuse, domestic violence, and homelessness. Her family attended the Presbyterian church when she was growing up, although her father was "Irish Catholic."

Mary was twenty-four years old. She was born in Connecticut and lived most of her life there, leaving to attend college at the University of California in northern California. While in college, she worked as a publicist for a local publishing company. Mary was scheduled to start graduate school in Georgia in fall 1994. She was raised Jewish but no longer practices the religion. Mary added that she wrote her senior thesis on racism in the women's movement.

Focus Group 7

Elaine was twenty-six years old. She was born in California but has lived most of her life in Seattle, Washington, except for a few years in Houston, Texas. She attended undergraduate school at a liberal arts college in Washington. Elaine is from a "non-specific, non-practicing" Protestant family.

Joan was age forty-one. She was born in Alberta, Canada, and moved to Oregon as a young child. She received a BA degree at a university in Oregon. Joan moved to central California in her mid-thirties and worked as a graphics artist at the time of the study. Joan did not identify any religious affiliation.

Violet was age twenty-four. She was born in California but moved to Kansas as a young child. She attended college in San Antonio, Texas, and returned to California to attend graduate school. Violet was raised Methodist but had no affiliation with any church when the study was underway.

Focus Group 8

Anita, age twenty-seven, was born in Los Angeles and has lived both there and in Illinois, where she attended the University of Chicago. She worked as a paralegal in a law firm in California when the study took place. Anita stated that she has been both agnostic and Christian.

Charlotte was twenty-seven years old, born in San Francisco, and raised in Berkeley, California. She did her undergraduate work at a liberal arts college in Ohio and was a graduate student when she decided to participate in the study. Charlotte was raised in the Jewish faith and has taught at Hebrew school.

Janice was age thirty-nine. She was born in northern California, where she has lived most of her life. She attended college in Arizona and spent one year at a university in Mexico City. She worked as a court interpreter at the time of the study. Janice grew up in a

Lutheran family and became affiliated with the Baptist church in high school. She was not affiliated with any religion when she participated in the study.

Researcher

Barbara was fifty-three years old when the focus groups were held. She was born in Texas, where she lived for fifty years before moving to California for graduate school. She was married for twenty-five years and raised four daughters with her former husband. Barbara was raised Catholic, attending Catholic schools for twelve years. She no longer practices religion.

Appendix C: Participants' Race Awareness

Very high race awareness

Martha
Lisa
Ruth

High race awareness

Anne
Jean
Loretta
Lucy
Mary
Violet

Moderate race awareness

Anita
Charlotte
Corrine
Elaine
Julie
Molly

Low race awareness

Heather
Karen
Kelly
Penny

Very low race awareness

Alyssa
Janice
Joan
Katie
Sharon
Vanessa

Appendix D: Antiracism Resources

Books and Videos

Historical Racism

Aptheker, Herbert. *American Negro Slave Revolts.* New York: International Publishers, 1983.

Bigelow, Bill, and Bob Petersen. Rethinking Columbus. Available at www.rethinkingschools.org/publication/columbus/columbus.shtml. An online resource depicting the other side of the discovery of America (the European invasion of North America).

Hampton, Henry (producer). *Eyes on the Prize I & II* (video). PBS Video, Kari Ostafinski, distributor. Kostafinski@pbs.org. A fourteen-part award-winning series about the civil rights movement.

Loewen, James. *Lies My Teacher Told Me.* New York: The New Press, 1995.

Riggs, Marlon. *Ethnic Notions.* California Newsreel, distributor. Contact@newsreel.org. An award-winning video portraying stereotypes about blacks throughout U.S. history.

———. *Color Adjustment.* California Newsreel, distributor. Contact@newsreel.org. A documentary video about how blacks were integrated into prime-time television, starting with *Amos 'n Andy.*

Takaki, Ronald. *A Different Mirror: A History of Multicultural America.* New York: author, 1993.

Williams, Juan. *Eyes on the Prize: America's Civil Rights Years, 1954–1965.* New York: Penguin, 1987.

Institutional Racism

Bell, Derrick. *Faces at the Bottom of the Well: The Permanence of Racism.* New York: Basic Books, 1992.

Bonilla-Silva, Eduardo. *Racism without Racists: Color-Blind Racism and the Persistence of Racial Inequality in the United States.* Lanham, MD: Rowman and Littlefield, 2003.

Doan, Ashley, and Eduardo Bonilla-Silva. *White Out: The Continuing Significance of Racism.* New York: Routledge, 2003.

Feagin, Joe. *Racist America: Roots, Current Realities, and Future Reparations.* New York: Routledge, 2001.

Fine, Michelle, Lois Weis, Linda C. Powell, and L. Mun Wong. *Off White: Readings on Power, Privilege, and Resistance.* New York: Routledge, 1996.

Hacker, Andrew. *Two Nations: Black and White, Separate, Hostile, Unequal.* New York: Charles Scribner's Sons, 1992.

Katz, Judith, Frederick Miller, Edith Seashore, and Elsie Cross. *The Promise of Diversity: Over 40 Voices Discuss Strategies for Eliminating Racism in Organizations.* New York: McGraw-Hill, 1995.

Public Broadcasting Service. *Frontline: A Class Divided.* Hollywood.com, distributor. www.hollywood.com. A video about Jane Elliott's "Blue-Eyed/Brown-Eyed" exercise, first tried in 1970.

Wah, Lee Wun (producer/director). *The Color of Fear.* StirFry Seminars & Consulting, distributor. www.stirfryseminars.com. A video in which eight men of various backgrounds (white, black, Asian, Latino, and Native American) discuss their experiences of racism and discrimination.

———. *Walking Each Other Home.* StirFry Seminars & Consulting, distributor. www.stirfryseminars.com. A video in which the eight men who participated in *The Color of Fear* discuss their visions of ending racism.

Williams, Patricia. *The Alchemy of Race and Rights: Diary of a Law Professor.* Cambridge, MA: Harvard University Press, 1991.

Wise, Tim. *White Like Me: Reflections on Race from a Privileged Son.* New York: Soft Skull Press, 2005.

Personal Racism

Barndt, Joseph. *Dismantling Racism: The Continuing Challenge to White America.* Minneapolis, MN: Augsburg Fortress, 1991.

Ford, Clyde. *We* Can *All Get Along: Fifty Steps You Can Take to Help End Racism.* New York: Dell, 1994.

Katz, Judith. *White Awareness: Handbook for Antiracism Training,* 2nd ed. Norman: University of Oklahoma Press, 2003.

Kivel, Paul. *Uprooting Racism: How White People Can Work for Racial Justice.* British Columbia: New Society Publishers, 2002.

Lester, Nora. *Blue Eyed: A Guide to Use in Organizations.* www.newsreel.org/guides/blueeyed.htm. An on-line resource for facilitating Jane Elliott's "Blue-Eyed/Brown-Eyed" exercise.

Mathias, Barbara, and Mary Ann French. *Forty Ways to Raise a Nonracist Child.* New York: HarperCollins, 1996.

Public Broadcasting Service. *Not in Our Town.* The Working Group, distributor. www.theworkinggroup.org. A video that features members from five northern California communities who stood up to racism and hatred.

———. *Frontline: A Class Divided.* Hollywood.com, distributor. www.hollywood.com. A video about Jane Elliott's Blue Eyed/Brown Eyed exercise, first tried in 1970.

Reid, Frances. *Skin Deep: College Students Confront Racism.* California Newsreel, distributor. Contact@newsreel.org. A video in which college students of differing racial and ethnic backgrounds discuss their feelings and attitudes about race and racism.

Leading Antiracism Workshops

Adams, Maurianne, Lee Ann Bell, and Pat Griffin. *Teaching for Diversity and Social Justice: A Sourcebook.* New York: Routledge, 1997.

Banks, James. *Teaching Strategies for Ethnic Studies,* 6th ed. New York: Allyn and Bacon.

Bigelow, Bill, *Rethinking Our Classrooms: Teaching for Equity and Justice.* Milwaukee, WI: Rethinking Schools, 1994.

Kailin, Julie. *Antiracist Education: From Theory to Practice.* Lanham, MD: Rowman and Littlefield, 2002.

Internet Resources

Jim Crow Museum, available at www.Ferris.edu/jimcrow.

Southern Poverty Law Center website on teaching tolerance, available at www.splcenter.org.

Tim Wise homepage, available at www.timwise.org.

References

Aaker, David, and George Day. 1986. *Marketing Research.* New York: John Wiley and Sons.

Adorno, Theodor, Else Frenkel-Brunswick, Daniel Levinson, and R. N. Sanford. 1950. *The Authoritarian Personality.* New York: Harper.

Alexander, Jeffery. 1987. "The 'Individualist Dilemma' in Phenomonology and Interactionism." In *The Micro-Macro Link,* edited by J. Alexander, B. Giesen, R. Munch, and N. Smelser. Berkeley: University of California Press.

Alexander, Jeffery, Bernhard Giesen, Richard Munch, and Neil Smelser. 1987. *The Micro-Macro Link.* Berkeley: University of California Press.

Allen, Walter, and Reynolds Farley. 1986. "The Shifting Social and Economic Tides of Black America, 1950–1980." *American Sociological Review* 12: 277–306.

Allport, Gordon. 1954. *The Nature of Prejudice.* Reading, PA: Addison-Wesley.

Andersen, Margaret. 2003. *Thinking about Women: Sociological Perspectives on Sex and Gender,* 6th ed. New York: Allyn and Bacon.

Apple, Michael. 1982. *Education and Power.* Boston: ARK Paperbacks.

Babbie, Earl. 2001. *The Practice of Social Research,* 9th ed. Belmont, CA: Wadsworth.

Ball, Donald. 1972. "The Definition of Situation." *Journal for the Theory of Social Behavior* 2: 24–36.

Bargh, John. 1999. "The Cognitive Monster: The Case Against the Controllability of Automatic Stereotype Effects." In *Dual-Process Theories in Social Psychology,* edited by S. Chaiken and Y. Trope. New York: Guilford.

Barnett, Victoria. 1999. *Bystanders: Conscience and Complicity during the Holocaust.* Westport, CT: Praeger.

Baron, James, and Jeffrey Pfeffer. 1994. "The Social Psychology of Organizations and Inequality." *Social Psychology Quarterly* 57(3): 190–209.

Becker, Howard. 1963. *Outsiders: Studies in the Sociology of Deviance.* New York: Free Press.

Belanger, Kathleen. 2002. "Examination of Racial Imbalance for Children in Foster Care: Implications for Training." *Journal of Health and Social Policy* 15: 163–176.

Belenky, Mary, Blythe Clinchy, Nancy Goldberger, and Jill Tarule. 1986. *Women's Ways of Knowing: The Development of Self, Voice, and Mind.* New York: Basic.

Bell, Derrick. 1992. *Races at the Bottom of the Well: The Permanence of Racism.* New York: Basic.

Benton, Sarah. 1994. "Feminism." In *Ideas That Shape Politics,* edited by M. Foley. Manchester: Manchester University Press.

Berg, Bruce. 2004. *Qualitative Research Methods for the Social Sciences.* New York: Allyn and Bacon.

Berger, Peter, and Thomas Luckmann. 1966. *The Social Construction of Reality: A Treatise in the Sociology of Knowledge.* New York: Doubleday.

Berube, Michael. 1994. *Public Access: Literary Theory and American Cultural Politics.* New York: Verso.

Bishop, Donna, and Charles Frazier. 1996. "Race Effects in Juvenile Justice Decision-Making: Findings of a Statewide Analysis." *Journal of Criminal Law and Criminology* 86: 404–429.

Black, James, and Dean Champion. 1976. *Methods and Issues in Social Research.* New York: John Wiley and Sons.

Blauner, Robert. 1972. *Racial Oppression in America.* New York: Harper and Row.

———. 1994. "Talking Past Each Other: Black and White Languages of Race." In *Race and Ethnic Conflict: Contending Views on Prejudice, Discrimination, and Ethnoviolence,* edited by F. Pincus and H. Ehrlich. Boulder, CO: Westview.

Blumer, Herbert. 1958a. "Research Trends in the Study of Race Relations." *International Social Science Bulletin* 10(3): 403–447.

———. 1958b. "Race Prejudice as a Sense of Group Position." *Pacific Sociological Review* 1(1): 3–7.

———. 1965. "The Future of the Color Line." In *The South in Continuity and Change,* edited by John McKinney and Edgar Thompson. Durham, NC: Duke University Press.

———. 1969. *Symbolic Interactionism: Perspective and Method.* Englewood Cliffs, NJ: Prentice-Hall.

Bobo, Lawrence. 1988. "Group Conflict, Prejudice, and the Paradox of Contemporary Attitudes." In *Eliminating Racism,* edited by Phyllis Katz and Dalmas Taylor. New York: Plenum.

———. 1999. "Prejudice as Group Position: Micro-foundations of a Sociological Approach to Racism and Race Relations." *Journal of Social Issues* 55(3): 445–472.

Bodenhausen, Galen, and Neil Macrae. 1996. "The Self-Regulation of Intergroup Perception: Mechanisms and Consequences of Stereotype

Suppression." In *Stereotypes and Stereotyping,* edited by Neil Macrae, Charles Stangor, and Miles Hewstone. New York: Guilford.

Bolton, Kenneth, Jr., and Joe Feagin. 2004. *Black in Blue: African-American Police Officers and Racism.* New York: Routledge.

Bonacich, Edna. 1972. "A Theory of Ethnic Antagonism: The Split Labor Market." *American Sociological Review* 37: 547–559.

———. 1976. "Advanced Capitalism and Black/White Relations in the United States: A Split Labor Market Interpretation." *American Sociological Review* 41: 34–51.

Bonilla-Silva, Eduardo. 1996. "Rethinking Racism: Toward a Structural Interpretation." *American Sociological Review* 62 (June): 465–480.

———. 1997. "Rethinking Racism: Toward a Structural Interpretation." *American Sociological Review* 62: 465–480.

———. 2001. *White Supremacy and Racism in the Post-Civil Rights Era.* Boulder, CO: Lynne Rienner.

———. 2003. *Racism Without Racists: Color-Blind Racism and the Persistence of Racial Inequality in the United States.* Lanham, MD: Rowman and Littlefield.

Bourdieu, Pierre. [1972] 1978. *Outline of a Theory of Practice.* Translated by Richard Nice. London: Cambridge University Press.

———. [1979] 1984. *Distinction: A Social Critique of the Judgment of Taste.* Translated by Richard Nice. Cambridge, MA: Harvard University Press.

———. 1989. "Social Space and Symbolic Power." *Sociological Theory* 7: 14–25.

———. [1980] 1990. *The Logic of Practice.* Translated by Richard Nice. Stanford, CA: Stanford University Press.

———. [1994] 1998. *Practical Reason: On the Theory of Action.* Stanford, CA: Stanford University Press.

Brandt, Godfrey. 1986. *The Realization of Anti-Racist Teaching.* London: Falmer.

Breaugh, James. 1981. "Relationships Between Recruiting Sources and Employee Performance, Absenteeism, and Work Attitudes." *Academy of Management Journal* 24: 142–147.

Brewer, Marilynn. 1996. "When Stereotypes Lead to Stereotyping: The Use of Stereotypes in Person Perception." In *Stereotypes and Stereotyping,* edited by Neil Macrae, Charles Stangor, and Miles Hewstone. New York: Guilford.

Brewer, Marilyn, and Roderick Kramer. 1985. "The Psychology of Intergroup Attitudes and Behavior." *Annual Review of Psychology* 36: 219–243.

Bristow, Ann, and Jodi Esper. 1988. "Feminist Research Ethos." In *A Feminist Ethic for Social Research,* edited by the Nebraska Sociological Feminist Collective. Lewiston, NY: Edwin Mellen.

Brown, Cynthia. 2002. *Refusing Racism: White Allies and the Struggle for Civil Rights.* New York: Teachers College Press.

Brown, Michael, Martin Carnoy, Elliott Currie, Troy Duster, David Oppenheimer, Marjorie Shultz, and David Wellman. 2003. *Whitewashing Race: The Myth of a Color-Blind Society.* Berkeley: University of California Press.

Bullock, Lyndal, and Gable, Robert. (eds.). 2004. *Quality Personnel Preparation in Emotional/Behavioral Disorders: Current Perspectives and Future Directions.* Denton, TX: University of North Texas Institute for Behavioral and Learning Differences.

Burawoy, Michael. 1991. "The Extended Case Method." In *Ethnography Unbound,* edited by M. Burawoy. Berkeley: University of California Press.

Burnham, Kenneth, John Connors, and Richard Leonard. 1969. "Racial Prejudice in Relation to Education, Sex, and Religion." *Journal for the Scientific Study of Religion* 8(2): 318.

Butler, Judith. 1990. *Gender Trouble.* New York: Routledge.

———. 1999. "Performativity's Social Magic." In *Bourdieu: A Critical Reader,* edited by R. Shusterman. Malden, MA: Blackwell.

Calder, Bobby. 1977. "Focus Groups and the Nature of Qualitative Marketing Research." *Journal of Marketing Research* 14: 353–364.

Camic, Charles. 2000. "The Matter of Habit." In *Pierre Bourdieu,* vol. 1, edited by D. Robbins. Thousand Oaks, CA: Sage.

Campbell, Angus. 1971. *White Attitudes Toward Black People.* Ann Arbor, MI: Institute for Social Research.

Carmichael, Stokely, and Charles Hamilton. 1967. *Black Power: The Politics of Liberation.* New York: Vintage.

Casey Family Programs. 2005. *Knowing Who You Are: Helping Youth in Care Develop their Racial and Ethnic Identity.* Seattle, WA: Casey Family Programs.

Casey Family Programs and Texas Child Protective Services. 2007. *Engaging Communities in Taking a Stand for Children and Families: Leadership Development and Strategic Planning in the Texas Child Welfare System.* Seattle, WA: Casey Family Programs.

Charon, Joel. 1998. *Symbolic Interactionism: An Introduction, An Interpretation, An Integration,* 6th ed. Upper Saddle River, NJ: Prentice-Hall.

Chibnall, Susan, and Nicole Dutch. 2003. "Children of Color in the Child Welfare System: Perspectives from the Child Welfare Community." *Administration for Children and Families.* Washington, DC: Department of Health and Human Services.

Child Welfare Information Gateway. 2003. "Major Federal Legislation Concerned with Child Protection, Child Welfare, and Adoption." Washington DC: Children's Bureau.

Churchill, Gilbert. 1988. *Basic Marketing Research.* Chicago: Dryden Press.

Clark, Stuart. 1991. "Fear of a Black Planet." *Socialist Review* 21 (3–4): 37–59.

Collins, Patricia Hill. 1986. "Learning from the Outside Within: The Sociological Significance of Black Feminist Thought." *Social Problems* 33(6): 14–32.

———. 1990. *Black Feminist Thought: Knowledge, Consciousness, and the Politics of Empowerment.* Boston: Unwin Hyman.

Collins, Randall. 1988. "The Micro Contribution to Macro Sociology." *Sociological Theory* 6 (Fall): 242–253.

Combahee River Collective. [1977] 1978. "A Black Feminist Statement." In *Groups in Contact: The Psychology of Desegregation,* edited by Z. Eisenstein. New York: Academic.

Cooley, Charles Horton. 1916. *Social Organization: A Study of the Larger Mind.* New York: Charles Scribner's Sons.

Coontz, Stephanie. 1992. *The Way We Never Were: American Families and the Nostalgia Trap.* New York: Basic.

Cose, Ellis. 1993. *The Rage of a Privileged Class.* New York: HarperCollins.

Crenshaw, Kimberlie. [1989] 1994. "Demarginalizing the Intersection of Race and Sex: A Black Feminist Critique of Anti-discrimination Doctrine, Feminist Theory, and Antiracist Politics." In *Living with Contradictions: Controversies in Feminist Social Ethics,* edited by A. Jaggar. Boulder, CO: Westview.

Daly, Mary. 1973. *Beyond God the Father: Toward a Philosophy of Women's Liberation.* Boston: Beacon.

———. 1978. *Gyn/Ecology: The Metaethics of Radical Feminism.* Boston: Beacon.

Davis, Angela. 1983. *Women, Race, and Class.* New York: Vintage.

Dennis, R. 1981. "Socialization and Racism: The White Experience." In *Impacts of Racism on White Americans,* edited by B. Bowser and R. Hunt. Beverly Hills, CA: Sage.

Denzin, Norman. 1989. *Interpretive Interactionism.* Newbury Park, CA: Sage.

———. 1992. *Symbolic Interactionism and Cultural Studies: The Politics of Interpretation.* Cambridge, MA: Blackwell.

Denzin, Norman, and Yvonna Lincoln. 1994. *Handbook of Qualitative Research.* Thousand Oaks, CA: Sage.

Derezotes, Denette, Brad Richardson, Connie Bear King, Julia Kleinschmit-Rembert, and Betty Pratt. 2008. "Evaluating Multisystemic Efforts to Impact Disproportionality Through Key Decision Points." *Child Welfare* 87: 241–254.

Derezotes, Dennette, and John Poertner. 2005. "Factors Contributing to the Overrepresentation of African American Children in the Child Welfare System." In *Race Matters in Child Welfare: The Overrepresentation of African American Children in the System,* edited by D. Derezotes, J. Poertner, and M. Testa. Washington, DC: Child Welfare League of America Press.

Devine, Patricia. 1989. "Stereotypes and Prejudice: Their Automatic and Controlled Components." *Journal of Personality and Social Psychology* 56: 5–18.

Dovidio, John, and Samuel Gaertner. 1998. "On the Nature of Contemporary Prejudice: The Causes, Consequences, and Challenges of Aversive Racism." In *Confronting Racism: The Problem and the Response,* edited by J. Eberhardt and S. Fiske. Newbury Park, CA: Sage.

Du Bois, Ellen Carol. 1978. *Feminism and Suffrage: The Emergence of an Independent Women's Movement in America, 1848–1869.* Ithaca, NY: Cornell University Press.

Du Bois, W. E. B. [1903] 1999. *The Souls of Black Folk.* In *W. E. B. Du Bois: The Souls of Black Folk,* edited by H. L. Gates Jr. and T. H. Oliver. New York: W. W. Norton.

Dumond, Dwight Lowell. 1961. *Antislavery: The Crusade for Freedom in America.* Ann Arbor: University of Michigan Press.

Dworkin, Anthony Gary, and Rosalind J. Dworkin. 1999. *The Minority Report: An Introduction to Racial, Ethnic, and Gender Relations.* 3d ed. Orlando, FL: Harcourt Brace.

Ebaugh, Helen, and Mary Curry. 2000. "Fictive Kin as Social Capital in New Immigrant Communities." *Sociological Perspectives* 43: 189–209.

Essed, Philomena. 1991. *Understanding Everyday Racism: An Interdisciplinary Theory.* Newbury Park, CA: Sage.

Fanon, Frantz. 1967. *Black Skin, White Masks.* New York: Grove.

Feagin, Joe. 2001. *Racist America: Roots, Current Realities, and Future Reparations.* New York: Routledge.

Feagin, Joe, and Clarice Feagin. 1994. "Theoretical Perspectives in Race and Ethnic Relations." In *Race and Ethnic Conflict: Contending Views on Prejudice, Discrimination, and Ethnoviolence,* edited by F. Pincus and H. Ehrlich. Boulder, CO: Westview.

Feagin, Joe, and Eileen O'Brien. 2003. *White Men on Race: Power, Privilege, and the Shaping of Cultural Consciousness.* Boston: Beacon.

Feagin, Joe, and Melvin Sikes. 1994. *Living with Racism: The Black Middle-Class Experience.* Boston: Beacon.

Feagin, Joe, and Hernán Vera. 1995. *White Racism: The Basics.* New York: Routledge.

———. 2002. "Confronting One's Own Racism." In *White Privilege: Essential Readings on the Other Side of Racism,* edited by P. Rothenberg. New York: Worth.

Feagin, Joe, Hernán Vera, and Pinar Batur. 2001. *White Racism: The Basics,* 2nd ed. New York: Routledge.

Feldstein, Richard. 1997. *Political Correctness: A Response from the Cultural Left.* Minneapolis: University of Minnesota Press.

Fine, Gary Alan. 2001. *Difficult Reputations: Collective Memories of the Evil, Inept, and Controversial.* Chicago: University of Chicago Press.

Fiske, Susan. 1989. "Examining the Role of Intent: Toward Understanding Its Role in Stereotyping and Prejudice." In *Unintended Thought,* edited by Jim Uleman and John Bargh. New York: Guilford.

Fiske, Susan, and Shelley Taylor. 1984. *Social Cognition.* New York: McGraw-Hill.

Flagg, Barbara. 1997. "The Transparency Phenomenon, Race-Neutral Decision-making, and Discriminatory Intent." In *Critical White Studies: Looking Behind the Mirror,* edited by R. Delgado and J. Stefancic. Philadelphia: Temple University Press.

Forte, James. 1998. "Power and Role-Taking: A Review of Theory, Research, and Practice." *Journal of Human Behavior in the Social Environment* 1 (4): 27–56.

Frankenberg, Ruth. 1993. *White Women, Race Matters: The Social Construction of Whiteness.* Minneapolis: University of Minnesota Press.

Fredrickson, George. 1971. *The Black Image in the White Mind.* New York: Harper and Row.

Frye, Marilyn. 1983. "On Being White." In *The Politics of Reality: Essays in Feminist Theory,* edited by Marilyn Frye. New York: Crossing Press.

———. 1992. *Willful Virgin: Essays in Feminism.* Freedom, CA: Crossing Press.

Gaertner, Samuel, and James Dovidio. 1986. *Prejudice, Discrimination, and Racism.* New York: Academic.

———. 2000. *Reducing Intergroup Bias: The Common In-group Identity Model.* New York: Taylor and Francis.

Garfinkel, Harold. 1967. *Studies in Ethnomethodology.* Englewood Cliffs, NJ: Prentice Hall.

Gelders, Emma. 1968. *They Took Their Stand.* New York: Crowell-Collier.

Genovese, Eugene. 1974. *Roll, Jordan, Roll: The World the Slaves Made.* New York: Random House.

George, Patrick Mark. 2004. "Race Traitors: Exploring the Motivation and Action of White Antiracists." Unpublished doctoral dissertation, University of New Mexico.

Giddens, Anthony. 1979. *Central Problems in Social Theory: Action, Structure, and Contradiction in Social Analysis.* Berkeley: University of California Press.

———. 1981. "Agency, Institution, and Time-Space Analysis." In *Advances in Social Theory and Methodology: Toward an Integration of Micro- and Macro-Sociologies,* edited by K. Knorr-Cetina and A. V. Cicourel. London: Routledge and Kegan Paul.

———. 1984. *The Constitution of Society.* Berkeley: University of California Press.

Giddings, Paula. 1984. *When and Where I Enter: The Impact of Black Women on Race and Sex in America.* New York: Bantam.

Giroux, Henry. 1983. *Theory and Resistance in Education: A Pedagogy for the Opposition.* New York: Bergin and Garvey.

———. 1994. "Insurgent Multiculturalism." In *Multiculturalism: A Critical Reader,* edited by D. Goldberg. Cambridge, MA: Blackwell.

Gitlin, Todd. 1985. *Inside Prime Time.* New York: Pantheon.

Glaser, Barney, and Anselm Strauss. 1967. *The Discovery of Grounded Theory: Strategies for Qualitative Research.* Chicago: Aldine de Gruyter.

Goffman, Erving. 1963. *Stigma: Notes on the Management of Spoiled Identity.* New York: Touchstone.

———. 1967. *Interaction Ritual: Essays on Face-to-Face Behavior.* New York: Pantheon.

Goldberg, David Theo. 1993. *Racist Culture: Philosophy and the Politics of Meaning.* Cambridge, MA: Blackwell.

Goleman, Daniel. 2003. "Studying the Pivotal Role of Bystanders." In *The Psychology of Good and Evil: Why Children, Adults, and Groups Help and Harm Others,* edited by E. Staub. New York: Cambridge University Press.

Gramsci, Antonio. 1971. *Selections from the Prison Notebooks.* Edited by Q. Hoare and G. Smith. New York: International.

Guba, Egon, and Yvonna Lincoln. 1998. "Competing Paradigms in Qualitative Research." In *The Landscape of Qualitative Research: Theories and Issues,* edited by N. Denzin and Y. Lincoln. Thousand Oaks, CA: Sage.

Gubrium, Jaber, and James Holstein. 1997. *The New Language of Qualitative Method.* New York: Oxford University Press.

Gutmann, Herbert. 1983. "Persistent Myths About the Afro-American Family." In *An American Family in Social-Historical Perspective,* 3rd ed., edited by M. Gordon. New York: St. Martin's Press.

Hacker, Andrew. 1992. *Two Nations: Black and White, Separate, Hostile, Unequal.* New York: Charles Scribner's Sons.

Hackman, Richard. 1976. "Group Influences on Individuals." In *Handbook of Industrial and Organizational Psychology,* edited by M. Dunnette. Chicago: Rand McNally.

Hall, Edward T. 1959. *The Silent Language.* New York: Doubleday.

Hansen, Karen, and Ilene Philipson. 1990. *Women, Class, and the Feminist Imagination: A Socialist-Feminist Reader.* Philadelphia: Temple University Press.

Harding, Sandra. 1991. *Whose Science? Whose Knowledge? Thinking from Women's Lives.* Ithaca, NY: Cornell University Press.

Harry, Beth, and Janette Klingner. 2006. *Why Are So Many Minority Students in Special Education?: Understanding Race and Disability in Schools.* New York: Teachers College Press, Columbia University.

Harry, Beth, Janette Klingner, Keith Sturges, and Robert Moore. 2002. "Of Rocks and Soft Places: Using Qualitative Methods to Investigate Disproportionality." In *Racial Inequity in Special Education,* edited by D. Losen and G. Orfield. Boston, MA: Harvard Education Press.

Hernton, Calvin. [1965] 1988. *Sex and Racism in America.* New York: Anchor.

Herrnstein, Richard, and Charles Murray. 1995. *The Bell Curve: Intelligence and Class Structure in American Life.* New York: Free Press.

Hill, Robert. 1998. "Understanding Black Family Functioning: A Holistic Perspective." *Journal of Comparative Family Studies* 29(1): 15–25.

Hill, Robert, Andrew Billingsley, Eleanor Engram, Michelene Malson, and

Roger Stack. 1993. *Research on the African American Family: A Holistic Perspective.* Westport, CT: Auburn House.

Hofstadter, Douglas. 1985. *Metamagical Themas: Questing for the Essence of Mind and Pattern.* New York: BasicBooks.

Holstein, James, and Jaber Gubruim. 1997. "Active Interviewing." In *Qualitative Research: Theory, Method, and Practice,* edited by D. Silverman. London: Sage.

hooks, bell. 1981. *Ain't I a Woman: Black Women and Feminism.* Boston: South End.

———. 1984. *Feminist Theory from Margin to Center.* Boston: South End.

———. 1989. *Talking Back: Thinking Feminist, Thinking Black.* Boston: South End Press.

———. 1990. *Yearning: Race, Gender, and Cultural Politics.* Boston: South End.

———. 1995. *Killing Rage: Ending Racism.* New York: Henry Holt.

———. 2001. *Salvation: Black People and Love.* New York: HarperCollins.

———. 2004. *Rock My Soul: Black People and Self-Esteem.* New York: Routledge.

Hosp, John, and Michelle Hosp. 2002. "Behavior Differences between African-American and Caucasian Students: Issues for Assessment and Intervention." *Education and Treatment of Children* 24(3): 336–350.

Hughes, J., and J. Sharock. 1997. *The Philosophy of Social Research.* London: Longman.

Hull, Gloria, Patricia Bell Scott, and Barbara Smith. 1982. *All the Women Are White, All the Blacks Are Men, But Some of Us Are Brave: Black Women and Feminism.* New York: Feminist Press.

Ibarra, Herminia, and Steven Andrews. 1993. "Power, Social Influence, and Sense Making: Effects of Network Centrality and Proximity on Employee Perceptions." *Administrative Science Quarterly* 38: 277–303.

Ignatiev, Noel, and John Garvey. 1996. *Race Traitor.* New York: Routledge.

Jackman, Mary. 1994. *The Velvet Glove: Paternalism and Conflict in Gender, Class, and Race Relations.* Berkeley: University of California Press.

Jackman, Mary, and Michael Muha. 1984. "Education and Intergroup Attitudes: Moral Enlightenment, Superficial Democratic Commitment, or Ideological Refinement?" *American Sociological Review* 49: 751–169.

Jacobs, David. 1981. "Toward a Theory of Mobility and Behavior in Organizations: An Inquiry into the Consequences of Some Relationships between Individual Performance and Organizational Success." *American Journal of Sociology* 87: 684–707.

Jaynes, Gerald D., and Robin M. Williams. 1989. *A Common Destiny: Blacks in American Society.* Washington, DC: National Academy.

Jenkins, Richard. 1992. *Key Sociologists: Pierre Bourdieu.* London: Routledge.

Johnson, Allan. 1997. *The Forest and the Trees: Sociology as Life, Practice, and Promise.* Philadelphia: Temple University Press.

———. 2000. *The Blackwell Dictionary of Sociology: A User's Guide to Sociological Language,* 2nd ed. Cambridge, MA: Blackwell.

Jussim, Lee, Leritam Coleman, and Lauren Lerch. 1987. "The Nature of Stereotypes: A Comparison and Integration of Three Theories." *Journal of Personality and Social Psychology* 56: 536–546.

Kailin, Julie. 2002. *Antiracist Education: From Theory to Practice.* Lanham, MD: Rowman and Littlefield.

Kaspersen, Lars. 1995. *Anthony Giddens: An Introduction to a Social Theorist.* Cambridge, MA: Blackwell.

Katz, Jack. 1975. "Essence as Moral Identities: Verifiability and Responsibility in Imputations of Deviance and Charisma." *American Journal of Sociology* 80(6): 1369–1390.

Kellner, Douglas. 1990. *Television and the Crisis of Democracy.* Boulder, CO: Westview.

Killian, Lewis M. 1990. "Race Relations and the Nineties: Where Are the Dreams of the Sixties?" *Social Forces* 69(1): 1–13.

King, Joyce. 1991. "Dysconscious Racism: Ideology, Identity, and Miseducation." *Journal of Negro Education* 60(2): 133–146.

Knowles, Lewis, and Kenneth Pruitt. 1969. *Institutional Racism in America.* Englewood Cliffs, NJ: Prentice Hall.

Kovel, Joel. 1970. *White Racism: A Psychohistory.* New York: Columbia University Press.

Lather, Patti. 1991. *Getting Smart: Feminist Research and Pedagogy within the Postmodern.* New York: Routledge.

Lin, Nan, John Vaughn, and Walter Ensel. 1981. "Social Resources and Occupational Status Attainment." *Social Forces* 59: 1163–1181.

Lincoln, Yvonne, and Egon Guba. 1985. *Naturalistic Inquiry.* Beverley Hills, CA: Sage.

Lipsitz, George. 1998. *The Possessive Investment in Whiteness: How White People Profit from Identity Politics.* Philadelphia: Temple University Press.

Losen, Daniel, and Gary Orfield. 2002. *Racial Inequity in Special Education.* Boston, MA: Harvard Education Press.

Macionis, John. 2001. *Society: The Basics.* 5th ed. Upper Saddle River, NJ: Prentice Hall.

MacLeod, Jay. 1987. *Ain't No Makin' It: Leveled Aspirations in a Low-Income Neighborhood.* Boulder, CO: Westview Press.

Manis, J., and B. Meltzer. 1972. *Symbolic Interaction: A Reader in Social Psychology,* 2nd ed. Boston: Allyn and Bacon.

Mannheim, Karl. [1936] 1952. *Essays on the Sociology of Knowledge.* London: Routledge and Kegan Paul.

Marcus, George. 1994. "What Comes (Just) After "Post"? The Case of Ethnography." In *Handbook of Qualitative Research,* edited by N. Denzin and Y. Lincoln. Thousand Oaks, CA: Sage.

Marger, Martin. 1994. *Race and Ethnic Relations: American and Global Perspectives.* Belmont, CA: Wadsworth.

Margolis, Joseph. 1999. "Pierre Bourdieu: Habitus and the Logic of Practice." In *Bourdieu: A Critical Reader,* edited by R. Shusterman. Malden, MA: Blackwell.

Marshall, Catherine, and Gretchen Rossman. 1999. *Designing Qualitative Research,* 3rd ed. Thousand Oaks, CA: Sage.

Matza, David. 1964. *Delinquency and Drift.* New York: John Wiley.

McConahay, John. 1982. "Self-Interest versus Racial Attitudes as Correlates of Anti-Busing Attitudes in Louisville: Is It the Buses or the Blacks?" *Journal of Politics* 44: 692–720.

McConahay, John, and Joseph Hough. 1976. "Symbolic Racism." *Journal of Social Issues* 32: 23–45.

McHugh, Peter. 1968. *Defining the Situation: The Organization of Meaning in Social Interaction.* New York: Bobbs-Merrill.

McIntosh, Peggy. [1988] 1992. "White Privilege and Male Privilege: A Personal Account of Coming to See Correspondences through Work in Women's Studies." In *Race, Class, and Gender: An Anthology,* edited by M. Andersen and P. H. Collins. Belmont, CA: Wadsworth.

McIntyre, Lisa. 2002. *The Practical Skeptic: Core Concepts in Sociology,* 2nd ed. New York: McGraw-Hill.

McKay, Nellie. 1993. "Acknowledging Differences: Can Women Find Unity through Diversity?" In *Theorizing Black Feminisms: The Visionary Pragmatism of Black Women,* edited by S. James and A. Busia. New York: Routledge.

Mead, George Herbert. 1934. *Mind, Self, and Society.* Chicago: University of Chicago Press.

Mehan, Hugh. 1992. "Understanding Inequality in Schools: The Contribution of Interpretive Studies." *Sociology of Education* 65: 1–20.

Melamed, Elissa. 1983. *Mirror, Mirror: The Terror of Not Being Young.* New York: Simon and Schuster.

Merton, Robert. 1967. *On Theoretical Sociology.* New York: Free Press.

Mills, C. Wright. 1959. *The Sociological Imagination.* London: Oxford University Press.

———. [1943] 1964. *Sociology and Pragmatism: The Higher Learning in America.* New York: Galaxy.

Monteith, Margo. 1991. "Self-Regulation of Stereotypic Responses: Implications for Prejudice Reduction Efforts." Unpublished doctoral dissertation, University of Wisconsin at Madison.

———. 1992. "Self Regulation of Prejudiced Responses: Implications for Progress in Prejudice Reduction Efforts." *Journal of Personality and Social Psychology* 65: 469–485.

Moraga, Cherrie, and Gloria Anzaldúa. 1983. *This Bridge Called My Back: Writings by Radical Women of Color.* New York: Kitchen Table Press.

Morton, Thomas. 1999. "The Increasing Colorization of America's Child Welfare System." *Policy and Practice* 57(4): 23–32.

Nemetz, Patricia, and Sandra Christensen. 1996. "The Challenge of Cultural Diversity: Harnessing a Diversity of Views to Understand Multiculturalism." *Academy of Management Review* 21(2): 434–462.

Newman, David. 2000. *Sociology: Exploring the Architecture of Everyday Life.* Thousand Oaks, CA: Pine Forge.

Oakley, Ann. 1981. "Interviewing Women: A Contradiction in Terms." In *Doing Feminist Research,* edited by H. Roberts. London: Routledge, Kegan, and Paul.

O'Brien, Eileen. 2001. *Whites Confront Racism: Antiracists and Their Paths to Action.* Lanham, MD: Rowman and Littlefield.

Okin, Susan. 1989. *Justice, Gender, and the Family.* New York: Basic.

Omi, Michael, and Howard Winant. 1986. *Racial Formation in the United States.* New York: Routledge.

———. 1994. *Racial Formation in the United States,* 2nd ed. New York: Routledge.

O'Reilly, Charles, III, David Caldwell, and William Barnett. 1989. "Work Group Demography, Social Integration, and Turnover." *Administrative Science Quarterly* 34(1): 21–37.

Ortner, Sherry. 1994. "Theory in Anthropology since the Sixties." In *Culture/Power/History: A Reader in Contemporary Social Theory,* edited by N. Dirks, G. Eley, and S. Ortner. Princeton, NJ: Princeton University Press.

Orum, Anthony, Joe Feagin, and Gideon Sjoberg. 1991. *The Case for the Case Study.* Chapel Hill: University of North Carolina Press.

Park, Robert. [1926] 1950. *Race and Culture.* New York: Free Press.

Parrish, Thomas. 2002. "Racial Disparities in the Identification, Funding, and Provision of Special Education." In *Racial Inequity in Special Education,* edited by D. Losen and G. Orfield. Boston, MA: Harvard Education Press.

Parrish, Thomas, and Christine Hikido. 1998. *Inequalities in Public School District Revenues* (NCES 98-210). Washington, DC: U.S. Department of Education, National Center for Education Statistics.

Parsons, Talcott. 1949. *The Structure of Social Action: A Study in Social Theory with Special Reference to a Group of Recent European Writers.* Glencoe, IL: Free Press.

Perry, Pamela. 2002. *Shades of White.* Durham, NC: Duke University Press.

Pfuhl, Erdwin, and Stuart Henry. 1993. *The Deviance Process,* 3rd ed. New York: Aldine de Gruyter.

Pincus, Fred. 2003. *Reverse Discrimination: Dismantling the Myth.* Boulder, CO: Lynne Rienner.

Pincus, Fred, and Howard Ehrlich. 1994. *Race and Ethnic Conflict: Contending Views on Prejudice, Discrimination, and Ethnoviolence.* Boulder, CO: Westview.

Poussaint, Alvin. 2001. "Is Extreme Racism a Mental Illness: Point Counterpoint." *Western Journal of Medicine* 176: 4.

Pratt, Minnie Bruce. 1984. "Identity: Skin Blood Heart." In *Yours in Struggle,* edited by E. Bulkin. Ithaca, NY: Firebrand.

Quarles, Benjamin. 1974. *Allies for Freedom: Blacks and John Brown.* New York: Oxford University Press.

Ritchie, Jane, and Jane Lewis. 2003. *Qualitative Research Practice.* London: Sage.

Ritzer, George. 1990. "Micro-Macro Linkage in Sociological Theory: Applying a Metatheoretical Tool." In *Frontiers of Sociological Theory,* edited by G. Ritzer. New York: Columbia University Press.

Ritzer, George, and Pamela Gindoff. 1994. "Agency-Structure, Micro-Macro, Individualism-Holism-Relationism: A Metatheoretical Explanation of Theoretical Convergence Between the United States and Europe." In *Agency and Structure: Reorienting Social Theory,* edited by Piotr Sztompka. New York: Gordon and Breach.

Roediger, David. 1991. *The Wages of Whiteness: Race and the Making of the American Working Class.* New York: Verso.

Rollins, Judith. 1985. *Between Women: Domestics and their Employers.* Philadelphia: Temple University Press.

Rolock, Nancy, and Mark Testa. 2005. "Indicated Child Abuse and Neglect Reports: Is the Investigation Process Racially Biased?" In *Race Matters in Child Welfare: The Overrepresentation of African American Children in the System,* edited by D. Derezotes, J. Poertner, and M. Testa. Washington, DC: CWLA Press.

Rorty, Richard. 1989. *Contingency, Irony, and Solidarity.* Cambridge, UK: Cambridge University Press.

Ross, Thomas. 1990. "Innocence and Affirmative Action." *Vanderbilt Law Review* 43: 297–316.

Sanjek, Roger. 1994. "The Enduring Inequalities of Race." In *Race,* edited by S. Gregory and R. Sanjek. New Brunswick, NJ: Rutgers University Press.

Schlesinger, Arthur, Jr. 1992. *The Disuniting of America: Reflections on a Multicultural Society.* New York: W. W. Norton.

Schuman, Howard, Charlotte Steeh, and Lawrence Bobo. 1985. *Racial Trends in America: Trends and Interpretations.* Cambridge, MA: Harvard University Press.

Schwalbe, Michael. 1983. "Language and the Self: An Expanded View from a Symbolic Interactionist Perspective." *Symbolic Interaction* 6: 291–306.

Seale, Clive. 1999. *The Quality of Qualitative Research.* Oxford: Blackwell.

Sears, David. 1988. "Symbolic Racism." In *Eliminating Racism: Profiles in Controversy,* edited by P. Katz and D. Taylor. New York: Plenum.

Sears, David, and P. J. Henry. 2003. "The Origins of Symbolic Racism." *Journal of Personality and Social Psychology* 85(2): 259–275.

Sears, David, and Donald Kinder. 1971. "Racial Tensions and Voting in Los

Angeles." In *Los Angeles: Viability and Prospects for Metropolitan Leadership,* edited by W. Hirsch. New York: Praeger.

Sears, David, and John McConahay. 1973. *The Politics of Violence.* Boston: Houghton Mifflin.

Sedlak, Andrea, and Dana Schulz. 2005. "Race Differences in Risk of Maltreatment in the General Child Population." In *Race Matters in Child Welfare: The Overrepresentation of African American Children in the System,* edited by D. Derezotes, J. Poertner, and M. Testa. Washington, DC: CWLA Press.

Shibutani, Tamotsu. 1955. "Reference Groups as Perspectives." *American Journal of Sociology* 60: 562–569.

Shott, Susan. 1979. "Emotion and Social Life: A Symbolic Interactionist Analysis." *American Journal of Sociology* 84: 1317–1334.

Sidel, Ruth. 1998. *Keeping Women and Children Last: America's War on the Poor.* New York: Penguin.

Sigelman, Lee, and Susan Welch. 1991. *Black Americans' Views of Racial Inequality: The Dream Deferred.* New York: Cambridge University Press.

———. 1993. "The Contact Hypothesis Revisited: Black-White Interaction and Positive Racial Attitudes." *Social Forces* 71(3): 781–795.

Silverman, David. 2004. *Qualitative Research: Theory, Method, and Practice,* 2nd ed. London: Sage.

Skiba, Russell, Ada Simmons, Shana Ritter, Kristin Kohler, Michelle Henderson, and Tony Wu. 2006. "The Context of Minority Disproportionality: Practitioner Perspectives on Special Education Referral." *Teachers College Record* 108(7): 1424–1459.

Smelser, Neil. 1998. *The Social Edges of Psychoanalysis.* Berkeley: University of California Press.

Smith, Barbara. 1982. "Racism and Women's Studies." In *All the Women Are White, All the Blacks Are Men, But Some of Us Are Brave: Black Women's Studies,* edited by B. Hull, P. Scott, and B. Smith. New York: Feminist Press.

Smith, Christopher. 1994. "Back and to the Future: The Intergroup Contact Hypothesis Revisited." *Sociological Inquiry* 64(4): 438–455.

Smith, Rolf. 2002. *The Seven Levels of Change: Different Thinking for Different Results,* 2nd ed. Irving, TX: Tapestry.

Sniderman, Paul, and Michael Hagen. 1985. *Race and Inequality: A Study in American Values.* Chatham, NJ: Chatham House.

Spacks, Patricia. 1981. "The Difference It Makes." In *A Feminist Perspective in the Academy,* edited by E. Langland and W. Gove. Chicago: University of Chicago Press.

Squires, Gregory, and Sally O'Connor. 2001. *Color and Money: Politics and Prospects for Community Reinvestment in Urban America.* Albany: State University of New York Press.

Stake, Robert. 1995. *The Art of Case Study Research.* Thousand Oaks, CA: Sage.

Staub, Ervin. 1992. *The Roots of Evil: The Origins of Genocide and Other Group Violence.* New York: Cambridge University Press.

———. 2003. *The Psychology of Good and Evil: Why Children, Adults, and Groups Help and Harm Others.* New York: Cambridge University Press.

Steinberg, Stephen. 1995. *Turning Back: The Retreat from Racial Justice in American Thought and Policy.* Boston: Beacon.

Sterne, Emma Gelders. 1968. *They Took Their Stand.* New York: Crowell-Collier Press.

Strauss, Anselm, and Juliet Corbin. 1991. *Basics of Qualitative Research: Grounded Theory Procedures and Techniques.* Newbury Park, CA: Sage.

Swain, Carol. 2002. *The New White Nationalism in America: Its Challenge to Integration.* New York: Cambridge University Press.

Sykes, Gresham, and David Matza. 1957. "Techniques of Neutralization: A Theory of Delinquency." *American Sociological Review* 22 (December): 664–670.

Tafjel, Henri, and John Turner. 1986. "The Social Identity Theory of Intergroup Behavior." In *The Psychology of Intergroup Relations,* edited by S. Worchel and W. Austin. Chicago: Nelson-Hall.

Tatum, Beverly. 1994. "Teaching White Students about Racism: The Search for White Allies and the Restoration of Hope." *Teachers College Record* 95: 463–476.

Thernstrom, Stephan, and Abigail Thernstrom. 1997. *America in Black and White: One Nation, Indivisible.* New York: Simon and Schuster.

Thomas, W. I. 1923. *The Unadjusted Girl.* New York: Little, Brown.

Thomas, W. I., and Dorothy Thomas. 1928. *The Child in America.* New York: Knopf.

Thompson, Becky. 2001. *A Promise and a Way of Life: White Antiracist Activism.* Minneapolis: University of Minnesota Press.

Trepagnier, Barbara. 1993. "The Social Psychology of Difference." Unpublished manuscript, University of California at Santa Barbara.

———. 2001. "Deconstructing Categories: The Exposure of Silent Racism." *Symbolic Interaction* 24(2): 141–163.

Turner, Jonathan, and Royce Singleton. 1978. "A Theory of Ethnic Oppression: Toward a Reintegration of Cultural and Structural Concepts in Ethnic Relations Theory." *Social Forces* 56(4): 1001–1018.

U.S. Census Bureau. 2000. *State and County QuickFacts: Texas.* Retrieved July 1, 2009, from http://quickfacts.census.gov/qfd/index.html Van der Berghe, Pierre. 1967. *Race and Racism.* New York: Wiley.

Van Dijk, Teum. 1984. *Prejudice in Discourse: An Analysis of Ethnic Prejudice in Cognition and Conversation.* Philadelphia: John Benjamins.

Wagner, Gary, Jeffrey Pfeffer, and Charles O'Reilly III. 1984. "Organizational Demography and Turnover in Top Management Groups." *Administrative Science Quarterly* 29: 74–92.

Wagner, Helmut. 1970. *Alfred Schutz: On Phenomenology and Social Relations.* Chicago: University of Chicago Press.

Waters, Malcolm. 1994. *Modern Sociological Theory.* Thousand Oaks, CA: Sage.

Weber, Max. [1918] 1958. "Inconvenient Facts." In *From Max Weber,* edited by H. Gerth and C. W. Mills. New York: Oxford University Press.

Wegner, Daniel. 1994. "Ironic Processes of Mental Control." *Psychological Review* 101(1): 34–52.

Weiner, Marli. 1985/1986. "The Intersection of Race and Gender: The Antebellum Plantation Mistress and Her Slaves." *Humboldt Journal of Social Relations* 13(1–2): 374–386.

Wellman, Barry. 1983. "Network Analysis: Some Basic Principles." In *Sociological Theory,* edited by R. Collins. San Francisco: Jossey-Bass.

Wellman, Barry, and Scot Wortley. 1990. "Different Strokes from Different Folks: Community Ties and Social Support." *American Journal of Sociology* 96(3): 558–588.

Wellman, David. 1977. *Portraits of White Racism,* 2nd ed. New York: Cambridge University Press.

———. 1993. *Portraits of White Racism,* 3rd ed. New York: Cambridge University Press.

West, Cornel. 1988. "Marxist Theory and the Specificity of Afro-American Oppression." In *Marxism and the Interpretation of Culture,* edited by C. Nelson and L. Grossberg. Urbana: University of Illinois Press.

Whitmeyer, Joseph. 1994. "Why Actor Models Are Integral to Structural Analysis." *Sociological Theory* 12(2): 153–165.

Williams, Patricia. 1991. *The Alchemy of Race and Rights: Diary of a Law Professor.* Cambridge, MA: Harvard University Press.

Winant, Howard. 2004. "Behind Blue Eyes: Whiteness and Contemporary U.S. Racial Politics." In *Off White: Readings on Power, Privilege, and Resistance,* 2nd ed., edited by M. Fine, L. Weis, L. Pruitt, and A. Burns. New York: Routledge.

Wise, Tim. 2002. "Racial Profiling and Its Apologists." *Z Magazine* (March): 40–44.

Wolf, Charlotte. 1994. "Dependency-Bond as Construct." *Symbolic Interaction* 17(4): 367–393.

X, Malcolm. 1965. *The Autobiography of Malcolm X.* New York: Grove.

Zeller, Richard. 1993. "Focus Group Research on Sensitive Topics: Setting the Agenda without Setting the Agenda." In *Successful Focus Groups: Advancing the State of the Art,* edited by D. Morgan. Newbury Park, CA: Sage.

Index

About the Author

Barbara Trepagnier is Professor of Sociology at Texas State University–San Marcos. She received a Ph.D. degree in sociology in 1996 from the University of California–Santa Barbara. She holds a B.A. in psychology and a M.A. in sociology from the University of Houston. In an effort to further the ideas in this book, she is currently engaged in a study titled "Conversations about Race."